The
Lancashire, Cumbria &
Bus Handboc

British Bus Publishing

Body codes used in the Bus Handbook series:

Type:
A	Articulated vehicle
B	Bus, either single-deck or double-deck
BC	Express - high-back seating in a bus body
C	Coach
M	Minibus with design capacity of 16 seats or less
N	Low-floor bus (*Niederflur*), either single-deck or double-deck
O	Open-top bus (CO = convertible - PO = Partial open-top)

Seating capacity is then shown. For double-decks the upper deck quantity is followed by the lower deck.

Door position:
C	Centre entrance/exit
D	Dual doorway.
F	Front entrance/exit
R	Rear entrance/exit (no distinction between doored and open)
T	Three or more access points

Equipment:
L	Lift for wheelchair		TV	Training Vehicle.
M	Mail compartment		RV	Used as tow bus or Engineers vehicle.
T	Toilet		w	Vehicle is withdrawn from service.

e.g. - B32/28F is a double-deck bus with thirty-two seats upstairs, twenty-eight down and a front entrance/exit. N43D is a low-floor bus with two doorways.

Re-registrations:
Where a vehicle has gained new index marks the details are listed at the end of each fleet showing the current mark, followed in sequence by those previously carried starting with the original mark.

Other books in the series:
The Scottish Bus Handbook
The Ireland & Islands Bus Handbook
The North East Bus Handbook
The Yorkshire Bus Handbook
The Lancashire, Cumbria and Manchester Bus Handbook
The Merseyside and Cheshire Bus Handbook
The West Midlands Bus Handbook
The East Midlands Bus Handbook
The Eastern Bus Handbook
The Welsh Bus Handbook
The South East Bus Handbook
The South West Bus Handbook

Annual books are produced for the major groups:
The Stagecoach Bus Handbook
The FirstBus Bus Handbook
The Arriva Bus Handbook
The National Express Handbook

Associated series:
The Hong Kong Bus Handbook
The Leyland Lynx Handbook
The Model Bus Handbook
The Postbus Handbook
The Overall Advert Book Volume 1
The Toy & Model Bus Handbook - Volume 1 - Early Diecasts
The Fire Brigade Handbook (fleet list of each local authority fire brigade)
The Fire Brigade Handbook - Special Appliances Volume 1
The Fire Brigade Handbook - Special Appliances Volume 2
The Police Range Rover Handbook

Some earlier editions of these books are still available. Please contact the publisher.

Contents

The Lancashire, Cumbria and Manchester Bus Handbook

This fourth edition of the Bus Handbook covering the northern part of The North West region is part of a series that details the fleets of bus and express coach operators from across Britain. A list of current editions is shown on page 2. The operators included in this edition cover those who provide tendered and commercial services in the counties and unitary areas within the region. Also included are a number of operators who provide significant coaching activities.

Quality photographs for inclusion in the series are welcome, for which a fee is payable. The publishers unfortunately cannot accept responsibility for any loss and request you show your name on each picture or slide.

To keep the fleet information up to date we recommend the Ian Allan publication, Buses, published monthly, or for more detailed information, the PSV Circle monthly news sheets.

The writer and publisher would be glad to hear from readers should any information be available which corrects or enhances that given in this publication.

Series Editor: Bill Potter
Principal Editors for *The Lancashire, Cumbria and Manchester Bus Handbook:* Stuart Martin and Malcolm Jones

Acknowledgments:
We are grateful to David Donati, Bob Downham, Keith Grimes, Mark Jameson, PSV Circle and the operating companies for their assistance in the compilation of this book.

The front cover photograph is by Richard Godfrey and shows the vehicle chosen to Blackburn Buses to celebrate the Golden Jubilee of Queen Elizabeth II. The fronticepiece also by Richard Godfrey illustrates the Pyoneer style of local body builder East Lancashire as seen on Preston Bus' Trident 184. Rear cover pictures are by Cliff Beeton and Richard Godfrey.

Earlier editions of the area covered by the Lancashire, Cumbria and Manchester Bus Handbook:

1st Edition (North West Bus Handbook) -1993 - ISBN 1-897990-00-6
2nd Edition (North West Bus Handbook) -1994 - ISBN 1-897990-07-3
1st Edition (Lancashire Cumbria and Manchester Bus Handbook) -1996 - ISBN 1-897990-13-8
2nd Edition (Lancashire Cumbria and Manchester Bus Handbook) -1999 - ISBN 1-897990-48-0
This Edition - 2002   ISBN 1-897990-77-4

ISBN 1 897990 77 4
Published by *British Bus Publishing Ltd*
16 St Margaret's Drive, Wellington, Telford, TF1 3PH

Telephone: 01952 255669 - Facsimile 01952 222397 - www.britishbuspublishing.co.uk
© British Bus Publishing Ltd, May 2002

ALFA

Alfa Coaches Ltd, Euxton Lane, Chorley, PR7 6AF

-11	DAF DE33WSSB3000	Ikarus Blue Danube 350	C53F	1997-1998

P211RUM	**4**	P214RUM	**6**	R116GNW	**8**	R118GNW	**10**	R120GNW	
P212RUM	**5**	P215RUM	**7**	R117GNW	**9**	R119GNW	**11**	R121GNW	
P213RUM									

T112AUA	DAF DE33WSSB3000	Ikarus Blue Danube 396	C49FT	1999	
T113AUA	DAF DE33WSSB3000	Ikarus Blue Danube 396	C49FT	1999	
W214CDN	DAF DE33WSSB3000	Ikarus Blue Danube 396	C49FT	2000	
W215CDN	DAF DE33WSSB3000	Ikarus Blue Danube 396	C53F	2000	
W217CDN	DAF DE33WSSB3000	Ikarus Blue Danube 396	C53F	2000	
02	Dennis R	Plaxton Paragon	C49FT	2002	
02	Dennis R	Plaxton Paragon	C49FT	2002	
02	Dennis R	Plaxton Paragon	C49FT	2002	
02	Dennis R	Plaxton Paragon	C49FT	2002	
K512RJX	DAF SB3000DKV601	Van Hool Alizée	C53F	1993	London Coaches, 1999
K513RJX	DAF SB3000DKV601	Van Hool Alizée	C53F	1993	London Coaches, 1999
R5BSL	Dennis Javelin	Plaxton Première 320	C53F	1998	
B10MHC	DAF SE33WSSB3000	Plaxton Première 350	C51FT	1998	Weaver, Newbury, 2001
B10MNC	DAF SE33WSSB3000	Plaxton Première 350	C51FT	1998	Weaver, Newbury, 2001

epots: Whitebirk Road, Blackburn and Bowesfield Lane, Stockton.
eb: www.alfatravel.co.uk

he principal coach employed by Alfa is the DAF SB3000, here with Ikarus bodywork. R117GNW is one of
xteen operated, though for the 2002 season Transbus' semi-integral Plaxton Paragon R are to join the fleet.
ob Downham

ARCHWAY TRAVEL

R M J & M Archer, Unit H Cocker Avenue, Poulton-le-Fylde, FY6 8JU

Reg	Chassis	Body	Seating	Year	History
ONF660R	Leyland Atlantean AN68A/1R	Northern Counties	B43/32F	1976	Metro, Blackpool, 1999
ONF698R	Leyland Atlantean AN68A/1R	Northern Counties	B43/32F	1977	Town Bus, Poulton-le-Fylde, 1996
RJA809R	Leyland Atlantean AN68A/1R	Northern Counties	B43/32F	1977	Town Bus, Poulton-le-Fylde, 1996
WVW901S	Leyland Atlantean AN68A/1R	Park Royal	B43/32F	1978	Broadway Stars, Leigh, 2001
BYX205V	MCW Metrobus DR101/9	MCW	B43/28D	1979	Packman & Vann, Cleveleys, 2001
BYX280V	MCW Metrobus DR101/12	MCW	B43/28D	1980	Packman & Vann, Cleveleys, 2001
BYX295V	MCW Metrobus DR101/12	MCW	B43/28D	1980	Packman & Vann, Cleveleys, 2001
EYE323V	MCW Metrobus DR101/12	MCW	B43/28D	1980	Packman & Vann, Cleveleys, 2001
GYE382W	MCW Metrobus DR101/12	MCW	B43/28D	1980	Packman & Vann, Cleveleys, 2001
GYE445W	MCW Metrobus DR101/12	MCW	B43/28D	1980	Packman & Vann, Cleveleys, 2001
RUT131W	DAF MB200DKTL600	Jonckheere Bermuda	C51F	1981	Reilly, Bootle, 2001
FIL4988	Volvo B10M-61	Jonckheere Jubilee P90	C50/7FT	1984	AG Executive, Pilling, 1997
A20JDA	Bedford YNT	Duple Laser	C53F	1985	Jackson, Chorley, 1992
C752CWX	Neoplan N722/3	Plaxton Paramount 4000	C53/18CT	1986	Flatt & Smith, Gowthorpe, 2001
D331VVV	Quest J	Jonckheere Piccolo P35	C33FT	1987	Goldenstand, Park Royal, 1994
F74SMC	Mercedes-Benz 609D	Reeve Burgess Beaver	B20F	1988	Ash, Woodburn Moor, 2001

Previous registrations:

A20JDA	B222OJU		RUT131W	OFP73W, 531PP
FIL4988	A318XHE			

Web: www.archwaytravel.com

Archway Travel operate local school and contract services on the Fylde using a fleet of Atlanteans and former London Metrobuses alongside coaches. Pictured in Poulton-le-Fylde is Duple-bodied Bedford A20JDA, which started life with Bexleyheath Transport in London. *Bill Potter*

ASHALLS

J A Ashall Ltd, 610 Ashton New Road, Manchester, M11 4SG

IIL3476	Volvo B10M-61	Caetano Algarve	C49Ft	1986	Belle Vue, Gorton, 2000
C857EML	Volvo B9M	Plaxton Bustler	BC35C	1986	Speedlink, 2001
C858EML	Volvo B9M	Plaxton Bustler	BC35C	1986	Speedlink, 2001
C888REG	Bedford YNV	Duple 320	C53FT	1986	Roys, Rochdale, 2002
D27XFL	Scania K113CRB	Van Hool Alizée	C53F	1986	Smyton, Omargh, 2002
G703AEF	DAF MB230DKFL615	Duple 320	C53F	1989	Go-Ahead, 1998
TJI4830	Scania K113CRB	Berkhof Excellence 2000	C53F	1991	First London, 2000
TJI4836	Scania K113CRB	Berkhof Excellence 2000	C53F	1991	First London, 2000
M68LAG	Scania K113CRB	Van Hool Alizée HE	C49FT	1995	East Yorkshire, 2001
N753VCY	DAF MB230LT615	Van Hool Alizée	C49FT	1996	Pullman, Crofty, 2001
R720EGD	Mercedes-Benz 814D	Mellor	BC33F	1997	
S582RGA	Mercedes-Benz Vario O814	Plaxton Beaver 2	B31F	1998	White Ribon, East Kilbride, 1999
T581KGB	Mercedes-Benz Vario O814	Plaxton Beaver 2	B27F	1999	
V20CBC	Mercedes-Benz Vario O814	Plaxton Beaver 2	B31F	1999	Coakley, Motherwell, 2002
V333ASH	Scania K124IB4	Irizar Century 12.35	C49FT	1999	
V387HGG	Dennis Dart SLF	Plaxton Pointer MPD	N28F	2000	
V389HGG	Dennis Dart SLF	Plaxton Pointer MPD	N28F	2000	
V390HGG	Dennis Dart SLF	Plaxton Pointer MPD	N28F	2000	
X301AKY	MAN 18.350 HOCL -R	Neoplan Transliner	C49FT	2001	

Previous registrations

D27XFL	D27XFL, LIW1830	TJI4830	J740TDP
IIL2379	C610KDS	TJI4836	J746TDP

Three low-floor Dennis Darts entered service with Ashalls in 2000 for use on services in the Stockport area. Pictured arriving at the bus station is V390HGG, illustrating the Plaxton Pointer 2 body. *Cliff Beeton*

ASPDEN OF BLACKBURN

J & F Aspden of Blackburn, Lancaster Street, Blackburn, BB2 1UA

FFR170S	Bristol VRT/SL3/6LXB	Eastern Coach Works	B43/31F	1977	Burnley & Pendle, 1993
GEY273	Leyland Leopard PSU3E/4R	Plaxton Paramount 3200 (1987)	C53F	1977	Cumberland, 1987
VHG357V	Leyland Leopard PSU3E/4R	Duple Dominant II	C53F	1979	
WCK124V	Leyland Leopard PSU3E/4R	Duple Dominant II Express	C51F	1979	Catteralls, Southam, 1994
OBV142	Leyland Leopard PSU3F/5R	Plaxton Supreme IV	C53F	1980	Brewers, 1989
ECB96W	Leyland Leopard PSU3F/5R	Plaxton Supreme IV	C53F	1980	
PRN424X	Leyland Tiger TRCTL11/2R	Plaxton Supreme V	C53F	1982	
RHG189X	Leyland Tiger TRCTL11/2R	Plaxton Supreme V	C53F	1982	
KBV310	Leyland Tiger TRCTL11/3R	Plaxton Paramount 3500	C51F	1982	Ebdon, Sidcup, 1985
PBV779	Leyland Tiger TRCTL11/3R	Plaxton Paramount 3500	C53F	1982	Ribble Buses, 1988
HBV682	Leyland Tiger TRCTL11/3R	Plaxton Paramount 3200	C53F	1983	
SBV703	Leyland Tiger TRCTL11/3R	Duple Carribean 2	C49FT	1985	Robinson's, Great Harwood, 1991
JBV529	Leyland Tiger TRCTL11/3RZ	Duple 320	C53F	1986	
E187PFV	DAF MB230LB615	Plaxton Paramount 3500 III	C51FT	1987	Powercraft, Blackburn, 1999
F341XFR	Leyland Tiger TRCTL11/3ARZ	Plaxton Paramount 3500 III	C51F	1989	Bradshaw, St Annes, 1999

Previous registrations

E187PFV	E646KCX, RIB8747	KBV310	FNM856Y
GEY273	THH618S	OBV142	ETC309W
HBV682	CRN587Y	PBV779	BRN1Y, NRN567, FFR738Y
JBV529	C794MCK	SBV703	B211AFV

Aspdens's fleet is represented by Duple 320-bodied Leyland Tiger JBV529 which has been with the company from new. It is seen outside Blackburn rail station in April 2002. *Bob Downham*

BATTERSBY SILVER GREY

Harrisons Coaches (Morecambe) Ltd, The Coach Station, Middlegate, Morecambe, LA3 3PE

D137NUS	Mercedes-Benz L608D	Alexander AM	B21F	1986	Highwayman, Errol, 1996
4148VZ	Mercedes-Benz 609D	North West CS	BC24F	1988	Travel Right, Morecambe, 2000
5108VX	Mercedes-Benz 609D	Reeve Burgess Beaver	BC23F	1988	
F220RSE	Mercedes-Benz 407D	Devon Conversions	M15	1989	Middlehurst, Lancaster, 1994
3267HX	Mercedes-Benz 811D	Whittaker Europa	BC23F	1989	
7845UG	Volvo B10M-60	Plaxton Paramount 3500 III	C57F	1989	Wallace Arnold, 1992
1359UP	Volvo B10M-60	Plaxton Paramount 3500 III	C49FT	1990	Wilson, Carnwath, 2001
7144FN	Mercedes-Benz 609D	Reeve Burgess Beaver	BC23F	1991	Pennine Way, Laneshawbridge, '94
8850WU	Mercedes-Benz 609D	Onyx	BC24F	1994	Russell, Strathaven, 1997
7017UN	Volvo B10M-62	Plaxton Première 350	C49FT	1995	
4360WF	Volvo B10M-62	Plaxton Première 350	C53FT	1996	
5096WF	Volvo B10M-62	Plaxton Première 350	C53FT	1996	
7622UK	Volvo B10M-62	Plaxton Première 350	C53FT	1996	
817GTA	Volvo B10M-62	Plaxton Première 350	C49FT	1997	
7121RU	Volvo B10M-62	Plaxton Première 350	C53FT	1997	
R901WEC	Volvo B10M-62	Plaxton Première 350	C49FT	1998	
R902WEC	Volvo B10M-62	Plaxton Première 350	C49FT	1998	
R434FWT	Volvo B10M-62	Plaxton Première 350	C49FT	1998	Wallace Arnold, 2002
S904LHG	Volvo B10M-62	Plaxton Première 350	C49FT	1998	
S905LHG	Volvo B10M-62	Plaxton Première 350	C49FT	1999	
T543EUB	Volvo B10M-62	Plaxton Première 350	C48FT	1999	Wallace Arnold, 2002
V301DRN	Mercedes-Benz Vario O814	Plaxton Cheetah	C25F	1999	
V302DRN	Mercedes-Benz Vario O814	Plaxton Cheetah	C33F	1999	
W912BEC	Volvo B10M-62	Plaxton Paragon	C49FT	2000	

The Plaxton Première 350 was the preferred coach supplied to Battersby's fleet in the second half of the 1990s. Pictured in Windsor, 7017UN illustrates the application of the two-tone blue livery. *Dave Heath*

W913BEC is one of five Scania K124LBs with Irizar Century bodies operated by Battersby Silver Grey of Morecambe. When pictured in Grasmere in June 2001 it carried the contract colours of Trafalgar Tours. *J C Walton*

W913BEC	Scania L94IB	Irizar Century	C49FT	2000	
W914BEC	Scania L94IB	Irizar Century	C49FT	2000	
W916BEC	Scania L94IB	Irizar Century	C49FT	2000	
W975BEC	Scania L94IB	Irizar Century	C49FT	2000	
X178XEC	Mercedes-Benz Vario O814	Plaxton Beaver 2	BC33F	2000	Dawson Rentals, 2001
Y917XEC	Volvo B10M-62	Plaxton Paragon	C49FT	2001	
Y918XEC	Volvo B10M-62	Plaxton Paragon	C49FT	2001	
Y919XEC	Scania L94IB	Irizar Century	C49FT	2001	
PF51KHB	Mercedes-Benz Vario O814	Plaxton Beaver 2	BC33F	2001	
PF51KHC	Mercedes-Benz Vario O814	Plaxton Beaver 2	BC33F	2001	
02	Volvo B12M	Plaxton Paragon	C49FT	2002	
02	Volvo B12M	Plaxton Paragon	C49FT	2002	

Previous registrations:

817GTA	P897EEC	7017UN	N890NNR
1359UP	G372REG	7121RU	P896EEC
3267HX	G840KET	7144FN	J505DBE
4148VZ	E564VHF	7622UK	P895EEC
4360WF	N891AEO	7845UG	F435DUG
5096WF	P894TCK	8850WU	L741NFS
5108VX	F102VFV		

BLACKBURN TRANSPORT

Blackburn Borough Transport Ltd, Intack Garage, Whitebirk Road, Blackburn, BB1 3JD

1-5		Dennis Trident		East Lancashire Lolyne		N53/37F	2002		
1		2		3		4		5	

10-22		Leyland Atlantean AN68C/1R		East Lancashire		B43/31F	1981-82		
10	UCW430X	15	UCW429X	18	VBV18Y	21	VBV21Y	22	VBV22Y
13	OCW13X	16	SBV16X						

24-29		Leyland Atlantean AN68D/1R		East Lancashire		B43/31F	1983		
24	FCK24Y	26	A26JBV	27	FCK27Y	28	A28JBV	29	A29JBV
25	FCK25Y								

30	D367JJD	Leyland Olympian ONLXB/1RH		Eastern Coach Works		B42/30F	1987	Stagecoach London, 2000	

31-40		Leyland Olympian ONTL11/2R		Eastern Coach Works		B50/33D*	1983-84	Lothian Buses, 2000-01 *Seating varies	
31	OFS684Y	33	A704YFS	35	A720YFS	37	B737GSC	39	B739GSC
32	A703YFS	34	A719YFS	36	A721YFS	38	B738GSC	40	B740GSC

41-45		Leyland Olympian ONLXB/1RH		Eastern Coach Works		B42/29F	1986	Stagecoach London, 2000	
41	D141FYM	42	D324YNO	43	D133FYM	44	D144FYM	45	D145FYM

46-55		Leyland Olympian ONTL11/2R		Eastern Coach Works		B50/33D	1984	Lothian Buses, 2002	
46	B741GSC	48		50		52		54	
47		49		51		53		55	

91-100		Leyland Titan TNLXB2RR		Leyland		B42/26D	1982	Stagecoach London, 2002	
91	KYV521X	93	KYV533X	95	KYV545X	97	KYV517X	99	KYV465X
92	KYV525X	94	KYV544X	96	KYV526X	98	KYV508X	100	KYN306X

206-210		Volvo B10BLE		Wright Renown		N44F	1999		
206	V206EBV	207	V207EBV	208	V208EBV	209	V209EBV	210	V210EBV

Recent arrivals at Blackburn Transport are ten Leyland Titans. These have been acquired for the expanding contract business. Seen shortly after repainting is 92, KYV525X.
Bob Downham

Blackburn Transport bought ten Olympians from Lothian in 2000 and a further nine are due soon. These are the longer version of the model which Eastern Coach Works built inserting an additional narrow body section similar to that seen in the Routemaster RML class. Seen with Blackburn's Cathedral in the background, 39, B739GSC illustrated the retention of the dual-door layout and the contrasting colour applied to the entrance door, just one of the features incorporated to aid the partially sighted. *Mark Doggett*

300	BCB340	Volvo B10M-62	Plaxton Première 320	C49F	1997	Excelsior, Bournemouth, 1999
301	W301GCW	Volvo B10M-62	Plaxton Première 350	C49FT	2000	
302	02	Volvo B12B	Van Hool Alizée T9	C49FT	2002	
326	LUF549	Volvo B10M-60	Plaxton Paramount 3500 III	C51F	1991	Ambassador Travel, 1994
327	PCB24	Volvo B10M-60	Plaxton Paramount 3500 III	C49F	1991	Dodsworth, Boroughbridge, 1995
328	213ONU	Volvo B10M-62	Plaxton Première 320	C49FT	1995	Excelsior, Bournemouth, 1996
329	428EXA	Volvo B10M-62	Plaxton Première 320	C49FT	1995	Excelsior, Bournemouth, 1996
330	YJY316	Volvo B10M-62	Plaxton Première 320	C49FT	1996	Excelsior, Bournemouth, 1998

418-422

		Volvo B10M-55	East Lancashire EL2000	BC51F	1991	
418	J418JBV	**419** J419JBV	**420** J420JBV	**421** J421JBV	**422** J422JBV	

423	BVP807V	Leyland National 2 NL116L11/1R	East Lancs Greenway (1993)	B49F	1980	North Western, 1992
424	LFR638W	Leyland National 2 NL116AL11/2R	East Lancs Greenway (1993)	B49F	1981	North Western, 1992
425	PJT267R	Leyland National 11351A/2R	East Lancs Greenway (1994)	B49F	1976	Solent Blue Line, 1994
426	TCW868T	Leyland National 11351A/2R	East Lancs Greenway (1994)	B49F	1979	North Devon, 1994
427	TOF694S	Leyland National 11351A/1R[V]	East Lancs Greenway (1995)	B49F	1978	Midland, Cannock, 1995
428	TJN505R	Leyland National 11351A/1R[V]	East Lancs Greenway (1995)	B49F	1977	Eastern National, 1995
429	YEV317S	Leyland National 11351A/1R[V]	East Lancs Greenway (1995)	B49F	1978	Thamesway, 1995
430	YEV324S	Leyland National 11351A/1R[V]	East Lancs Greenway (1995)	B49F	1978	Thamesway, 1995
431	EXI2455	Leyland National 1151/1R/2802[V]	East Lancs Greenway (1995)	B49F	1973	Express Motors, Bontnewydd, 1997
525	BFV861R	Leyland National 10351A/2R	East Lancs Greenway (1993)	B41F	1977	London Buses, 1992
526	BYW361V	Leyland National 10351A/2R	East Lancs Greenway (1993)	B41F	1979	Evag-Cannon, Bolton, 1992
527	LRN552N	Leyland National 10351/2R	East Lancs Greenway (1993)	B41F	1975	Isle of Man Road Services, 1992
528	JDT432N	Leyland National 10351/2R	East Lancs Greenway (1993)	B41F	1975	Isle of Man Road Services, 1992
529	JWG191P	Leyland National 10351/2R	East Lancs Greenway (1993)	B41F	1975	Isle of Man Road Services, 1992
530	HPF313N	Leyland National 10351/1R/SC	East Lancs Greenway (1993)	B41F	1975	Birmingham Omnibus, 1992
531	AYR324T	Leyland National 10351A/2R	East Lancs Greenway (1994)	B41F	1979	CMT Buses, Aintree, 1994
532	JJG907P	Leyland National 10351/1R	East Lancs Greenway (1994)	B41F	1975	Busylink, Hemel Hempstead, 1994
533	M533RCW	Volvo B6-9.9m	East Lancashire	B41F	1994	
534	M534RCW	Volvo B6-9.9m	East Lancashire	B41F	1994	
535	M535RCW	Volvo B6-9.9m	East Lancashire	B41F	1994	
536	M536RCW	Volvo B6-9.9m	East Lancashire	B41F	1994	

The Lancashire, Cumbria and Manchester Bus Handbook

The minibus element of Blackburn Transport's fleet is migrating to Mini Pointer Darts, displacing the Optare MetroRider. The highest number to date is 667, PK51LJY, seen with the latest livery styling. *Richard Godfrey*

611-615

	Optare MetroRider MR03		Optare			B29F	1992	London Central, 1998	
611	J701CGK	612	J708CGK	613	J703CGK	614	J694CGK	615	K223MGT

627	M627WBV	Optare MetroRider MR15	Optare	B29F	1995
628	M628WBV	Optare MetroRider MR15	Optare	B29F	1995
629	M629WBV	Optare MetroRider MR15	Optare	B29F	1995
630	M630WBV	Optare MetroRider MR15	Optare	B29F	1995

631-644

	Optare MetroRider MR17		Optare			B29F	1995-98		
631	M631WFR	634	N634LFR	637	P637ARN	640	P640ARN	643	R643OBV
632	M632WFR	635	N635LFR	638	P638ARN	641	R641OBV	644	R644OBV
633	N633LFR	636	N636LFR	639	P639ARN	642	R642OBV		

651-667

	Dennis Dart SLF		Plaxton Pointer MPD			N29F	1999-2002		
651	V651HEC	655	V655HEC	658	V658HEC	661	PK51LJN	664	PK51LJV
652	V652HEC	656	V656HEC	659	V659HEC	662	PK51LJO	665	PK51LJX
653	V653HEC	657	V657HEC	660	V660HEC	663	PK51LJU	667	PK51LJY
654	V654HEC								

Ancillary vehicle:

402	PUS158W	Leyland Leopard PSU3F/4R	Alexander AYS		TV	1981

Previous Registrations:

13ONU	XEL31, L345ERU	JWG191P	JWG191P, 4648MAN
28EXA	A14EXC, M351MRU	LRN552N	JDT437N, 3176MAN
CB340	P526BLJ	LUF549	PTF743L
FV861R	OJD880R	PCB24	H724VWU
324YNO	D262FYL, VLT14	TCW868T	AFJ757T
367JJD	D263FYL, VLT9	UCW429X	OCW15X
XI2455	BCD801L	UCW430X	OCW10X
OT432N	JDT432N, 4647MAN	YJY316	A13EXC, N224THO

Web: www.blackburntransport.co.uk; Depot also at Burton Road, Blackpool.

BLACKPOOL

Blackpool Buses - Blackpool & Fleetwood Tramway - Metro

Blackpool Transport Services Ltd, Rigby Road, Blackpool, FY1 5DD

101-133 DAF SB220LC550 Optare Delta BC46F* 1990-93 *131-3 are BC48F

101	G101NBV	108	G108NBV	115	H115YHG	122	H122CHG	128	K128UFV
102	G102NBV	109	H109YHG	116	H116YHG	123	J123GRN	129	K129UFV
103	G103NBV	110	H110YHG	117	H117YHG	124	J124GRN	130	K130UFV
104	G104NBV	112	H112YHG	118	H118CHG	125	J125GRN	131	H1FBT
105	G105NBV	113	H113YHG	119	H119CHG	126	J126GRN	132	H2FBT
106	G106NBV	114	H114YHG	120	H120CHG	127	K127UFV	133	H3FBT
107	G107NBV						

210-218 Optare Excel L1070 Optare N40F 1999

210	T210HCW	212	T212HCW	214	T214HCW	216	T216HCW	218	T218HCW
211	T211HCW	213	T213HCW	215	T215HCW	217	T217HCW		

261-276 Optare Solo M850 Optare N28F 1999

261	V261HEC	264	V264HEC	267	V267HEC	271	V271HEC	274	V274HEC
262	V262HEC	265	V265HEC	268	V268HEC	272	V272HEC	275	V275HEC
263	V263HEC	266	V266HEC	269	V269HEC	273	V273HEC	276	V276HEC

301-309 Dennis Trident East Lancashire Lolyne N51/31F 2002

301	PJ02PYD	303	PJ02PYG	305	PJ02PYL	307	PJ02PYP	309	PJ02PYT
302	PJ02PYF	304	PJ02PYH	306	PJ02PYO	308	PJ02PYS		

324-340 Leyland Atlantean AN68A/2R East Lancashire B50/36F 1979-80

324	URN324V	328	URN328V	331	AHG331V	334	AHG334V	338	AHG338V
325	URN325V	329	URN329V	332	AHG332V	336	AHG336V	339	AHG339V
326	URN326V	330	URN330V	333	AHG333V	337	AHG337V	340	AHG340V
327	URN327V						

341-350 Leyland Atlantean AN68C/2R East Lancashire B50/36F 1981

341	GHG341W	344	GHG344W	346	GHG346W	348	GHG348W	350	GHG350W
343	GHG343W	345	GHG345W	347	GHG347W	349	GHG349W		

351-364 Leyland Atlantean AN68D/2R East Lancashire B49/36F* 1982-84 *363/4 are BC45/29F

351	UHG351Y	354	UHG354Y	357	A357HHG	360	A360HHG	363	B363UBV
352	UHG352Y	355	A355HHG	358	A358HHG	361	A361HHG	364	B364UBV
353	UHG353Y	356	A356HHG	359	A359HHG	362	A362HHG		

365	UWW5X	Leyland Olympian ONLXB/1R	Roe	B47/29F	1982	West Yorkshire PTE, 1986
366	UWW11X	Leyland Olympian ONLXB/1R	Roe	B47/29F	1982	West Yorkshire PTE, 1986
367	UWW15X	Leyland Olympian ONLXB/1R	Roe	B47/29F	1982	West Yorkshire PTE, 1986

368-373 Leyland Olympian ONCL10/1RZ East Lancashire B45/31F 1989

368	F368AFR	370	F370AFR	371	F371AFR	372	F372AFR	373	F373AFR
369	F369AFR						

374-379 Volvo Olympian YN2RC16Z4 Northern Counties Palatine 2 B43/29F 1994

374	M374SCK	376	M376SCK	377	M377SCK	378	M378SCK	379	M379SCK
375	M375SCK						

401-410 Leyland Olympian ONLXB/1R Eastern Coach Works B43/32F* 1983-84 Trent, 1996 *407-10 are B45/30F

401	XAU701Y	403	XAU703Y	405	XAU705Y	407	A707DAU	409	A709DAU
402	XAU702Y	404	XAU704Y	406	XAU706Y	408	A708DAU	410	A710DAU

During the last two years more buses have received colours for particular routes and adopted *Metro* branding. The new livery is shown here on Optare MetroRider 594, N594LFV, seen in Lancaster at the northern end of Lancashire County service 88. This route is expected to be shortened to Knott End following the resumption of the Fleetwood - Knott End ferry. *Stuart Martin*

441	HIL5341	Leyland Atlantean AN68C/2R	Northern Counties	BC43/33F	1981	
442	HIL5342	Leyland Atlantean AN68C/2R	Northern Counties	BC43/33F	1982	
443	HIL5943	Leyland Atlantean AN68D/2RF	Northern Counties Palatine (1992)	BC43/33F	1983	
444	NJI5504	Leyland Atlantean AN68D/2R	Northern Counties	BC43/33F	1983	
445	NJI5505	Leyland Atlantean AN68D/2R	Northern Counties	BC43/33F	1984	
469w	SRJ757R	Leyland Atlantean AN68A/1R	Northern Counties	B43/32F	1977	GM Buses, 1989
471	OJI4371	Leyland Atlantean AN68A/1R	Northern Counties (1990)	B43/31F	1977	
472	OJI4372	Leyland Atlantean AN68M/1RF	Northern Counties (1990)	B43/31F	1977	
473	OJI4373	Leyland Atlantean AN68A/1R	Northern Counties (1990)	B43/31F	1977	
474	OJI4374	Leyland Atlantean AN68A/1R	Northern Counties (1990)	B43/31F	1977	
475	SIB8405	Leyland Atlantean AN68M/1RF	Northern Counties (1990)	B43 /31F	1976	
480w	HRN100N	Leyland Atlantean AN68/1R	NCME/Willowbrook	B43/31F	1975	
483w	HRN103N	Leyland Atlantean AN68/1R	NCME/Willowbrook	B43/31F	1975	
495	RHG95T	Leyland Atlantean AN68A/1R	Northern Counties	B43/31F	1979	

501-518   Optare MetroRider MR37   Optare   B25F   1996-98

501	P501UFR	505	S505LHG	509	S509LHG	513	S513LHG	516	S516LHG
502	P502UFR	506	S506LHG	510	S510LHG	514	S514LHG	517	S517LHG
503	P503UFR	507	S507LHG	511	S511LHG	515	S515LHG	518	S518LHG
504	P504UFR	508	S508LHG	512	S512LHG				

584	M924TYG	Optare MetroRider MR37	Optare	B25F	1995	Optare demonstrator, 1995

585-596   Optare MetroRider MR37   Optare   B25F   1995-96

585	N585GRN	588	N588GRN	591	N591GRN	593	N593LFV	595	N595LFV
586	N586GRN	589	N589GRN	592	N592GRN	594	N594LFV	596	N596LFV
587	N587GRN	590	N590GRN						

One of the early recipients of Metro yellow and grey was Optare Delta 132, H2FBT, which was new to Lytham St Annes before the fleets were amalgamated. New services under the *Metro Coastlines* name have been introduced with route branding being applied to most buses. *Dave Heath*

Special event vehicle:

934	BTB928	Leyland Lion LT7	Leyland	B34F	1936

Ancillary vehicles:

922	URN322V	Leyland Atlantean AN68A/2R	East Lancashire	TV	1979
923	URN323V	Leyland Atlantean AN68A/2R	East Lancashire	TV	1979

Trams:

8		BET M4d	Blackpool Corporation (1974)	ST48D	1935
147		Preston McGuire	Hurst Nelson	ST46/32D	1924	Vintage car

600-607
English Electric M4d — English Electric — OST56C* 1934-35 — *602 is OST52C

600	602	604	605	607

619		English Electric M4d	Bolton Group (1987)	toastrack 58-seat	1973

621-637
EMB M4d — Brush — ST48C* 1937 — *626 is ST46C, 633 is a Trawler

621	623	626	630	631	632	633	634	636	637
622	625	627							

641-647
Primrose/Brush M4d — East Lancashire — ST52D 1984-88 — 641/2/6 is ST53D

641	642	643	644	645	646	647

648		Maley & Taunton/Brush M4d	East Lancashire	ST52D	1985
660		Maley & Taunton M4d	Roberts	ST56C	1953

671-677
English Electric, 1935 M4s — English Electric (refurb 1958-62) — ST53C 1935

671	672	673	674	675	676	677

The future of the tram line and possible extension to cover the Fylde is under consideration. Meanwhile the stalwarts continue to ply between Fleetwood and Starr Gate, with street operation between Ash Street and the Ferry in Fleetwood. Now carrying the livery applied after the war is number 700. Over the years many combinations of green and cream have been used. *David Longstaff*

678		English Electric, 1935 M4d		English Electric		ST48C	1961			
679		English Electric, 1935 M4d		English Electric		ST48C	1961			
680		English Electric, 1935 M4d		English Electric		ST48C	1960			

681-687		Maley & Taunton M4d		MCW		ST61C	1960			
681	682	683	684	685	686	687				

700-726		English Electric M4d		English Electric		DT54/40C*	1934-35	*706 is ODT54/40C, seating varies		
700	703	707	710	713	716	718	720	722	724	
701	704	708	711	715	717	719	721	723	726	
702	706	709	712							

732w		Dick Kerr M4s		Blackpool Corporation		48-seat	1960	*Moon Rocket*
733w		English Electric M4d		Blackpool Corporation		35-seat	1962	*Wild West Loco*
734w		Dick Kerr B4s		Blackpool Corporation		60-seat	1962	*Wild West coach*
735		English Electric M4d		Blackpool Corporation		57/42	1963	*Hovercraft*
736		Dick Kerr M4d		Blackpool Corporation		71-seat	1965	*Frigate*
761		English Electric (1934) M4d		Blackpool/East Lancs		DT56/44F	1979	
762		English Electric (1934) M4d		Blackpool/East Lancs		DT56/34D	1982	

Previous Registrations:

IL5341	HBV97W	OJI4371	EBV85S
IL5342	PCW98X	OJI4372	EBV86S
IL5943	ACK99Y	OJI4373	EBV87S
JI5504	A74LHG	OJI4374	EBV88S
JI5505	B75URN	SIB8405	OCK84P

BLUE BUS

Blue Bus & Coach Services Ltd; Blue Bus (Lancashire) Ltd, Unit 4a Horwich Business Park,
Chorley New Road, Horwich, Bolton, BL6 5UE

0	X13LUE	Dennis Dart SLF	Plaxton Pointer MPD	N29F	2000	
1	K1BLU	Dennis Dart 9.8SDL3017	East Lancashire EL2000	B40F	1993	
2	M2BLU	Dennis Dart 9.8SDL3043	East Lancashire EL2000	B40F	1994	
4	N4BLU	Dennis Dart 9.8SDL3054	Alexander Dash	B40F	1995	
6	R6BLU	Dennis Dart SLF	Plaxton Pointer 2	N36F	1998	
7	R7BLU	Dennis Dart SLF	Plaxton Pointer 2	N36F	1998	
8	R8BLU	Dennis Dart SLF	Plaxton Pointer 2	N36F	1998	
9	S9BLU	Dennis Dart SLF	Plaxton Pointer 2	N36F	1998	
10	T10BLU	Dennis Dart SLF	Plaxton Pointer MPD	N28F	1999	
11	T11BLU	Dennis Dart SLF	Plaxton Pointer MPD	N28F	1999	
12	W12LUE	Dennis Dart SLF	Plaxton Pointer MPD	N29F	2000	
14	X14LUE	Dennis Dart SLF	Plaxton Pointer MPD	N29F	2000	
15	MF51TVV	Dennis Dart SLF	Plaxton Pointer MPD	N29F	2002	
16	MF51TVW	Dennis Dart SLF	Plaxton Pointer MPD	N29F	2002	
17	MF51TVX	Dennis Dart SLF	Plaxton Pointer MPD	N29F	2002	
18	MF51TVY	Dennis Dart SLF	Plaxton Pointer MPD	N29F	2002	
19	MV02XYH	Dennis Dart SLF	Plaxton Pointer MPD	N29F	2002	
20	Y20BLU	DAF DE12CSSB120	Wrightbus Cadet	N36F	2001	
21	Y21BLU	DAF DE12CSSB120	Wrightbus Cadet	N36F	2001	
22	V22BLU	Volvo B10BLE	Wright Renown	N42F	1999	
23	X23BLU	DAF DE12CSSB120	Wrightbus Cadet	N36F	2000	
27	T222MTB	MAN 18.220 HOCL - R	Alexander ALX300	N42F	1999	MAN demonstrator, 2000
28	V928FMS	Dennis Dart SLF	Alexander ALX200	N40F	1999	Alexander demonstrator, 2000
29	T674TSG	Dennis Dart SLF	Alexander ALX200	N26D	1999	Connex, 2002
33	V33BLU	DAF DE02GSSB220	East Lancashire Myllennium	N42F	1999	
34	V34ENC	DAF DE02GSSB220	Ikarus Citibus 481	N42F	1999	
35	V35ENC	DAF DE02GSSB220	Ikarus Citibus 481	N42F	1999	
36	Y36KNB	DAF DE02GSSB220	Ikarus Polaris	N42F	2001	
37	Y37KNB	DAF DE02GSSB220	Ikarus Polaris	N42F	2001	
38	Y38KNB	DAF DE02GSSB220	Ikarus Polaris	N42F	2001	
39	R33GNW	DAF DE02GSSB220	Plaxton Prestige	N42F	1998	Arriva Bus and Coach, 2002
41	V41DJA	Volvo Olympian	East Lancashire Pyoneer	B47/30F	1999	
42	T42PVM	Volvo Olympian	East Lancashire Pyoneer	B47/30F	1999	
43	S43BLU	Volvo Olympian	East Lancashire Pyoneer	B47/30F	1998	
44	R44BLU	Volvo Olympian	East Lancashire Pyoneer	BC45/30F	1998	
45	S45BLU	Volvo Olympian	East Lancashire Pyoneer	B47/30F	1998	

Two DAF SB120s
with Wrightbus
Cadet bodywork
joined the fleet in
2000 following the
arrival of a similar
bus the previous
year. Lettered for
route 111 between
Preston and Wigan,
21, Y21BLU, is seen
arriving in Preston in
April 2002.
Bob Downham

An unusual body style currently operating in England is the Ikarus Polaris. Supplied on the DAF SB220, three operate for Blue Bus. Many of the low-floor buses carry *Blue Buggy Bus* titles on their front panels. Wigan is the location for this view of 36, Y36KNB. *David Longbottom*

46	Y46ABA	Dennis Trident	Plaxton President	N47/28F	2001	
47	Y47ABA	Dennis Trident	Plaxton President	N47/28F	2001	
48	Y48ABA	Dennis Trident	Plaxton President	N47/28F	2001	
51	LDZ2951	Leyland Leopard PSU3E/4R [D]	East Lancashire EL2000 ('92)	B51F	1980	Trent, 1992
52	HIL9152	Leyland Leopard PSU3F/4R [D]	East Lancashire EL2000 ('92)	B51F	1982	Trent, 1992
53	WIB4053	Leyland Leopard PSU3F/4R [D]	East Lancashire EL2000 ('94)	B51F	1982	National Welsh, 1993
54	WIB4054	Leyland Leopard PSU3F/4R [D]	East Lancashire EL2000 ('95)	B51F	1982	United, 1995
60	F816OVU	Leyland Tiger TRCTL11/2RP	Duple Dominant	B53F	1988	Stagecoach Red & White, 1999
61	RJI2161	Volvo B58-56	East Lancashire EL2000 ('95)	BC49F	1980	Pride of the Road, 1994
62	F902JBB	Leyland Tiger TRBTL11/2RP	Duple 300	B55F	1989	Go-Gateshead, 1999
63	H163DJU	Dennis Javelin 11SDA1914	Duple 300	B55F	1991	Go-Gateshead, 1999
70	CSF160W	Leyland Leopard PSU3G/4R	Alexander AYS	B53F	1981	Fife Scottish, 1998
71	LBZ4071	Leyland Tiger TRCTL11/2R(V)	East Lancashire EL2000 ('94)	B51F	1982	Burman, Dordon, 1994
72	WJI9072	Leyland Tiger TRBTL11/2R	East Lancashire EL2000 ('98)	B51F	1983	Fife Scottish, 1998
74	WJI9074	Leyland Tiger TRBTL11/2R	East Lancashire EL2000 ('98)	B51F	1983	Red & White (Parfitts), 1997
1	V951KAG	Mercedes-Benz Vario O814	Plaxton Beaver 2	B27F	2000	Plaxton demonstrator, 2001
2	MV02XYJ	Mercedes-Benz Vario O814	Plaxton Beaver 2	B27F	2002	
3	MV02XYK	Mercedes-Benz Vario O814	Plaxton Beaver 2	B27F	2002	
4	N94BNF	Mercedes-Benz 709D	Plaxton Beaver	B25F	1996	
5	N95BNF	Mercedes-Benz 709D	Plaxton Beaver	B25F	1996	
6	L654MYG	Mercedes-Benz 711D	Plaxton Beaver	B27F	1996	Gibson, Renfrew, 2002
101	F701ENE	Leyland Tiger TRCL10/3ARZA	Plaxton Paramount 3200 III	C53F	1989	Shearings, 1992
200	N200BLU	DAF DE33WSSB3000	Van Hool Alizée HE	C53F	1996	
300	R300BLU	DAF DE33WSSB3000	Plaxton Première 320	C53F	1998	

Previous registrations:

816OVU	F311RMH, A17RBL		RJI2161	PYD984V
HIL9152	SCH150X		WIB4053	KWO563X
			WIB4054	LPY460W
LBZ4071	ESU157X, 403EXH, RDV903, HGD802X		WJI9072	MNS6Y
LDZ2951	KVO143W		WJI9074	EWR657Y

BLUEBIRD

MTG, TA & M Dunstan, Alexander House, Greengate, Middleton, Rochdale, M24 1RU

1	R1BLU	Dennis Dart SLF	Wright Crusader	N32F	1997	
2	T2BLU	Dennis Dart SLF	Wright Crusader	N39F	1999	
3	V3BLU	Scania N113DRB	East Lancashire Citizen	BC45/33F	1999	
4	V4BLU	Scania N113DRB	East Lancashire Cityzen	BC45/31F	1999	
5	W5BLU	Dennis Dart SLF	East Lancashire Spryte	N37F	2000	
6	W6BLU	Dennis Dart SLF	East Lancashire Spryte	N37F	2000	
7	X7BLU	Dennis Dart SLF	East Lancashire Spryte	N37F	2000	
8	Y8BLU	Dennis Dart SLF	East Lancashire Spryte	N37F	2001	
9	MD02BLU	Dennis Dart SLF	East Lancashire Spryte	N37F	2002	
10	M10BLU	Iveco TurboDaily 59.12	Marshall C31	B19F	1995	
11	S11BLU	Mercedes-Benz Vario O814	Plaxton Beaver 2	B31F	1998	Universal, Chadderton, 2000
12	MC02BLU	Dennis Dart SLF	Transbus Pointer MPD	N29F	2002	
13	P13BLU	Dennis Dart SLF	East Lancashire Spryte	N44F	1996	Dunn-Line, Nottingham, 2000
14	P14BLU	Dennis Dart SLF	East Lancashire Spryte	N44F	1996	Dunn-Line, Nottingham, 2000
15	R15BLU	Iveco TurboDaily 59.12	Marshall C31	B26F	1998	
16	R16BLU	Iveco TurboDaily 59.12	Marshall C31	B26F	1998	
17	N17BLU	Iveco TurboDaily 59.12	UVG Citistar	B27F	1995	
18	R18BLU	Mercedes-Benz Vario O810	UVG Citistar	B27F	1998	
19	R19BLU	Mercedes-Benz Vario O810	UVG Citistar	B27F	1998	
20	P20BLU	Dennis Dart SLF	Wright Crusader	N32F	1997	
23	G813RNC	Leyland Tiger TR2R62C21Z5	Plaxton Paramount 3200 III	C53F	1990	Blackpool, 1999
24	L4BLU	Iveco TurboDaily 59.12	Marshall C31	B27F	1994	
27	N7BLU	Iveco TurboDaily 59.12	UVG Citistar	B27F	1995	
28	M8BLU	Iveco TurboDaily 59.12	Marshall C31	B19F	1995	
30	P30BLU	Dennis Dart SLF	Wright Crusader	N32F	1997	
40	P40BLU	Dennis Dart SLF	Wright Crusader	N32F	1997	
50	P50BLU	Dennis Dart SLF	Wright Crusader	N32F	1997	

Bluebird have recently added a further East Lancashire-bodied Dart to their fleet based in Middleton. Numbered 9, MD02BLU is seen in the local bus station shortly after entering service. *Bill Potter*

Just three double-deck buses carry Bluebird colours, all interesting buses in themselves. Number 77 is the only Iveco double-deck bus in the country arriving from north Devon where it plied between Ilfracombe and Barnstaple. Seen in Manchester's Piccadilly, V3BLU is one of thirty Scania N113s fitted with East Lancashire Cityzen bodywork built in 1999 for the chassis dealer's stock. These were the last non-low-floor double-deck buses from Scania. All of the type are fitted with high-back seating as shown here. *Richard Godfrey*

52	S2BLU	Mercedes-Benz Vario O814	Plaxton Beaver 2	B27F	1998	
53	S3BLU	Mercedes-Benz Vario O814	Plaxton Beaver 2	B27F	1998	
54	S4BLU	Mercedes-Benz Vario O814	Plaxton Beaver 2	B27F	1998	
55	S5BLU	Dennis Dart SLF	Wright Crusader	N39F	1999	
56	S6BLU	Dennis Dart SLF	Wright Crusader	N39F	1999	
59	MAZ4969	Leyland Leopard PSU4E/4R	East Lancashire EL2000 (1996)	B45F	1980	Burnley & Pendle, 1993
70	MAZ4970	Leyland Leopard PSU4E/4R	East Lancashire EL2000 (1996)	B45F	1980	Burnley & Pendle, 1993
71	E107DJR	Volvo B10M61	Duple 300	B55F	1987	Go-Ahead Northern, 2000
80	TIL1180	Volvo B10M-55	Plaxton Derwent II	B54F	1993	Tillingbourne, Cranleigh, 2001
82	TIL1182	Volvo B10M-55	Plaxton Derwent II	B54F	1993	Tillingbourne, Cranleigh, 2001
77	J227OKX	Iveco EuroRider 480.12.21	Alexander RH	B50/31F	1991	Filer, Ilfracombe, 2001

Special event vehicle

| | TXJ540K | Leyland Leopard PSU3B/4R | Duple Viceroy | C49F | 1972 | Catholic CRS, East Didsbury, 1998 |

Ancillary vehicles

| B1 | HCS807N | Leyland Leopard PSU3/3R | Alexander AYS | TV | 1975 | Plymouth Citybus, 1998 |
| B2 | OSJ610R | Leyland Leopard PSU3C/4R | Alexander AY | TV | 1976 | Plymouth Citybus, 1998 |

Previous registrations:

AZ4969	YHG15V		P14BLU	P352EAU
AZ4970	YHG16V, LBU607V		S11BLU	S925SVM
			TIL1180	F280HOD
V3BLU	P351EAU		TIL1182	F282HOD

Web: www.bluebirdbus.co.uk

BROWNRIGGS

S H Brownrigg Ltd, 53 Main Street, Egremont, CA22 2DB

SIW2805	Volvo B58-61	Plaxton Supreme IV	C55F	1979	Stephenson, Maryport, 1998
RIW9059	Volvo B10M-61	Plaxton Supreme VI	C53F	1982	Stephenson, Maryport, 1998
CYJ492Y	Leyland Tiger TRCTL11/3R	Plaxton Paramount 3200	C50F	1983	Stagecoach South, 1994
TIL3971	Leyland Tiger TRCTL11/3R	Plaxton Paramount 3200	C50F	1983	Stagecoach South, 1994
A227MDD	Leyland Tiger TRCTL11/3R	Plaxton Paramount 3200	C51F	1984	Cheltenham & Gloucester, 1994
A70KDU	Leyland Tiger TRCTL11/3R	Plaxton Paramount 3200 E	C53F	1984	Stagecoach South Midlands, 2001
C110OHH	Leyland Tiger TRCTL11/3RH	Plaxton Paramount 3500 II	C48FT	1986	
C472CAP	Leyland Tiger TRCTL11/3RH	Plaxton Paramount 3200 II	C51F	1986	Stagecoach South Midlands, 2001
E755VJO	MCW MetroRider MF150/26	MCW	B25F	1987	City of Oxford, 1998
E46HFE	MCW MetroRider MF150/94	MCW	B23F	1988	East Midland, 1996
E57HFE	MCW MetroRider MF150/94	MCW	BC23F	1988	East Midland, 1998
ESU913	Scania K92CRB	Van Hool Alizée H	C53F	1988	Stagecoach Manchester, 1998
ESU920	Scania K92CRB	Van Hool Alizée H	C53F	1988	Stagecoach Manchester, 1998
TAZ5004	Scania K113CRB	Plaxton Paramount 3500 III	C48FT	1988	Stagecoach Manchester, 1998
RAZ7353	Scania K113CRB	Plaxton Paramount 3500 III	C49FT	1988	Stagecoach Manchester, 1998
NIL8663	Volvo B10M-61	Plaxton Paramount 3500 III	C49FT	1988	Moxon, Oldcoats, 1997
F767FDV	Mercedes-Benz 709D	Reeve Burgess Beaver	B25F	1989	Stagecoach Oxford, 1999
F769FDV	Mercedes-Benz 709D	Reeve Burgess Beaver	B25F	1989	Stagecoach Oxford, 1999
F770FDV	Mercedes-Benz 709D	Reeve Burgess Beaver	B25F	1989	Stagecoach Oxford, 1999

Brownriggs minibus fleet includes N976LWR, a Mercedes-Benz 814 with Mellor Solo bodywork. The bus had just returned to Egremont from undertaking a school duty when pictured. *Bill Potter*

Pictured in Middleton-in-Teesdale with the local Dearham Band is NIL6108 in the Brownriggs fleet. The model features a rear trailing axle, thus the 'T' in this model's code. Volvo use the 'T' in the B7, however, to indicates a transverse engine. *J C Walton*

NIL6108	Volvo B10MT	Van Hool Alizée H	C49FT	1989	Dover, Hetton-le-Hole, 1997
RIL1744	Volvo B10M-60	Plaxton Paramount 3500 III	C48FT	1991	Stagecoach Cambus, 1999
PIL7395	Volvo B10M-60	Plaxton Paramount 3500 III	C48FT	1991	Stagecoach Cambus, 1999
YAZ6510	Volvo B10M-60	Plaxton Paramount 3500 III	C48FT	1991	Stagecoach Cambus, 1999
WDA1T	Volvo B10M-60	Plaxton Excalibur	C44FT	1992	Stagecoach Red & White, 2000
K339ADB	Mercedes-Benz 711D	Plaxton Beaver	BC25F	1993	Coussens & Castleton, 2001
L225LRM	Ford Transit VE6	Ford	M8	1994	
L547KRE	Ford Transit VE6	Ford	M8	1994	United Rentals, 1998
L506MAO	Ford Transit VE6	Ford	M8	1994	United Rentals, 1998
L510MAO	Ford Transit VE6	Ford	M8	1994	United Rentals, 1998
M204VWF	Mercedes-Benz 814D	Plaxton Beaver	BC33F	1994	Armstrong, Inverkeithing, 1997
N744VRM	LDV 400	LDV	M16	1995	Lakeland SD, Egremont, 1999
N976LWR	Mercedes-Benz 814D	Mellor Solo	BC33F	1996	Cropper, Kirkstall, 1998
N30SHB	Volvo B10M-62	Plaxton Excalibur	C53F	1996	Logan, Dunlyne, 2002
N109HRH	Ford Transit VE6	Advanced Vehicle Bodies	M11	1996	TLS Rentals, 1999

'revious registrations:

,70KDU	A70KDU, BIW4977		
,227MDD	A71KDU, 552OHU, A873MRW, YJV806	PIL7395	H652UWR
110OHH	C110OHH, WLT824	RAZ7353	F948NER
472CAP	YDK917, JPU817, C472CAP, 6253VC	RIL1744	H649UWR
YJ492Y	XUF531Y, 401DCD	RIW9059	CJV943X, BAZ4772, NSC754X
SU913	F951NER	SIW2805	GGD662T, ESU933, KGE46T
SU920	F950NER	TAZ5004	F947NER
30SHB	N96BHL	TIL3971	?
,L6108	G200XAC, GIL4271	WDA1T	J424HDS, KSU464, J424HDS
L8663	E588VTH, GIL4271, E850AHL	YAZ6510	H653UWR

BU-VAL

M Bull, 5 Paragon Industrial Estate, Smithybridge, Littleborough, OL15 8QF

T22	YNC22X	Bedford YNT	Plaxton Supreme IV	C57F	1982	Whitehead, Smithybridge, 2001
449	G449LKW	Iveco Daily 49.10	Reeve Burgess Beaver	B25F	1989	Citibus, Middleton, 1996
275	G275MWU	Iveco Daily 49.10	Reeve Burgess Beaver	B25F	1990	Citibus, Middleton, 1996
276	G276MWU	Iveco Daily 49.10	Reeve Burgess Beaver	B25F	1990	Citibus, Middleton, 1996
918	H918XUA	Iveco Daily 49.10	Reeve Burgess Beaver	B25F	1990	Citibus, Middleton, 1996
228	J228OKX	Iveco TurboDaily 59.12	Marshall C31	B29F	1992	Iveco demonstrator, 2001
529	K529EFL	Iveco Daily 49.10	Marshall C29	B23F	1993	Stagecoach Midland Red, 1999
803	L803FBA	Iveco TurboDaily 59.12	Mellor	B27F	1994	
804	L804FBA	Iveco TurboDaily 59.12	Mellor	B27F	1994	Crichton, Low Fell, 2001
367	M367CUF	Iveco TurboDaily 59.12	Mellor	B29F	1995	
905	M5BLU	Iveco TurboDaily 59.12	Marshall C31	B19F	1995	Bluebird, Middleton, 2001
906	M6BLU	Iveco TurboDaily 59.12	Marshall C31	B19F	1995	Bluebird, Middleton, 2001
909	M9BLU	Iveco TurboDaily 59.12	Marshall C31	B19F	1995	Bluebird, Middleton, 2001
912	M12BLU	Iveco TurboDaily 59.12	Marshall C31	B19F	1995	Bluebird, Middleton, 2000
913	N13BLU	Iveco TurboDaily 59.12	Mellor	B27F	1995	Bluebird, Middleton, 2000
914	N14BLU	Iveco TurboDaily 59.12	Mellor	B27F	1995	Bluebird, Middleton, 2000
219	R219AOR	Iveco TurboDaily 59.12	Marshall C31	B27F	1997	Jacobs, Horton Heath, 2001
801	R801WJA	Iveco TurboDaily 59.12	Mellor Solo	B27F	1997	
805	R805WJA	Iveco TurboDaily 59.12	Mellor Solo	B27F	1997	
807	R807WJA	Iveco TurboDaily 59.12	Mellor Solo	B27F	1997	Universal, Chadderton, 2000
946	R946AMB	Mercedes-Benz Vario O814	Plaxton Beaver 2	B31F	1997	Mitchell, Plean, 2001
933	S933SVM	Iveco TurboDaily 59.12	Mellor Solo	B27F	1997	
934	S934SVM	Iveco TurboDaily 59.12	Mellor Solo	B27F	1997	
309	S309DLG	Mercedes-Benz Vario O814	Plaxton Beaver 2	B31F	1997	Connex, 2001

Previous registrations:

H918XUA	H281SWW, H12SDW	YNC22X	479DKH

Bu-Val is a minibus operator whose main area of operation is Rochdale, a town that has seen many operators arrive after the Greater Manchester depot closed. The Bu-val fleet comprises mostly Iveco products, and its S933SVM was bodied in the town by Mellor Coachcraft. *Mark Doggett.*

R BULLOCK

R Bullock & Co (Transport) Ltd, Commercial Garage, Stockport Road, Cheadle, SK8 2AG

	Reg	Chassis	Body	Code	Year	Notes
w	JIL8204	Leyland Leopard PSU5/4R	Plaxton Panorama Elite III	C57F	1975	
	NDE916R	Bristol LH6L	Eastern Coach Works	B45F	1977	Vickers, Worksop, 1999
w	JIL8205	AEC Reliance 6U2R	Duple Dominant II Express	C53F	1979	Bibby, Ingleton, 1994
	BYW379V	Leyland National 10351A/2R (Volvo)		B44F	1979	Arriva North West, 1999
w	BUI1675	Leyland Leopard PSU3F/4R	East Lancashire (1993)	B51F	1981	Go-Ahead Northern, 1990
	A280ROW	Leyland Olympian ONLXB/1R	East Lancashire	B45/31F	1983	Stephenson, Rochford, 1998
w	BUI1610	Dennis Dorchester SDA805	Plaxton Paramount 3200	C57F	1984	
	BUI1133	Dennis Dorchester SDA805	Plaxton Paramount 3200	C57F	1985	
	BUI1484	Leyland Tiger TRCLXCT/3RZ	Plaxton P'mount 3500 III (1993)	C51FT	1986	
	C281BBP	Dennis Dominator DDA1008	East Lancashire	B45/31F	1986	Southampton Citybus, 1991
	C285BBP	Leyland Olympian ONLXB/1R	East Lancashire	BC43/27F	1986	Southampton Citybus, 1992
	BUI1424	Scania N112DRB	Van Hool Alizée L	BC49F	1987	Speedlink, 1996
	E758OWY	Mercedes-Benz 709D	Made-to-Measure	BC20F	1988	
	E928KYR	Leyland Olympian ONLXB/1RH	Northern Counties	B43/30F	1988	Arriva North West, 2001
	F439AKB	Leyland Olympian ONCL10/2RZ	Northern Counties	B47/34F	1988	Arriva North West, 2001
w	F452FDB	Leyland Tiger TRBTL11/2RP	Duple 300	B55F	1989	
	F682SRN	Leyland Tiger TRCL10/3RZA	Plaxton Paramount 3500 III	C51FT	1989	D Coaches, Morriston, 1994
	F231YTJ	Leyland Olympian ONCL10/1RZ	Alexander RL	B45/30F	1989	Arriva North West, 2001
	F232YTJ	Leyland Olympian ONCL10/1RZ	Alexander RL	B45/30F	1989	Arriva North West, 2001
	F233YTJ	Leyland Olympian ONCL10/1RZ	Alexander RL	B45/30F	1989	Arriva North West, 2001
	F235YTJ	Leyland Olympian ONCL10/1RZ	Alexander RL	B45/30F	1989	Arriva North West, 2001
	F236YTJ	Leyland Olympian ONCL10/1RZ	Alexander RL	B45/30F	1989	Arriva North West, 2001
	F237YTJ	Leyland Olympian ONCL10/1RZ	Alexander RL	B45/30F	1989	Arriva North West, 2001
	F238YTJ	Leyland Olympian ONCL10/1RZ	Alexander RL	B45/30F	1989	Arriva North West, 2001
	F239YTJ	Leyland Olympian ONCL10/1RZ	Alexander RL	B45/30F	1989	Arriva North West, 2001
	F240YTJ	Leyland Olympian ONCL10/1RZ	Alexander RL	B45/30F	1989	Arriva North West, 2001
	G423SNF	Leyland Tiger TRBTL11/2RP	Duple 300	B55F	1990	
	G918DVX	Ford Transit 190	Dormobile	B16F	1990	Marton Community Bus, 1998

The year 2000 saw considerable investment in new double-decks for R Bullock, sourcing a mix of low-floor Dennis Tridents and standard Scania buses. Seen waiting time in Piccadilly is X939NBU which features East Lancashire Lolyne bodywork. *Richard Godfrey*

J200BUL	Leyland Tiger TRCL10/3ARZA	Plaxton Paramount 3200 III	C57F	1991
L10BUL	Leyland Olympian ON2R50C13Z4	East Lancashire	B45/31F	1993
L20BUL	Leyland Olympian ON2R50C13Z4	East Lancashire	B45/31F	1993
L800BUL	Volvo B10M-60	Van Hool Alizée HE	C51FT	1994
L8SLT	Dennis Javelin	Berkhof Excellence 1000	C51F	1994
L42DBC	Toyota Coaster HZB50R	Caetano Optimo III	C18F	1994	Hertz, Heathrow, 1998
M786NBA	Dennis Javelin 12SDA2131	Berkhof Excellence 1000	C51FT	1995
M788NBA	Volvo Olympian YN2RV18Z4	East Lancashire	B45/30F	1995
M789NBA	Volvo Olympian YN2RV18Z4	East Lancashire	B45/30F	1995
M790NBA	Volvo Olympian YN2RC16Z5	East Lancashire	B45/31F	1994
N621XBU	Volvo B10M-62	Caetano Algarve II	C53F	1996
N634XBU	Scania L113CRL	Wright Axcess-ultralow	N42F	1996
P480HBA	Volvo B10M-62	Van Hool Alizée HE	C51FT	1996
P481HBA	Volvo B10M-62	Caetano Algarve II	C49FT	1997
P482HBA	Volvo B10M-62	Caetano Algarve II	C53F	1997
P483HBA	Volvo Olympian YN2RV18Z4	Northern Counties Palatine	B47/30F	1996
P484HBA	Volvo Olympian YN2RV18Z4	Northern Counties Palatine	B47/30F	1996
P485HBA	Volvo Olympian YN2RV18Z4	Northern Counties Palatine	B47/30F	1996
P486HBA	Volvo Olympian YN2RV18Z4	Northern Counties Palatine	B47/30F	1996
R290CVM	DAF DE02RSDB250	Optare Spectra	B50/27F	1998
R291CVM	DAF DE02RSDB250	Optare Spectra	B50/27F	1998
R292CVM	Volvo B10M-62	Caetano Algarve II	C53FT	1998
R293CVM	Volvo B10M-62	Caetano Algarve II	C53FT	1998
S957URJ	Volvo Olympian	Northern Counties Palatine 2	B47/30F	1999
S958URJ	Volvo Olympian	Northern Counties Palatine 2	B47/30F	1999
S959URJ	Volvo Olympian	Northern Counties Palatine 2	B47/30F	1999
S960URJ	Volvo Olympian	Northern Counties Palatine 2	B47/30F	1999
T68FBN	Volvo B10M-62	Caetano Enigma	C53F	1999
T69FBN	Volvo B10M-62	Caetano Enigma	C49FT	1999
W663PTD	Volvo B10M-62	Caetano Enigma	C53F	2000
W664PTD	Volvo B10M-62	Caetano Enigma	C53F	2000
W671PTD	Dennis Trident	East Lancashire Lolyne	N51/31F	2000
W672PTD	Dennis Trident	East Lancashire Lolyne	N51/31F	2000
W673PTD	Dennis Trident	East Lancashire Lolyne	N51/31F	2000
W674PTD	Dennis Trident	East Lancashire Lolyne	N51/31F	2000
W675PTD	Scania N113DRB	East Lancashire Cityzen	BC47/31F	2000
W676PTD	Scania N113DRB	East Lancashire Cityzen	BC47/31F	2000
W677PTD	Scania N113DRB	East Lancashire Cityzen	BC47/31F	2000
W678PTD	Scania N113DRB	East Lancashire Cityzen	BC47/31F	2000
X939NBU	Dennis Trident	East Lancashire Lolyne	N51/31F	2000
ML02RWF	Volvo B12M	Caetano Enigma	C53F	2002

Special Event Vehicle:

LMA284	Foden PVSC6	Lawson	C35F	1949	Stevens, Crewe, 1970
GFW476	Foden PVSC6	Plaxton	FC37F	1950	Fieldsend, Salford, 1956

Previous registrations:

BUI1133	B593SNC	BUI1675	FNL687W
BUI1424	E213FLD	JIL8204	HFM804M
BUI1484	C33EVM	JIL8205	YPL88T, BIB7667, SWH271T
BUI1610	A530OBU	JIL8209	SDA832S

Recent arrivals for the double-deck fleet are nine Olympians from Arriva North West, and part of that fleet expected to be sold along with the Speke depot but subsequently sold on the market. Now carrying R Bullock colours, F232YTJ is seen in Stockport.
Cliff Beeton

BURNLEY & PENDLE

Burnley & Pendle Travel Ltd, Prospect Park, Broughton Way, Starbeck, Harrogate, HG2 7NY

Part of the Blazefield Group

108	L659MYG	Mercedes-Benz 711D	Plaxton Beaver	B27F	1993	Harrogate & District, 2001

200-214		Volvo B6LE		Alexander ALX200		N36F	1997	Stagecoach Lancashire, 2001
200	P335JND	**203**	P338JND	**208**	P343JND	**209**	P344JND	**214** P349JND
202	P337JND	**205**	P340JND					

418	H418FGS	Mercedes-Benz 811D	Reeve Burgess Beaver	B31F	1990	Harrogate & District, 2000
426	K26WBV	Volvo B10M-50	East Lancashire EL2000	B45F	1993	Stagecoach Lancashire, 2001
427	K27WBV	Volvo B10M-50	East Lancashire EL2000	B45F	1993	Stagecoach Lancashire, 2001
442	M799PRS	Volvo B10M-55	Alexander PS	BC48F	1995	Stagecoach Lancashire, 2001
453	M453VCW	Volvo B10M-55	Alexander PS	BC48F	1995	Stagecoach Lancashire, 2001
664	M384VWX	Volvo B6-9.9M	Alexander Dash	B40F	1995	Harrogate & District, 2002
665	M385VWX	Volvo B6-9.9M	Alexander Dash	B40F	1995	Harrogate & District, 2002
681	J41GGB	Leyland Lynx LX2R11C15Z4S	Leyland Lynx 2	B51F	1991	Stagecoach Lancashire, 2001
682	J42GGB	Leyland Lynx LX2R11C15Z4S	Leyland Lynx 2	B51F	1991	Stagecoach Lancashire, 2001
683	F168SMT	Leyland Lynx LX112L10ZR1S	Leyland Lynx	B49F	1989	Stagecoach Lancashire, 2001
693	E63WDT	Leyland Lynx LX112TL11ZR1R	Leyland Lynx	B49F	1987	Stagecoach Lancashire, 2001
694	D109NDW	Leyland Lynx LX112TL11ZR1	Leyland Lynx	B48F	1987	Stagecoach Lancashire, 2001
697	E115SDW	Leyland Lynx LX112TL11ZR1	Leyland Lynx	B48F	1988	Stagecoach Lancashire, 2001

940-967		Dennis Javelin 11SDA2133		Plaxton Interurban		BC47F	1994	Stagecoach Lancashire, 2001
943	M943JBO	**947**	M947JBO	**948**	M948JBO	**966**	L149BFV	**967** L107SDY
944	M944JBO							

1042-1072		Volvo B10BLE		Wrightbus Renown		NC44F	2001-02	
1042	Y142HRN	**1048**	Y148HRN	**1054**	Y154HRN	**1062**	Y162HRN	**1067** Y167HRN
1043	Y143HRN	**1049**	Y149HRN	**1057**	Y157HRN	**1063**	Y163HRN	**1068** Y168HRN
1044	Y144HRN	**1051**	Y151HRN	**1058**	Y158HRN	**1064**	Y164HRN	**1069** Y169HRN
1046	Y146HRN	**1052**	Y152HRN	**1059**	Y159HRN	**1065**	Y165HRN	**1071** Y171HRN
1047	Y147HRN	**1053**	Y153HRN	**1061**	Y161HRN	**1066**	Y166HRN	**1072** Y172HRN

Blazefield placed several orders for buses once they had acquired four depots from Stagecoach. Clitheroe, Blackburn and Bolton were branded Lancashire United and the fleet will be found under that heading. The Burnley allocation reverted to the Burnley & Pendle name. Seen in Colne in March 2002 is 1052, Y152HRN, a Volvo B10BLE with Wrightbus bodywork. Wrightbus is the successor builder to Wright, the name changing at the of 2000. *Richard Godfrey*

A pair of Stagecoach-standard Volvo B10Ms with Alexander PS bodywork now operate at Burnley & Pendle, and both are fitted with high-back seating. Pictured while passing through Blackburn, 442, M799PRS was heading for Preston on trunk route 152. *Mark Doggett*

1301	E101JFV	Volvo Citybus B10M-50	Alexander RV	BC47/35F	1988	Stagecoach Lancashire, 2001
1302	E102JFV	Volvo Citybus B10M-50	Alexander RV	BC47/35F	1988	Stagecoach Lancashire, 2001
1313	H113ABV	Volvo Citybus B10M-50	Alexander RV	B47/37F	1991	Stagecoach Lancashire, 2001
1314	H114ABV	Volvo Citybus B10M-50	Alexander RV	BC47/35F	1991	Stagecoach Lancashire, 2001
1315	H115ABV	Volvo Citybus B10M-50	Alexander RV	BC47/35F	1991	Stagecoach Lancashire, 2001

2102	A584HDB	Leyland Olympian ONLXCT/1R	Northern Counties	B43/30F	1983	Stagecoach Lancashire, 2001

2105-2132

		Leyland Olympian ONLXB/1R	Eastern Coach Works	B45/32F	1981-83	Stagecoach Lancashire, 2001

2105	JFR5W	2110	JFR10W	2115	OFV15X	2122	OFV22X	2130	VRN830Y
2107	JFR7W	2111	JFR11W	2119	OFV19X	2123	OFV23X	2132	DBV132Y
2108	JFR8W	2113	JFR13W	2121	OFV21X				

2136	CWR526Y	Leyland Olympian ONLXB/1R	Eastern Coach Works	B45/32F	1983	Stagecoach Lancashire, 2001
2158	A158OFR	Leyland Olympian ONLXB/1R	Eastern Coach Works	BC41/26F	1984	Stagecoach Lancashire, 2001
2211	A975OST	Leyland Olympian ONLXB/1R	Alexander RL	B45/32F	1984	Stagecoach Lancashire, 2001

2701-2716

		Volvo B7TL	Plaxton President	NC43/28F	2001	

2701	Y701HRN	2704	Y704HRN	2707	Y707HRN	2711	Y711HRN	2714	Y714HRN
2702	Y702HRN	2705	Y705HRN	2708	Y708HRN	2712	Y712HRN	2715	Y715HRN
2703	Y703HRN	2706	Y706HRN	2709	Y709HRN	2713	Y713HRN	2716	Y716HRN

2943	H143GGS	Leyland Olympian ON2R50C13Z4	Northern Counties Palatine	B47/30F	1991	BTS, Borehamwood, 1994
2945	H145GGS	Leyland Olympian ON2R50C13Z4	Northern Counties Palatine	B47/30F	1991	BTS, Borehamwood, 1994

Special event vehicle:

2101	GFR101W	Leyland Olympian ONLXB/1R*	Eastern Coach Works	B45/32F	1981	Stagecoach Lancashire, 2001

Ancillary vehicles:

449	L449HTM	Mercedes-Benz 811D	Plaxton Beaver	TV	1993	Sovereign, 2001
945	M945JBO	Dennis Javelin 11SDL2133	Plaxton Interurban	TV	1993	Stagecoach Lancashire, 2001

Now in its third colour scheme - having been new to the municipally-owned Burnley & Pendle, then to Stagecoach - E101JFV now carries Blazefield's Burnley & Pendle colours. The bus is a Volvo B10M Citybus with Alexander bodywork, from a batch of fifteen that are now shared with Lancashire United who operate the bus-seated examples. The new Burnley & Pendle operate to Preston on route 152 and the vehicle was in Blackburn when pictured. *Bob Downham*

Fifteen Volvo B7TLs with Plaxton Pointer bodywork were early arrivals with the new Burnley & Pendle and these are used on the express services between the commuting districts of east Lancashire and Manchester. Pictured in Colne, 2708, Y708HRN illustrates the route branding applied for route X43. *Richard Godfrey*

BUZY BUZ

D Bailey, 5 Appleby Business Park, Appleby Street, Blackburn, BB1 3BL

C221HJN	Mercedes-Benz L608D	Reeve Burgess	B20F	1985	Phil Henderson, Penygraig, 2001
C419VVN	Mercedes-Benz L608D	Reeve Burgess	B21F	1986	Darwen Mini Coaches, 2001
D116NUS	Mercedes-Benz L608D	Alexander AM	B21F	1986	Orion, Wemmys Bay, 2001
D118NUS	Mercedes-Benz L608D	Alexander AM	B21F	1986	Orion, Wemmys Bay, 2001
E142ERA	Renault-Dodge S56	Northern Counties	B25F	1987	City of Nottingham, 1999
E514HHN	Renault-Dodge S56	Alexander AM	B25F	1987	Blenkinsop, West Cornforth, 1999
E426AFT	Mercedes-Benz 709D	Reeve Burgess Beaver	B20F	1988	Stagecoach North East, 2002
F119JTO	Renault-Dodge S56	Reeve Burgess	B25F	1988	City of Nottingham, 1999
G24CSG	Renault-Dodge S56	Reeve Burgess	B25F	1989	Compass, Worthing, 2000
G51BEL	Mercedes-Benz 811D	Wadham Stringer	B31F	1989	Brighton & Hove, 2001
G57BEL	Mercedes-Benz 811D	Wadham Stringer	B31F	1989	Brighton & Hove, 2001
H406BVR	Mercedes-Benz 709D	Carlyle	B27F	1990	Vale of Manchester, 2001
HDZ5436	Renault S75	Wright NimBus	B31F	1990	Orion, Wemmys Bay, 2001
HDZ5490	Renault S75	Wright NimBus	B31F	1990	Orion, Wemmys Bay, 2001
J753MFP	Renault-Dodge S56	Northern Counties	BC25F	1992	First Leicester, 2000
J754MFP	Renault-Dodge S56	Northern Counties	BC25F	1992	First Leicester, 2000
N255DUR	Mercedes-Benz 709D	Marshall C19	B27F	1996	Isle of Wight CC, 2001
P501HEG	Marshall Minibus	Marshall MM	N26F	1997	Marshalls,Cambridge, 2002

Buzy Buz is the new operating name for D Bailey who is well advanced on applying the new colour Interesting among the fleet is integral Marshall Minibus P501HEG, seen here running route 214 f Sunnybower. *Bob Downham*

COASTLINKS EXPRESS

Fyrefield Ltd, Unit F West End Business Park, Blackburn Road, Oswaldtwistle, BB5 4WE

Reg	Chassis	Body	Seating	Year	Previous owner
XJI1302	Volvo B10M-61	Jonckheere Bermuda	C49FT	1981	Rigby's, Patricroft, 1995
NIW6515	Volvo B10M-61	Van Hool Alizée H	C49FT	1981	Haydock, Intack, 1997
GIL3112	Volvo B10M-61	Berkhof Everest 370	C49FT	1983	M C, Melksham, 1998
GBZ8304	Volvo B10M-61	LAG Panoramic	C49FT	1984	Pygall, Easington, 1999
TJI4823	Volvo B10M-60	Jonckheere Jubilee P50	C51FT	1989	First Cymru, 2001
TJI4826	Volvo B10M-60	Jonckheere Jubilee P50	C51FT	1989	First Cymru, 2001
XJI1301	Volvo B10M-61	Plaxton Expressliner	C46FT	1989	Newline, Melling, 1998
G164LWN	Volvo B10M-60	Plaxton Expressliner	C50FT	1990	Dover, Hetton-le-Hole, 2001
G911UPP	Mercedes-Benz 709D	Reeve Burgess Beaver	B25F	1989	Rossendale, 2001
F621OHD	Mercedes-Benz 709D	Reeve Burgess Beaver	B25F	1989	Rossendale, 2001

Previous registrations:

164LWN	G164LWN, OIL8656	TJI4823	F753OJH
GBZ8304	A990JJU	TJI4826	F756OJH
GIL3112	A135GTA	XJI1301	G563VHY
NIW6515	STT604X, 942AYA, 170BHR	XJI1302	WNV822W, 1656RU, SVM171W, PJI2668, SVM171W

Coastlkinks Express is a summer service between east Lancashire towns and the Fylde Coast. Pictured in Blackburn while running route X81 to Fleetwood, XJI1301 spent its early life on National Express. The Plaxton Expressliner uses the Paramount frame but has many different fitments inside, most notable being the drivers compartment. *Bob Downham*

COLLINSONS COACHES

J J & J M Collinson, Simmy Nook, Longridge, Preston, PR3 3BU

HWT64N	Leyland Atlantean AN68/1R	Roe	B43/33F	1975	Whittaker, Penwortham, 2001
LJA474P	Daimler Fleetline CRG6LXB	Northern Counties	B43/32F	1976	Finch, Higher Ince, 1998
MBR438T	Leyland Atlantean AN68A/1R	Eastern Coach Works	B43/23F	1979	Go-Northern, 2002
ENJ917V	Leyland National 11351A/1R		B52F	1981	Dart Buses, Paisley, 2000
OBV161X	Leyland Atlantean AN68C/2R	East Lancashire	B50/36F	1981	Cunningham, Upholland, 2001
OBV162X	Leyland Atlantean AN68C/2R	East Lancashire	B50/36F	1981	Cunningham, Upholland, 2001
GSC636X	Leyland Atlantean AN68C/1R	Alexander D	B45/30F	1982	Lothian Buses, 2000
GSC637X	Leyland Atlantean AN68C/1R	Alexander D	B45/30F	1982	Lothian Buses, 2000
HTU671X	Bova EL26/581	Bova Europa	C52F	1982	Four Girls, Pontybodkin, 1998
NST162Y	Volvo B10M-61	Van Hool Alizée H	C46FT	1983	Rapsons, Inverness, 1998
SJI5589	Scania K112TRS	Jonckheere Bermuda	C55/19FT	1986	Gath, Dewsbury, 2001
C875CYX	Volvo B10M-61	Plaxton Paramount 3500 II	C53F	1986	Ing, Pemberton, 1998
F57YCW	Leyland Tiger TRCTL11/3ARZ	Plaxton Paramount 3500 III	C50FT	1989	Hampson's Travel, Fleetwood, 2000
F927YWY	Mercedes-Benz 811D	Optare StarRider	B26F	1989	HMB, Gateshead, 1998
G330XRE	Mercedes-Benz 811D	PMT Ami	B28F	1989	First in the Potteries, 2002
R62MEW	LDV Convoy	Concept	M16	1998	van conversion, 2001
S884AGD	LDV Convoy	LDV	M16	1999	?, 2001

Previous registrations:

ENJ917V	ENJ917, WJI9367		HWT64N	PAZ7425, HWT64N	
F57YCW	F57YCW, EIB1647, 524FUP		NST162Y	WWA47Y, 9637EL	
HTU671X	SMY620X, 224ASV, XBC272X, VIB822		SJI5589	C366SVV	

April sees the transfer of Collinsons operation to new premises nearer Ribchester. The operation now includes contracts for Lancashire County including the link between Preston and Ribchester. Pictured on the service in April 2002, F927YWY is a StarRider the model based on a Mercedes-Benz 811D, but with Optare's own frontal styling. *Bob Downham*

COSGROVE'S

Cosgrove Hire Services, 133 Woodplumpton Road, Fulwood, Preston, PR2 2LS

C659PCX	DAF SB2300DHS585	Duple 340	C53FT	1986	
D765XFR	Volvo B10M-61	Plaxton Paramount 3500 III	C49F	1987	
E331EVH	DAF SB2300DHS585	Plaxton Paramount 3200 III	C53F	1988	
G225HCP	DAF SB3000DKV601	Van Hool Alizée	C51FT	1990	
G226HCP	DAF SB3000DKV601	Van Hool Alizée	C51FT	1990	
M639RCP	DAF DE33WSSB3000	Van Hool Alizée	C51FT	1995	
M827RCP	DAF DE33WSSB3000	Van Hool Alizée	C51FT	1995	
N596DWY	DAF DE33WSSB3000	Van Hool Alizée	C51FT	1995	
N990KUS	Mercedes-Benz 711D	Plaxton Beaver	BC25F	1995	Redline, Penwortham, 1997
W387WGE	Mercedes-Benz Vario O814	Plaxton Cheetah	C33F	2000	McKinnon Coaches, Neilston, 2000

The Cosgrove fleet is represented by DAF SB3000 G226HCP. The rear-engined DAF is the principle model of the fleet. This example was seen on rail replacement duties. *Bob Downham*

DARWEN COACH SERVICES

D R Russell, 5 West View, Knowle Lane, Darwen, BB3 0NP

CTT826T	Mercedes-Benz 307D	Devon Conversions	M12	1979	Dreamline, Blackburn, 2000
B931YCW	Mercedes-Benz L307D	Rovanne	M12	1985	private owner, 1986
D672SHH	Mercedes-Benz 609D	Ribble / Cumbria Commercials	B25F	1986	Ribble, 1997
D239NCS	Renault-Dodge S56	Alexander AM	B25F	1987	Blue Bus, Horwich, 1996
D682SEM	Renault-Dodge S56	Alexander AM	B23F	1987	MTL (Merseybus), 1997
D683SEM	Renault-Dodge S56	Alexander AM	B23F	1987	MTL (Merseybus), 1997
D685SEM	Renault-Dodge S56	Alexander AM	B23F	1987	MTL (Merseybus), 1997
D689SEM	Renault-Dodge S56	Alexander AM	B23F	1987	MTL (Heysham Travel), 1997
E177UWF	Renault-Dodge S56	Reeve Burgess Beaver	B25F	1987	Mainline, 1995
E88HRN	Mercedes-Benz 811D	Robin Hood	B29F	1987	Stagecoach Ribble, 1999
E602TBS	Renault-Dodge S56	Alexander AM	B25F	1988	Blue Bus, Horwich, 1999
E101EVM	Mercedes-Benz 811D	Reeve Burgess	BC21F	1988	East Yorkshire, 1998
E102EVM	Mercedes-Benz 811D	Reeve Burgess	BC21F	1988	East Yorkshire, 1998
F905YWY	Mercedes-Benz 811D	Optare StarRider	B26F	1988	Boomerang Bus, Tewkesbury, 1998
F915YWY	Mercedes-Benz 811D	Optare StarRider	B29F	1988	Boomerang Bus, Tewkesbury, 1998
F840HAP	MCW MetroRider MF158/3	MCW	B33F	1988	Bird, Skelmersdale, 2001
G156NRC	Renault-Dodge S56	Northern Counties	B25F	1989	Travelspeed, Oswaldtwistle, 2000
H688YGO	Optare MetroRider MR03	Optare	B26F	1991	Reading Buses, 2000
J966JNL	Optare MetroRider MR03	Optare	B25F	1991	Reading Buses, 2000
J176WAX	Optare MetroRider MR01	Optare	B31F	1992	Cardiff Bus, 2000
J179WAX	Optare MetroRider MR01	Optare	B31F	1992	Cardiff Bus, 2000
J180WAX	Optare MetroRider MR01	Optare	B31F	1992	Cardiff Bus, 2000
J181WAX	Optare MetroRider MR01	Optare	B31F	1992	Cardiff Bus, 2000
J182WAX	Optare MetroRider MR01	Optare	B31F	1992	Cardiff Bus, 2000

Previous registrations:
F840HAP   E518YWF, 418DCD

Depot: Provident Yard, Cotton Street, Darwen.

An injection of Metrorider from Cardiff Bus and Reading Buses has added to the Darwen Coach Services fleet. Painted in the traditional red and cream colours of the erstwhile Darwen Corporation, J966JNL was latterly with Reading. *Bob Downham*

DENNIS'S

R & M Cooper, 4 Charles Street, Dukinfield, Tameside, SK16 4SD

	RAZ8628	Volvo B10M-60	Plaxton Expressliner	C53F	1989	Easson, Southampton, 1997
EL1	Y951XRN	Dennis Dart SLF	East Lancashire Spryte	N37F	2001	
EL2	Y952XRN	Dennis Dart SLF	East Lancashire Spryte	N37F	2001	

P1-6

		Dennis Dart SLF		Plaxton Pointer		N37F	1996		
	P978LNB	**1**	P980LNB	**4**	P547HVM	**5**	P112OJA	**6**	P113OJA
	P979LNB								

P7	R103BDB	Dennis Dart SLF	Plaxton Pointer	N39F	1998
P8	R572ABA	Dennis Dart SLF	Plaxton Pointer	N36F	1997
P9	R573ABA	Dennis Dart SLF	Plaxton Pointer	N36F	1997
P10	R574ABA	Dennis Dart SLF	Plaxton Pointer	N39F	1997
P11	R575ABA	Dennis Dart SLF	Plaxton Pointer	N39F	1997
P12	T63AUA	Dennis Dart SLF	Plaxton Pointer 2	N39F	1999

T1-6

		Dennis Trident		East Lancashire Lolyne		N51/31F	2000-02	
	W531GCW	**3**	X793JHG	**4**	02	**5**	02	**5**	02
	X792JHG								

W1-17

		Dennis Dart 9.8SDL3017		Wright Handy-bus		B40F	1991-92	Go-Ahead Northern, 2001
	J610KCU	**5**	J640KCU	**9**	K865PCN	**12**	J952MFT	**15**	K368RTY
	J944MFT	**6**	J606KCU	**10**	J630KCU	**13**	J623KCU	**16**	K857PCN
	J622KCU	**7**	J633KCU	**11**	J951MFT	**14**	K366RTY	**17**	K369RTY
	J942MFT	**8**	J628KCU						

B1-11

		Mercedes-Benz 709D		Plaxton Beaver		B27F	1994-95	
B1	L680GNA	**MB4**	L683GNA	**MB7**	M729MBU	**MB9**	N320YNC	**MB11**	N322YNC
B2	L681GNA	**MB6**	M728MBU	**MB8**	M730MBU	**MB10**	N321YNC		

Previous registrations:

RAZ8628	G554SSP

Depot: Platt Street, Dukinfield

Representing the seventeen Darts acquired from the Go-Ahead group is DW12, J952MFT. The batch carry Wright bodywork to the Handy-bus style. Route 216 connects Ashton with Manchester where the bus is seen.
Dave Heath

Recent new buses for Dennis's fleet comprise a Dennis/East Lancashire combination. Two more Darts with Spryte bodies were added to the fleet and one is illustrated on the rear cover, while the Dennis Trident with Lolyne bodies are entering service on route 216, with three more yet to arrive. Pictured in Piccadilly is DT3, X793JHG. *Richard Godfrey*

Finglands 1743, N743VBA, is one of five Alexander-bodied Olympians to the Royale design. Pictured in the south Manchester district of Withington, it was operating one of the 40 series of routes that travel Wilmslow Road and pass the depot. *Richard Godfrey*

FINGLANDS

Finglands Coachways Ltd, 261 Wilmslow Road, Rusholme, Manchester, M14 5LJ

Part of EYMS Holdings

301	F301JNC	Leyland Tiger TRBTL11/2RP	Duple 300	BC55F	1989	
302	F302JNC	Leyland Tiger TRBTL11/2RP	Duple 300	BC55F	1989	
360	NJI1250	Mercedes-Benz 0303-15R	Mercedes Benz	C49FT	1990	
363	KAZ1363	Volvo B10M-61	Plaxton Paramount 3500 III	C53FT	1991	Park's of Hamilton, 1993
364	647JOE	Volvo B10M-61	Berkhof Excellence 1000LD	C49FT	1995	
365	HIL7745	Volvo B10M-62	Plaxton Première 320	C53F	1996	
366	HIL7746	Volvo B10M-62	Plaxton Première 320	C53F	1995	Excelsior, Bournemouth, 1997
367	RYV77	Volvo B10M-62	Van Hool Alizée	C33FT	1997	
368	SIA6180	Volvo B10M-62	Plaxton Première 320	C53F	1997	Excelsior, Bournemouth, 1998
369	S369SND	Toyota Coaster BB50R	Caetano Optimo IV	C21F	1998	
370	T370JVR	Volvo B10M-6200	Plaxton Première 350	C49FT	1999	
371	X371AVU	Volvo B10M-6200	Plaxton Première 350	C53F	2000	
372	10RU	Volvo B10M-62	Plaxton Panther	C34FT	2001	
373	MF51MBU	Volvo B10M-62	Plaxton Panther	C49FT	2002	
1422	M422RRN	Volvo B10M-55	Alexander PS	BC48F	1994	Stagecoach Manchester, 1995
1423	M423RRN	Volvo B10M-55	Alexander PS	BC48F	1994	Stagecoach Manchester, 1995
1424	M424RRN	Volvo B10M-55	Alexander PS	BC48F	1994	Stagecoach Manchester, 1995
1425	M425RRN	Volvo B10M-55	Alexander PS	BC48F	1994	Stagecoach Manchester, 1995
1426	M426RRN	Volvo B10M-55	Alexander PS	BC48F	1994	Stagecoach Manchester, 1995
1427	M427RRN	Volvo B10M-55	Alexander PS	BC48F	1994	Stagecoach Manchester, 1995
1428	V428DNB	Mercedes-Benz O405	Mercedes-Benz	N40F	1999	
1429	V429DNB	Mercedes-Benz O405	Mercedes-Benz	N40F	1999	
1706	F610GVO	Volvo Citybus B10M-50	Alexander RV	B45/37F	1989	Trent, 2000
1707	F611GVO	Volvo Citybus B10M-50	Alexander RV	B45/37F	1989	Trent, 2000
1708	F608GVO	Volvo Citybus B10M-50	Alexander RV	B45/37F	1989	Trent, 2000
1709	F609GVO	Volvo Citybus B10M-50	Alexander RV	B45/37F	1989	Trent, 2000
1710	F242MBA	Volvo Citybus B10M-50	Alexander RV	BC47/35F	1989	
1713	G613OTV	Volvo Citybus B10M-50	Alexander RV	B45/37F	1989	Trent, 1999
1716	G616OTV	Volvo Citybus B10M-50	Alexander RV	B45/37F	1989	Trent, 1999
1717	G617OTV	Volvo Citybus B10M-50	Alexander RV	B45/37F	1989	Trent, 1999
1718	G618OTV	Volvo Citybus B10M-50	Alexander RV	B45/37F	1989	Trent, 1999
1726	E473SON	MCW Metrobus DR102/63	MCW	B45/30F	1987	Metroline, 1992
1727	E474SON	MCW Metrobus DR102/63	MCW	B45/30F	1987	Metroline, 1992
1728	E476SON	MCW Metrobus DR102/63	MCW	B45/30F	1988	Metroline, 1992
1730	E480UOF	MCW Metrobus DR102/63	MCW	B45/30F	1988	Metroline, 1992

With Finingland's parent fleet operating sixteen Mercedes-Benz full-size buses the choice of a pair for the Manchester fleet was not unusual, though these were integral O405s. Seen crossing the tramline in Piccadilly 1428, V428DNB, illustrates the recognisable Mercedes styling found across most of Europe.
Richard Godfrey

New-generation buses from both Dennis and Volvo are used by Finglands. In 2000 a pair of Alexander-boded Tridents and a pair of Plaxton-bodied Volvo B7TLs joined the fleet with the latter being chosen for the 2002 delivery. Pictured in the city is 1762, X762ABU. *Richard Godfrey*

1739	M832HVC	Volvo Olympian YN2RV18Z4	Alexander Royale	B45/29F	1994	Volvo demonstrator, 1995
1740	N740VBA	Volvo Olympian YN2RV18Z4	Alexander Royale	B45/29F	1995	
1741	N741VBA	Volvo Olympian YN2RV18Z4	Alexander Royale	B45/29F	1995	
1742	N742VBA	Volvo Olympian YN2RV18Z4	Alexander Royale	B45/29F	1995	
1743	N743VBA	Volvo Olympian YN2RV18Z4	Alexander Royale	B45/29F	1995	
1744	N744ANE	Volvo Olympian YN2RV18Z4	Northern Counties Palatine II	B47/30F	1996	
1745	N745ANE	Volvo Olympian YN2RV18Z4	Northern Counties Palatine II	B47/30F	1996	
1746	N746ANE	Volvo Olympian YN2RV18Z4	Northern Counties Palatine II	B47/30F	1996	
1747	N47ANE	Volvo Olympian YN2RV18Z4	Northern Counties Palatine II	B47/30F	1996	
1748	N748ANE	Volvo Olympian YN2RV18Z4	Northern Counties Palatine II	B47/30F	1996	
1756	A671HNB	Leyland Atlantean AN68D/1R	Northern Counties	B43/32F	1983	Stagecoach Manchester, 1998
1761	X761ABU	Volvo B7TL	Plaxton President	N45/28F	2000	
1762	X762ABU	Volvo B7TL	Plaxton President	N45/28F	2000	
1763	X763ABU	Dennis Trident	Alexander ALX400	N45/29F	2000	
1764	X764ABU	Dennis Trident	Alexander ALX400	N45/29F	2000	
1765	MF51LZW	Volvo B7TL	Plaxton President	N45/28F	2002	
1766	MF51LZZ	Volvo B7TL	Plaxton President	N45/28F	2002	
1767	MF51MBV	Volvo B7TL	Plaxton President	N45/28F	2002	
1768	MF51MBX	Volvo B7TL	Plaxton President	N45/28F	2002	

Previous Registrations:

10RU	Y372KNB	KAZ1363	H907AHS
647JOE	M364SNB, RYV77	NJI1250	10RU
HIL7745	N365BNF	RYV77	R367WNC, 647JOE
HIL7746	A12XEL, M516NCG	SIA6180	A15XEL, P533CLJ

FIRST

First Manchester Ltd, Wallshaw Street, Oldham, OL1 3TR

102-115   Scania L94UB   Wright Axcess Floline   N40F   1998

102	S102TNB	105	S105TNB	108	S108TNB	111	S651RNA	114	S114TNB
103	S103TNB	106	S106TNB	109	S109TNB	112	S112TNB	115	S115TNB
104	S104TNB	107	S107TNB	110	S110TNB	113	S113TNB		

116-142   Scania L94UB   Wright Axcess Floline   N42F*   1999-2000   *116-119 are N40F

116	T916SSF	123	V330DBU	128	V128DND	133	V133DND	138	V138DND
117	T917SSF	124	V124DND	129	V129DND	134	V134DND	139	V139DND
118	T918SSF	125	V125DND	130	V130DND	135	V135DND	140	V140DND
119	T919SSF	126	V126DND	131	V131DND	136	V136DND	141	V141DND
121	V142DND	127	V127DND	132	V132DND	137	V137DND	142	W142PSH
122	V122DND								

151-170   Scania L94UB   Wright Axcess Floline   N43F   2001

151	Y343XBN	155	X271USH	159	Y623RTD	163	Y961XBU	167	Y962XBU
152	Y597KNE	156	X256USH	160	X272USH	164	Y347XBN	168	Y633RTD
153	X253USH	157	X257USH	161	X261USH	165	X265USH	169	X269USH
154	Y344XBN	158	Y364XBN	162	Y598KNE	166	X266USH	170	Y634RTD

171-178   Scania L94UB   Wright Axcess Floline   N40F   1999   First Aberdeen, 2001

171	S561JSE	173	T563BSS	175	T565BSS	177	T567BSS	178	S560JSE
172	T562BSS	174	T564BSS	176	T566BSS				

Following recent internal transfers, Bolton's allocation is where the entire fleet of Scania buses is now based. Seen on the trunk route from there into Manchester, 156, X271USH was from a batch some of which were registered in Scotland before delivery to the fleet. *Mark Doggett*

First operate all sixty-one of their Citaro fleet from Oldham depot, with high frequency route 409 from Rochdale to Ashton using them from new. Seen on that service is 305, W335JND. *Cliff Beeton*

301-360

Mercedes-Benz O530 Citaro   Mercedes-Benz   N38F   2000

301	W301JND	313	W313JND	325	W378JNE	337	W337RJA	349	W349RJA
302	W302JND	314	W314JND	326	W326JND	338	W338RJA	350	W362RJA
303	W303JND	315	W315JND	327	W327JND	339	W339RJA	351	W351RJA
304	W304JND	316	W334JND	328	W379JNE	340	W361RJA	352	W352RJA
305	W335JND	317	W317JND	329	W329JND	341	W341RJA	353	W353RJA
306	W336JND	318	W338JND	330	W331JND	342	W342RJA	354	W354RJA
307	W307JND	319	W319JND	331	W331RJA	343	W343RJA	355	W366RJA
308	W308JND	320	W337JND	332	W332RJA	344	W365RJA	356	W356RJA
309	W309JND	321	W341JND	333	W363RJA	345	W345RJA	357	W357RJA
310	W332JND	322	W322JND	334	W334RJA	346	W346RJA	358	W358RJA
311	W311JND	323	W339JND	335	W335RJA	347	W347RJA	359	W359RJA
312	W312JND	324	W324JND	336	W336RJA	348	W348RJA	360	W364RJA

361	W179BVP	Mercedes-Benz O530 Citaro	Mercedes-Benz	N38F	2000	Evobus demonstrator, 2001
407	G65RND	Leyland Tiger TR2R62C16Z4	Alexander N	B55F	1989	Timeline, 1998
409	G67RND	Leyland Tiger TR2R62C16Z4	Alexander N	B55F	1989	First PMT, 2001
412	G70RND	Leyland Tiger TR2R62C16Z4	Alexander N	B55F	1989	Timeline, 1998
421	G109YRE	Scania K93CRB	Alexander PS	B51F	1989	The Coachmasters, Rochdale, 2000

501-556

Volvo B10B   Wright Endurance   BC50F   1994-96

501	M501PNA	512	M512PNA	523	N523WVR	534	N534WVR	545	N545WVR
502	M502PNA	513	M513PNA	524	N524WVR	535	N535WVR	546	N546WVR
503	M503PNA	514	M514PNA	525	N525WVR	536	N536WVR	547	N547WVR
504	M504PNA	515	M515PNA	526	N526WVR	537	N537WVR	548	N548WVR
505	M505PNA	516	M516PNA	527	N527WVR	538	N538WVR	549	N549WVR
506	M506PNA	517	M517PNA	528	N528WVR	539	N539WVR	550	N550WVR
507	M507PNA	518	M518PNA	529	N529WVR	540	N540WVR	551	N551WVR
508	M508PNA	519	M519PNA	530	N530WVR	541	N541WVR	552	N552WVR
509	M509PNA	520	M520PNA	531	N531WVR	542	N542WVR	553	N553WVR
510	M510PNA	521	N521WVR	532	N532WVR	543	N543WVR	554	N554WVR
511	M511PNA	522	N522WVR	533	N533WVR	544	N544WVR	556	N556WVR

557-562

Volvo B10L — Wright Liberator — NC41F — 1996

557	N557BNF	558	N558BNF	559	N559BNF	561	N561BNF	562	N562BNF

563-568

Volvo B10L — Alexander Ultra — N43F — 1995-96 — Timeline, 1998

563	N301WNF	565	N303WNF	566	N304WNF	567	N305WNF	568	N306WNF
564	N302WNF								

571-583

Volvo B10BLE — Wright Renown — N42F — 1997

571	R571YNC	574	R574SBA	577	R577SBA	580	R580SBA	582	R582SBA
572	R572SBA	575	R575SBA	578	R578SBA	581	R581SBA	583	R583SBA
573	R573SBA	576	R576SBA	579	R579SBA				

601	J461OVU	Volvo B10M-50	Northern Counties Paladin	B49F	1991	
602	D497NYS	Volvo B10M-61	Duple Dominant	B55F	1986	First PMT, 2001

608-618

Dennis Dart 9.8SDL3054 — Northern Counties Paladin — B39F — 1995

608	M608SBA	610	M610SBA	612	M612SBA	614	M614SBA	618	M618SBA
609	M609SBA	611	M611SBA	613	M613SBA	617	M617SBA		

621-656

Volvo B10BLE — Wright Renown — N41F* — 1998-99 — *645-55 are N42F

621	R621CVR	626	R626CVR	631	R631CVR	647	R647CVR	653	S653RNA
622	R622CVR	627	R627CVR	632	R632CVR	648	R648CVR	652	S652RNA
623	R623CVR	628	R654CVR	633	R633CVR	649	R649CVR	654	S654RNA
624	R624CVR	629	R629CVR	645	R645CVR	650	R650CVR	655	S655RNA
625	R625CVR	630	R630CVR	646	R646CVR	651	R651CVR	656	S656RNA

668	S668SVU	Volvo B10BLE	Wright Renown	N40F	1999
669	S669SVU	Volvo B10BLE	Wright Renown	N40F	1999
670	S670SVU	Volvo B10BLE	Wright Renown	N40F	1999
671	S671SVU	Volvo B10BLE	Wright Renown	N40F	1999
699	W699RND	Volvo B10BLE	Wrightbus Eclipse	N41F	2000
701	Y774TNC	Volvo B7L	Wrightbus Eclipse	N41F	2001

711-785

Volvo B7L — Wrightbus Eclipse — N41F — 2002

711	MV02VCM	726	MV02VCF	741	MV02VAX	756	MV02VAJ	771	MV02VDA
712	MV02VCN	727	MV02VCG	742	MV02VAY	757	MV02VAK	772	MV02VDC
713	MV02VCO	728	MV02VCJ	743	MV02VBA	758	MV02VAM	773	MV02VDD
714	MV02VCP	729	MV02VCK	744	MV02VBB	759	MV02VAO	774	MV02VDE
715	MV02VCT	730	MV02VCL	745	MV02VBC	760	MV02VAU	775	MV02VDF
716	MV02VCU	731	MV02VBK	746	MV02VBD	761	MV02VDN	776	MV02VDG
717	MV02VCW	732	MV02VBL	747	MV02VBE	762	MV02VDO	777	MV02VDJ
718	MV02VCX	733	MV02VBM	748	MV02VBF	763	MV02VDP	778	MV02VDK
719	MV02VCY	734	MV02VBN	749	MV02VBG	764	MV02VDR	779	MV02VDL
720	MV02VCZ	735	MV02VBO	750	MV02VBJ	765	MV02VDT	780	MV02VDM
721	MV02VBZ	736	MV02VBP	751	MV02VAA	766	MV02VDX	781	MV02VEF
722	MV02VCA	737	MV02VBT	752	MV02VAD	767	MV02VDY	782	MV02VEH
723	MV02VCC	738	MV02VBU	753	MV02VAE	768	MV02VDZ	783	MV02VEK
724	MV02VCD	739	MV02VBX	754	MV02VAF	769	MV02VEA	784	MV02VEL
725	MV02VCE	740	MV02VBY	755	MV02VAH	770	MV02VEB	785	MV02VEM

901-914

Mercedes-Benz O405 — Wright Endurance — B49F — 1993 — First Aberdeen, 2001

901	L501KSA	904	L504KSA	907	L507KSA	910	L510KSA	913	L513KSA
902	L502KSA	905	L505KSA	908	L508KSA	911	L511KSA	914	L514KSA
903	L503KSA	906	L506KSA	909	L509KSA	912	L512KSA		

915-924

Mercedes-Benz O405 — Optare Prisma — B49F — 1995 — First Aberdeen, 2001

915	M586TSO	917	M517RSS	919	M519RSS	921	M521RSS	923	M523RSS
916	M516RSS	918	M518RSS	920	M520RSS	922	M522RSS	924	M524RSS

925-949

Mercedes-Benz O405 — Optare Prisma — B47F — 1995-97 — First Aberdeen, 2001

925	N525VSA	929	N529VSA	933	N533VSA	942	P542BSS	946	P546BSS
926	N526VSA	930	N530VSA	934	N534VSA	943	P543BSS	947	P547BSS
927	N527VSA	931	N531VSA	940	P540BSS	944	P544BSS	948	P548BSS
928	N528VSA	932	N532VSA	941	P541BSS	945	P545BSS	949	P549BSS

951-959

| | | | | | | | | | Mercedes-Benz O405 | Optare Prisma | B49F | 1995 | First in Leicester, 2002 |

951	M501GRY	**953**	M503GRY	**956**	M506GRY	**958**	M508GRY	**950**	M510GRY
952	M502GRY	**954**	M504GRY	**957**	M507GRY	**959**	M509GRY		

1043	N343CJA	Volvo B6-9.9m	Alexander Dash	B40F	1996
1044	N344CJA	Volvo B6-9.9m	Alexander Dash	B40F	1996
1047	N347CJA	Volvo B6-9.9m	Alexander Dash	B40F	1996
1048	N348CJA	Volvo B6-9.9m	Alexander Dash	B40F	1996
1049	M947OVC	Volvo B6-9.9m	Alexander Dash	B40F	1995	Volvo demonstrator, 1996
1050	M260KWK	Volvo B6-9.9m	Alexander Dash	B40F	1995	Volvo demonstrator, 1996

1051-1070

Volvo B6-9.9m · Northern Counties Paladin · B40F · 1994-95

1051	M251NVM	**1055**	M255NVM	**1059**	M259NVM	**1063**	M263SVU	**1067**	M267SVU
1052	M252NVM	**1056**	M256NVM	**1060**	M260NVM	**1064**	M264SVU	**1068**	M268SVU
1053	M253NVM	**1057**	M257NVM	**1061**	M261SVU	**1065**	M265SVU	**1069**	M269SVU
1054	M254NVM	**1058**	M258NVM	**1062**	M262SVU	**1066**	M266SVU	**1070**	M270SVU

1071	N71YNF	Volvo B6LE	Northern Counties Paladin	N37F	1995

1072-1086

Volvo B6LE · Wright Crusader · N38F* · 1996 · *1072/3/7 are N36F
1081-6 are N35F

1072	N372CJA	**1075**	N375CJA	**1078**	N378CJA	**1081**	N381CJA	**1084**	N384CJA
1073	N373CJA	**1076**	N376CJA	**1079**	N379CJA	**1082**	N382CJA	**1085**	N385CRJ
1074	N374CJA	**1077**	N377CJA	**1080**	N380CJA	**1083**	N383CJA	**1086**	N386CRJ

1087-1091

Volvo B6-9.9M · Alexander Dash · B40F · 1995 · First Wessex, 2000

1087	N787EUB	**1088**	N788EUB	**1089**	N789EUB	**1090**	N391EUG	**1091**	N325HUA

1093-1098

Volvo B6-9.9m · Alexander Dash · B38F · 1994-95 · Timeline, 1998

1093	N207WBA	**1095**	N209WBA	**1096**	N210WBA	**1097**	N211WBA	**1098**	N212WBA
1094	N208WBA								

1101-1106

Dennis Dart 9.8SDL3054 · Northern Counties Paladin · B39F · 1995

1101	M101RRJ	**1103**	M103RRJ	**1104**	M104RRJ	**1105**	M105RRJ	**1106**	M106RRJ
1102	M102RRJ								

1119-1138

Dennis Dart 9.8SDL3054 · Northern Counties Paladin · B39F · 1996

1119	N619CDB	**1123**	N623CDB	**1127**	N627CDB	**1131**	N631CDB	**1135**	N635CDB
1120	N620CDB	**1124**	N624CDB	**1128**	N628CDB	**1132**	N632CDB	**1136**	N636CDB
1121	N621CDB	**1125**	N625CDB	**1129**	N629CDB	**1133**	N633CDB	**1137**	N637CDB
1122	N622CDB	**1126**	N626CDB	**1130**	N630CDB	**1134**	N634CDB	**1138**	N638CDB

1139	N742GKH	Dennis Dart 9.8SDL3054	Plaxton Pointer	B39F	1996	Plaxton demonstrator, 1996

1140-1153

Dennis Dart 9.8SDL3054 · Plaxton Pointer · B40F · 1996

1140	N640CDB	**1143**	N643CDB	**1146**	N646CDB	**1149**	N649CDB	**1152**	N652CDB
1141	N641CDB	**1144**	N644CDB	**1147**	N647CDB	**1150**	N650CDB	**1153**	N653CDB
1142	N642CDB	**1145**	N645CDB	**1148**	N648CDB	**1151**	N651CDB		

1171	P871TAV	Dennis Dart	Marshall C37	B40F	1996	Pioneer, Rochdale, 1998
1172	P872TAV	Dennis Dart	Marshall C37	B40F	1996	Pioneer, Rochdale, 1998
1173	M944SRE	Dennis Dart 9SDL3040	Marshall C37	BC39F	1994	First PMT, 2001
1174	M946SRE	Dennis Dart 9SDL3040	Marshall C37	BC39F	1994	First PMT, 2001
1175	M947SRE	Dennis Dart 9SDL3040	Marshall C37	BC39F	1994	First PMT, 2001
1176	M948SRE	Dennis Dart 9SDL3040	Marshall C37	BC39F	1994	First PMT, 2001
1177	M965XVT	Dennis Dart 9.8SDL3054	Plaxton Pointer	BC36F	1995	First PMT, 2001
1178	M966XVT	Dennis Dart 9.8SDL3054	Plaxton Pointer	BC36F	1995	First PMT, 2001
1179	M963XVT	Dennis Dart 9.8SDL3054	Plaxton Pointer	BC36F	1995	First PMT, 2001

1181-1190

Dennis Dart 9.8SDL3054 · Plaxton Pointer · B37F · 1996 · First Centrewest, 2001

1181	N601XJM	**1183**	N603XJM	**1186**	N606XJM	**1188**	N608XJM	**1190**	N610XJM
1182	N602XJM	**1184**	N604XJM	**1187**	N607XJM	**1189**	N609XJM		

Having taken stock of all the Citaro buses it was planned that, when the vehicle maintenance at Aberdeen depot was out-sourced to Volvo and new buses were delivered, the mid-life Mercedes-Benz O405s were also moved to the Manchester area. Bodywork on these originated with three coachbuilders, Optare, Wright and Alexander, whose sole example was articulated and remained in the 'Granite City'. Pictured in Bury where several of the type have been allocated, 912, L512KSA carries Wright Endurance bodywork. *Mark Doggett*

1401	D501LNA	Leyland Lynx LX563.6LXCTZR1	Leyland	B48F	1986	
1404	D504LNA	Leyland Lynx LX112LXCTZR1	Leyland	B48F	1986	
1405	D752DLO	Leyland Lynx LX112TL11ZR1S	Leyland Lynx	B49F	1987	First PMT, 2001
1406	F102GRM	Leyland Lynx LX112L10ZR1R	Leyland Lynx	B48F	1988	First PMT, 2001
1407	F362YTJ	Leyland Lynx LX112L10ZR1R	Leyland Lynx	B51F	1988	First PMT, 2001
1408	F608WBV	Leyland Lynx LX112L10ZR1S	Leyland Lynx	B52F	1988	First PMT, 2001
1409	H851GRE	Leyland Lynx LX2R11C15Z4S	Leyland Lynx	BC48F	1990	First PMT, 2001
1410	M410RND	Iveco TurboDaily 59.12	Marshall C 31	B27F	1995	Citibus, Middleton, 1995
1481	C481CBU	Volvo Citybus B10M-50	Northern Counties	B46/33F	1986	
1482	C482CBU	Volvo Citybus B10M-50	Northern Counties	B46/33F	1986	
1483	C483CBU	Volvo Citybus B10M-50	Northern Counties	B46/33F	1986	
1511	L269GBU	Optare MetroRider	Optare	B28F	1993	First PMT, 2001
1512	L323NRF	Optare MetroRider MR17	Optare	B29F	1994	First PMT, 2001
1601	V41DTE	Optare Solo M850	Optare	N24F	1999	
1602	V42DTE	Optare Solo M850	Optare	N24F	1999	
1603	V43DTE	Optare Solo M850	Optare	N24F	1999	
1606	V71GEH	Optare Solo M850	Optare	N27F	1999	First in the Potteries, 2002
1607	V472GBF	Optare Solo M850	Optare	N27F	1999	First in the Potteries, 2002

1611-1620

		Optare Solo M850	Optare	N28F	2000	

1611	X611OBN	1613	X613OBN	1615	X615OBN	1617	X617OBN	1619	X619OBN
1612	X612OBN	1614	X614OBN	1616	X616OBN	1618	X618OBN	1620	X627OBN

1621-1625

		Optare Solo M920	Optare	N28F	2000	

1621	Y901KNB	1622	Y902KNB	1623	Y903KNB	1624	Y904KNB	1625	Y905KNB

1631	MA51AET	Optare Solo M850	Optare	N24F	2001	
1632	MA51AEU	Optare Solo M850	Optare	N24F	2001	
1633	MA51AEV	Optare Solo M850	Optare	N24F	2001	
1634	MA51AEW	Optare Solo M850	Optare	N24F	2001	

At the time of going to press the ten tri-axle double decks from New World First Bus were based at Queens Road depot and generally found on the high-frequency route 17 to Rochdale. Pictured on Rochdale Road in Manchester is 3001, K481EUX. *Richard Godfrey*

1706	J606HMF	Mercedes-Benz 811D	Plaxton Beaver	B28F	1992	Citibus, Middleton, 1995
1708	J608HMF	Mercedes-Benz 811D	Plaxton Beaver	B28F	1992	Citibus, Middleton, 1995
1709	J609HMF	Mercedes-Benz 811D	Plaxton Beaver	B28F	1992	Citibus, Middleton, 1995
1714	J614HMF	Mercedes-Benz 811D	Plaxton Beaver	B28F	1992	Citibus, Middleton, 1995
1721	M158LNC	Mercedes-Benz 811D	Alexander Sprint	B31F	1994	Timeline, 1998
1722	M159LNC	Mercedes-Benz 811D	Alexander Sprint	B31F	1994	Timeline, 1998
1724	M161LNC	Mercedes-Benz 811D	Alexander Sprint	B31F	1994	Timeline, 1998
1754	F672XMS	Mercedes-Benz 811D	Alexander Sprint	B26F	1988	Centrewest, 1998
1761	H357HVT	Mercedes-Benz 811D	Reeve Burgess Beaver	B33F	1990	First PMT, 2001
1762	H358JRE	Mercedes-Benz 811D	PMT Ami	B29F	1990	First PMT, 2001
1763	H360JRE	Mercedes-Benz 811D	PMT Ami	B29F	1990	First PMT, 2001
1764	K375BRE	Mercedes-Benz 811D	Autobus Classique	B29F	1992	First PMT, 2001

1801-1821

		Mercedes-Benz 709D			Plaxton Beaver			B23F	1995	Yorkshire Rider, 1996-97
1801	M234VWU	1805	M239VWU	1809	M218VWU	1812	M223VWU	1819	M215VWU	
1803	M237VWU	1806	M248VWU	1810	M247VWU	1815	M209VWU	1821	M207VWU	
1804	M238VWU	1808	M211VWU	1811	M245VWU	1818	M213VWU			

1831	N173WNF	Mercedes-Benz 811D	Alexander Sprint	B31F	1994	Timeline, 1998
1833	N175WNF	Mercedes-Benz 811D	Alexander Sprint	B31F	1994	Timeline, 1998
1834	N176WNF	Mercedes-Benz 811D	Alexander Sprint	B31F	1994	Timeline, 1998
1835	N177WNF	Mercedes-Benz 811D	Alexander Sprint	B31F	1994	Timeline, 1998

1852-1862

		Mercedes-Benz 709D		Reeve Burgess Beaver		B23F	1988-91	First Centrewest, 2000	
1852	F245MVW	1855	F258RHK	1857	F254RHK	1858	H302LPU	1862	H388MAR
1853	F256RHK	1856	F246MVW						

1871-1878

		Mercedes-Benz 709D		Plaxton Beaver		B22F	1996	First PMT, 2001	
1871	N405HVT	1873	P422MEH	1875	P424MEH	1877	P426MEH	1878	P427MEH
1872	N410HVT	1874	P423MEH	1876	P425MEH				

1880	K488CVT	Mercedes-Benz 709D	Dormobile Routemaker	B27F	1993	First PMT, 2001

The Lancashire, Cumbria and Manchester Bus Handbook

2001-2015

Volvo B10LA   Wright Fusion   AN50D   1999

2001	S111FML	2004	S994UJA	2007	T507JNA	2010	T510JNA	2013	T513JNA
2002	S992UJA	2005	S995UJA	2008	T508JNA	2011	T511JNA	2014	T514JNA
2003	S993UJA	2006	T506JNA	2009	T509JNA	2012	T512JNA	2015	T515JNA

| 2201 | X401CSG | Scania L94UA | | Wrightbus Fusion Eclipse | | AN58D | 2001 | | |

3001-3010

Leyland Olympian ON3R49C18Z4   Alexander RH   B53/31F   1993   First PMT, 2001

3001	K481EUX	3003	K483EUX	3005	K485EUX	3007	K487EUX	3009	K489EUX
3002	K482EUX	3004	K484EUX	3006	K486EUX	3008	K488EUX	3010	K480EUX

| 3016 | K174EUX | Volvo Olympian YN2RV18V3 | | Alexander RH | | B42/32F | 1994 | First PMT, 2001 | |

3037-3152

Leyland Olympian ONLXB/1R   Northern Counties   B43/30F   1984-85

3037	B37PJA	3054	B54PJA	3090	B90PJA	3108	B108SJA	3130	B130WNB
3038	B38PJA	3061	B61PJA	3092	B92PJA	3109	B109SJA	3131	B131WNB
3040	B40PJA	3062	B62PJA	3093	B93PJA	3111	B111SJA	3134	B134WNB
3041	B41PJA	3064	B64PJA	3096	B96SJA	3112	B112SJA	3136	B136WNB
3042	B42PJA	3066	B66PJA	3098	B98SJA	3113	B113SJA	3140	B140WNB
3043	B43PJA	3068	B68PJA	3101	B101SJA	3116	B116TVU	3141	B141WNB
3044	B44PJA	3071	B71PJA	3103	B103SJA	3120	B120TVU	3142	B142WNB
3045	B45PJA	3076	B76PJA	3104	B104SJA	3123	B123TVU	3144	B144WNB
3047	B47PJA	3078	B78PJA	3105	B105SJA	3127	B127TVU	3148	B148XNA
3051	B351PJA	3081	B81PJA	3106	B106SJA	3128	B128WNB	3152	B152XNA
3052	B52PJA	3083	B83PJA	3107	B107SJA	3129	B129WNB		

3159-3235

Leyland Olympian ONLXB/1R   Northern Counties   B43/30F*   1985-86   *3218 is BC43/26F

3159	C159YBA	3183	C183YBA	3200	C200CBU	3211	C211CBU	3227	C227ENE
3160	C160YBA	3186	C186YBA	3201	C201CBU	3217	C217CBU	3229	C229ENE
3161	C161YBA	3187	C187YBA	3202	C202CBU	3218	C218CBU	3231	C231ENE
3163	C163YBA	3188	C188YBA	3203	C203CBU	3219	C219CBU	3232	C232ENE
3168	C168YBA	3189	C189YBA	3204	C204CBU	3220	C220CBU	3233	C233ENE
3171	C171YBA	3190	C190YBA	3206	C206CBU	3223	C223CBU	3235	C235ENE
3177	C177YBA	3192	C192YBA	3209	C209CBU	3225	C225CBU		

3237-3276

Leyland Olympian ONLXB/1R   Northern Counties   B43/30F*   1986-87   *several are BC43/26F

3237	C237EVU	3245	C245EVU	3252	C252FRJ	3261	D261JVR	3270	D270JVR
3238	C238EVU	3246	C246FRJ	3253	C253FRJ	3262	D262JVR	3271	D271JVR
3239	C239EVU	3247	C247FRJ	3254	C254FRJ	3263	D263JVR	3273	D273JVR
3240	C240EVU	3248	C248FRJ	3256	D256JVR	3264	D264JVR	3274	D274JVR
3241	C241EVU	3249	C249FRJ	3257	D257JVR	3265	D265JVR	3275	D275JVR
3243	C243EVU	3250	C250FRJ	3258	D258JVR	3266	D266JVR	3276	D276JVR
3244	C244EVU	3251	C251FRJ	3259	D259JVR	3267	D267JVR		

3278-3305

Leyland Olympian ONLXB/1RZ   Northern Counties   B43/30F   1988-89

3278	F278DRJ	3281	F281DRJ	3287	F287DRJ	3292	F292DRJ	3302	F302DRJ
3279	F279DRJ	3284	F284DRJ	3288	F288DRJ	3293	F293DRJ	3303	F303DRJ
3280	F280DRJ	3286	F286DRJ	3290	F290DRJ	3299	F299DRJ	3305	F305DRJ

3311-3315

Leyland Olympian ON2R56C16Z4   Northern Counties Palatine   B44/32F   1992   First Bristol, 2000

311	K601LAE	3312	K602LAE	3313	K603LAE	3314	K604LAE	3315	K605LAE

3321-3327

Leyland Olympian ON2R50C13Z4   Northern Counties Palatine   B47/30F   1992   First Capital, 2001

321	K888TTT	3323	K888TWY	3325	K888PFD	3326	K888BFG	3327	K888BWU
322	K888ELR	3324	K888LAD						

| 328 | K888TKS | Leyland Olympian ON2R50C13Z4 | | Northern Counties Palatine II | | B46/29F | 1993 | First Capital, 2001 | |

3371-3377

Leyland Olympian ON2R50C13Z4   Leyland   B47/29F   1991   First in London, 2002

371	J158YRM	3373	J153YRM	3375	J155YRM	3376	J156YRM	3377	J157YRM
372	J152YRM	3374	J154YRM						

Eccles, more famous for its current cakes than buses, is the location of this view of Olympian 3252, C252FRJ. The vehicle was new in pink GM Express livery and retains the high-back seating in the lower saloon.
Mark Doggett

3381	F152XYG	Leyland Olympian ONCL10/1RZ	Northern Counties	B39/24F	1988	First in Yorkshire, 2002
3382	G176JYG	Leyland Olympian ONCL10/1RZ	Northern Counties	B47/29F	1990	First in Yorkshire, 2002
3383	G177JYG	Leyland Olympian ONCL10/1RZ	Northern Counties	B47/29F	1990	First in Yorkshire, 2002
3384	G178JYG	Leyland Olympian ONCL10/1RZ	Northern Counties	B47/29F	1990	First in Yorkshire, 2002

3401-3410
Volvo Olympian   Alexander Royale RV   B43/29F   1998

| 3401 | S654NUG | 3403 | S656NUG | 3405 | S658NUG | 3407 | S660NUG | 3409 | S662NUG |
| 3402 | S655NUG | 3404 | S657NUG | 3406 | S659NUG | 3408 | S661NUG | 3410 | S663NUG |

4801-4810
Scania N113DRB   East Lancashire   B51/37F*   1989-90   *809-16 are B47/37F
The Coachmasters, Rochdale, 2000

| 4801 | G801JRH | 4803 | G803JRH | 4805 | G805JRH | 4807 | H813WKH | 4809 | H815WKH |
| 4802 | G802JRH | 4804 | G804JRH | 4806 | H812WKH | 4808 | H814WKH | 4810 | H816WKH |

| 4811 | OTO555M | Scania N112DRB | Alexander RH | B47/29F | 1988 | The Coachmasters, Rochdale, 2000 |
| 4812 | F705JCN | Scania N112DRB | Alexander RH | B47/29F | 1988 | The Coachmasters, Rochdale, 2000 |

4821-4826
Dennis Dominator DDA1027   East Lancashire   B47/33F   1989   The Coachmasters, Rochdale, 2000

| 4821 | F152HAT | 4823 | F154HAT | 4824 | F155HAT | 4825 | F156HAT | 4826 | F157HAT |
| 4822 | F153HAT | | | | | | | | |

5015	GBU15V	MCW Metrobus DR102/10	MCW	B43/30F	1980
5035	MRJ35W	MCW Metrobus DR102/21	MCW	B43/30F	1981
5050	MRJ50W	MCW Metrobus DR102/21	MCW	B43/30F	1981

5114-5187
MCW Metrobus DR102/23   MCW   B43/30F   1981-83

5114	SND114X	5129	SND129X	5149	SND149X	5172	ANA172Y	5183	ANA183Y
5115	SND115X	5138	SND138X	5151	ANA151Y	5181	ANA181Y	5187	ANA187Y
5126	SND126X	5140	SND140X						

Following the transfer of Excels to Bolton from Leicester, and the withdrawal of the four in London, all the group's Excels are now at the one depot. Most are being refurbished with former Timeline 6602, R214SBA now carrying Barbie 2 as its interior is not to first's corporate scheme. It is seen on the Eccles service though the type are also common on the Edgworth and Egerton services. *Mark Doggett*

| 5203 | C203FVU | MCW Metrobus DR132/8 | Northern Counties | BC43/30F | 1986 | |
| 5208 | C208FVU | MCW Metrobus DR132/8 | Northern Counties | BC43/30F | 1986 | |

5301-5320

MCW Metrobus DR102/51 — Northern Counties — BC43/30F* 1986-87 *seating varies

5301	D301JVR	5305	D305JVR	5309	D309JVR	5313	D313LNB	5317	D317LNB
5302	D302JVR	5306	D306JVR	5310	D310JVR	5314	D314LNB	5318	D318LNB
5303	D303JVR	5307	D307JVR	5311	D311LNB	5315	D315LNB	5319	D319LNB
5304	D304JVR	5308	D308JVR	5312	D312LNB	5316	D316LNB	5320	D320LNB

5401-5405

MCW Metrobus DR102/72 — MCW — B46/31F 1989 First Glasgow, 2000

5401	G384OGD	5402	G385OGD	5403	G386OGD	5404	G387OGD	5405	G388OGD

5411-5415

MCW Metrobus DR102/69 — MCW — B46/31F 1988 First Yorkshire, 2001

5411	F601XWY	5412	F602XWY	5413	F603XWY	5414	F604XWY	5415	F605XWY

5421-5440

MCW Metrobus DR102/72 — MCW — B46/31F 1989 First in Glasgow, 2001-02

5421	G389OGD	5425	G393OGD	5428	G396OGD	5431	G399OGD	5437	G405OGD
5422	G390OGD	5426	G394OGD	5429	G397OGD	5432	G400OGD	5438	G406OGD
5424	G392OGD	5427	G395OGD	5430	G398OGD	5435	G403OGD	5439	G407OGD

| 5481 | G107FJW | MCW Metrobus DR102/70 | MCW | B43/30F | 1989 | First in London, 2002 |
| 5482 | E470SON | MCW Metrobus DR102/63 | MCW | B45/30F | 1989 | First in London, 2002 |

5483-5497

MCW Metrobus DR102/71 — MCW — B46/31F 1988 First in London, 2002

5483	F279NHJ	5486	F282NHJ	5489	F285NHJ	5492	F288NHJ	5495	F291NHJ
5484	F280NHJ	5487	F283NHJ	5490	F286NHJ	5493	F289NHJ	5496	F293NHJ
5485	F281NHJ	5488	F284NHJ	5491	F287NHJ	5494	F290NHJ	5497	F294NHJ

| 5571 | B571RWY | MCW Metrobus DR102/38 | MCW | B43/30F | 1984 | Yorkshire Rider, 1996 |
| 5572 | B572RWY | MCW Metrobus DR102/38 | MCW | B43/30F | 1984 | Yorkshire Rider, 1996 |

6001-6025 — Dennis Dart SLF — Plaxton Pointer — N41F* — 1996-97 — *6006 is N37F

6001	P301LND	6006	P306LND	6011	P311LND	6016	P316LND	6021	P321LND
6002	P302LND	6007	P307LND	6012	P312LND	6017	P317LND	6022	P322LND
6003	P303LND	6008	P308LND	6013	P313LND	6018	P318LND	6023	P323LND
6004	P304LND	6009	P309LND	6014	P314LND	6019	P319LND	6024	P324LND
6005	P305LND	6010	P310LND	6015	P315LND	6020	P320LND	6025	P325LND

6034-6080 — Dennis Dart SLF — Plaxton Pointer 2 — N37F* — 1997 — *6063-6073 are N34F

6034	R234SBA	6044	R244SBA	6054	R254SBA	6063	R263SBA	6072	R272SBA
6035	R235SBA	6045	R245SBA	6055	R255SBA	6064	R264SBA	6073	R273SBA
6036	R236SBA	6046	R246SBA	6056	R256SBA	6065	R265SBA	6074	R274SBA
6037	R237SBA	6047	R247SBA	6057	R257SBA	6066	R266SBA	6075	R275SBA
6038	R238SBA	6048	R248SBA	6058	R258SBA	6067	R267SBA	6076	R276SBA
6039	R239SBA	6049	R249SBA	6059	R259SBA	6068	R268SBA	6077	R277SBA
6040	R240SBA	6050	R250SBA	6060	R260SBA	6069	R269SBA	6078	R278SBA
6041	R241SBA	6051	R251SBA	6061	R261SBA	6070	R270SBA	6079	R279SBA
6042	R242SBA	6052	R252SBA	6062	R262SBA	6071	R271SBA	6080	R280SBA
6043	R243SBA	6053	R253SBA								

6201	S764RNE	Dennis Dart SLF	Plaxton Pointer MPD	N28F	1999	Springfield Coaches, Wigan, 2001
6203	S766RNE	Dennis Dart SLF	Plaxton Pointer MPD	N28F	1999	Springfield Coaches, Wigan, 2001

6501-6530 — Dennis Dart SLF — Wright Crusader — NC41F* — 1996-97 — *seating varies

6501	P501LND	6507	P507LND	6513	P513LND	6519	P519LND	6525	P525LND
6502	P502LND	6508	P508LND	6514	P514LND	6520	P520LND	6526	P526LND
6503	P503LND	6509	P509LND	6515	P515LND	6521	P521LND	6527	P527LND
6504	P504LND	6510	P510LND	6516	P516LND	6522	P522LND	6528	P528LND
6505	P505LND	6511	P511LND	6517	P517LND	6523	P523LND	6529	P529LND
6506	P506LND	6512	P512LND	6518	P518LND	6524	P524LND	6530	P530LND

6601-6610 — Optare Excel L1070 — Optare — N38F — 1996-97 — Timeline, 1998

6601	P213HRJ	6603	R215SBA	6605	R217SBA	6607	R219SBA	6609	R221SBA
6602	R214SBA	6604	R216SBA	6606	R218SBA	6608	R220SBA	6610	R223SBA

6621-6630 — Optare Excel L1150 — Optare — N38F — 1997 — First in Leicester, 2002

6621	R1LCB	6623	R3LCB	6625	R5LCB	6627	R7LCB	6629	R9LCB
6622	R2LCB	6624	R4LCB	6626	R6LCB	6628	R8LCB	6630	R10LCB

6701-6708 — Volvo B6BLE — Wright Crusader — N36F — 1999

6701	T701PND	6703	T703PND	6705	T705PND	6707	T707PND	6708	T708PND
6702	T702PND	6704	T704PND	6706	T706PND				

6711	X611NBU	Volvo B6BLE	Wrightbus Crusader 2	N38F	2001
6712	Y394RTD	Volvo B6BLE	Wrightbus Crusader 2	N38F	2001
6713	Y395RTD	Volvo B6BLE	Wrightbus Crusader 2	N38F	2001

7001-7010 — Volvo Citybus B10M-50 — Northern Counties — B45/31F* — 1991-92 — *7009/10 are B45/26FL

7001	H701GVM	7003	H703GVM	7005	H705GVM	7007	J707ONF	7009	J709ONF
7002	H702GVM	7004	H704GVM	7006	H706GVM	7008	J708ONF	7010	J710ONF

Transferred into the First fleet in Manchester saw former Glasgow Citybuses displacing the last of the Atlanteans. Pictured waiting time in Leigh bus station is 7046, G689PNS. *Mark Doggett*

7021-7062   Volvo Citybus B10M-50   Alexander RV   B47/37F 1989   First in Glasgow, 2002

7021	F792LSU	7030	G282OGE	7039	G297OGE	7047	G690PNS	7055	G701PNS
7022	F793LSU	7031	G283OGE	7040	G298OGE	7048	G691PNS	7056	G523RDS
7023	F795LSU	7032	G284OGE	7041	G299OGE	7049	G694PNS	7057	G524RDS
7024	G412OGD	7033	G286OGE	7042	G301OGE	7050	G695PNS	7058	G525RDS
7025	G410OGD	7034	G287OGE	7043	G302OGE	7051	G696PNS	7059	G526RDS
7026	G411OGD	7035	G291OGE	7044	G687PNS	7052	G697PNS	7060	G530RDS
7027	G414OGD	7036	G293OGE	7045	G688PNS	7053	G698PNS	7061	G532RDS
028	G280OGE	7036	G294OGE	7046	G689PNS	7054	G699PNS	7062	G533RDS
029	G281OGE	7038	G296OGE						

Ancillary vehicles:-

02	G58RND	Leyland Tiger TR2R62C16Z4	Alexander N	TV	1989	Timeline, 1998
03	G60RND	Leyland Tiger TR2R62C16Z4	Alexander N	TV	1989	Timeline, 1998
04	G62RND	Leyland Tiger TR2R62C16Z4	Alexander N	TV	1989	Timeline, 1998
06	G64RND	Leyland Tiger TR2R62C16Z4	Alexander N	TV	1989	Timeline, 1998
11	G69RND	Leyland Tiger TR2R62C16Z4	Alexander N	TV	1989	Timeline, 1998
415	M415RND	Iveco TurboDaily 59.12	Marshall C 31	TV	1995	Citibus, Middleton, 1995
416	M416RND	Iveco TurboDaily 59.12	Marshall C 31	TV	1995	Citibus, Middleton, 1995
842	H373OHK	Mercedes-Benz 709D	Reeve Burgess Beaver	B23F	1991	Essex Buses, 1999
061	MRJ61W	MCW Metrobus DR102/21	MCW	TV	1981	

Previous registration

586TSO	M1GRT	OTO555M	F702JCN

Note: Full details of vehicle allocations to depots and outstations are provided each year in the First Bus Handbook. Please see page 2 for more information.

FISHWICK

John Fishwick & Sons Ltd, Golden Hill Garage, Golden Hill Lane, Leyland, PR5 2LE

1	L1JFS	DAF DE12CSSB120	Wright Cadet	N42F	2000	
2	A462LFV	Leyland Atlantean AN69/2L	Eastern Coach Works	B47/35F	1983	
3	J7JFS	Leyland Lynx LX2R11C15Z4R	Leyland Lynx 2	B47F	1991	
4	H64CCK	Leyland Lynx LX2R11C15Z4R	Leyland Lynx 2	B47F	1991	
5	H65CCK	Leyland Lynx LX2R11C15Z4R	Leyland Lynx 2	B51F	1991	
6	NFR559T	Leyland National 11351A/1R		B49F	1979	
7	GCK428W	Leyland National 2 NL116AL11/1R		B49F	1981	
8	GCK429W	Leyland National 2 NL116AL11/1R		B49F	1981	
9	WRN412V	Leyland National 2 NL116L11/1R		B49F	1980	
10	WRN413V	Leyland National 2 NL116L11/1R		B49F	1980	
· 11	NFR560T	Leyland National 11351A/1R [DAF]		B49F	1979	
12	GCK430W	Leyland National 2 NL116AL11/1R		B49F	1981	
13	UHG147V	Leyland Atlantean AN68A/2R	East Lancashire	B49/36F	1980	Preston Bus, 2000
14	J14JFS	Leyland Lynx LX2R11C15Z4R	Leyland Lynx 2	B51F	1992	
15	R845VEC	Dennis Dart SLF	Wright Crusader	N41F	1997	
16	OFV620X	Leyland National 2 NL116AL11/1R		B49F	1981	
17	R846VEC	Dennis Dart SLF	Wright Crusader	N41F	1997	
18	R847VEC	Dennis Dart SLF	Wright Crusader	N41F	1997	
19	R848VEC	Dennis Dart SLF	Wright Crusader	N41F	1997	
20	UHG150V	Leyland Atlantean AN68A/2R	East Lancashire	B49/36F	1980	Preston Bus, 2000
21	UHG144V	Leyland Atlantean AN68A/2R	East Lancashire	B49/36F	1980	Preston Bus, 2000
22	UHG149V	Leyland Atlantean AN68A/2R	East Lancashire	B49/36F	1980	Preston Bus, 2000
23	GRN895W	Leyland Atlantean AN69/1L	Eastern Coach Works	B43/31F	1981	
24	UHG148V	Leyland Atlantean AN68A/2R	East Lancashire	B49/36F	1980	Preston Bus, 2000
25	D25VCW	Leyland Lynx LX112TL11ZR1	Leyland	B47F	1986	
26	OFV621X	Leyland National 2 NL116AL11/1R		B49F	1981	
27	ABV939Y	Leyland National 2 NL116TL11/1R		B49F	1982	
28	FBV524S	Leyland National 11351A/1R		B49F	1978	
29	T154AUA	Mercedes-Benz Vario O814	Alexander ALX100	B27F	1999	Arden, Cumbernauld, 2001

Though the fleet has seen the arrival of several Atlanteans recently, the core services use single-decks. Twelve Nationals are currently operated including National 2 8, GCK429W, which was delivered in 1981. It is seen in Lancaster Road in Preston while returning to Leyland on route 111. *Richard Godfrey*

With an operating base adjacent to the former Leyland factory, the use of that companies products has been loyally consistent. The factory now produces the DAF range of trucks and, interestingly, Fishwick were the first operator to place into service the Wrightbus Cadet that is based on the SB120 unit. Pictured as it sets out for home, 37, X822NWX is one of four Cadets now operated. *David Longbottom*

30	D30VCW	Leyland Lynx LX112TL11ZR1	Leyland	B47F	1986	
32	D32YCW	Leyland Lynx LX112TL11ZR1S	Leyland	B47F	1987	
33	D33YCW	Leyland Lynx LX112TL11ZR1S	Leyland	B47F	1987	
34	XCW957R	Leyland National 11351A/1R		B49F	1977	
35	R32GNW	DAF DE02GSSB220	Northern Counties Paladin	B42F	1997	Arriva Bus & Coach, 2000
36	X821NWX	DAF DE12CSSB120	Wrightbus Cadet	N42F	2001	
37	X822NWX	DAF DE12CSSB120	Wrightbus Cadet	N42F	2001	
38	X823NWX	DAF DE12CSSB120	Wrightbus Cadet	N42F	2001	
	T58AUA	DAF DE33WSSB3000	Van Hool Alizée 2	C48FT	1999	
	T59AUA	DAF DE33WSSB3000	Van Hool Alizée 2	C48FT	1999	
	W223CDN	EOS E180Z	EOS 90	C48FT	2000	
	W224CDN	EOS E180Z	EOS 90	C48FT	2000	
	Y477HUA	EOS E180Z	EOS 90	C48FT	2001	
	Y448HUA	EOS E180Z	EOS 90	C48FT	2001	
	YD02RHF	EOS E180Z	EOS 90	C48FT	2002	
M10	E100MFV	Mercedes-Benz 609D	Reeve Burgess Beaver	BC19F	1988	

FRAZER EAGLE

Frazer Eagle Ltd, Ewbank House, Cannon Street, Accrington, BB5 0RE

5692FM	Volvo B10M-60	Van Hool Alizée	C49FT	1989	Clyde Coast, Ardrossan, 1997
5287FM	Volvo B10M-60	Van Hool Alizée	C49FT	1993	Shearings, 2000
7501FM	Volvo B10M-60	Van Hool Alizée	C51FT	1993	Shearings, 2000
7974FM	Volvo B10M-60	Van Hool Alizée	C46FT	1993	Shearings, 2000
3402FM	Volvo B10M-62	Van Hool Alizée	C46FT	1995	Shearings, 2001
7345FM	Volvo B10M-62	Van Hool Alizée	C46FT	1995	Shearings, 2001
RJI8711	Volvo B10M-62	Van Hool Alizée (1995)	C49FT	1995	Shearings, 2001
S324JNW	Volvo B10M-62	Van Hool T9 Alizée	C49FT	1998	
S325JNW	Volvo B10M-62	Van Hool T9 Alizée	C49FT	1998	
T991JNW	Volvo B10M-62	Van Hool T9 Alizée	C49FT	1999	
T992JNW	Volvo B10M-62	Van Hool T9 Alizée	C49FT	1999	
Y716SUB	Bova FHD12.370	Bova Futura	C48FT	2001	
Y717SUB	Bova FHD12.370	Bova Futura	C48FT	2001	
YT51KPT	Bova FHD12.370	Bova Futura	C48FT	2002	
02	Bova FHD12.370	Bova Futura	C48FT	2002	

Previous Registrations

3402FM	M666KVU, SPR35, M260TRJ	7501FM	K459VVR
5287FM	K456VVR	7974FM	K457VVR
5692FM	G164ECS, RJI8711	RJI8711	M670KVU
7345FM	M683KVU		

Depots: Tanpits Road, Church, Accrington.

The latest four Van Hool Alizée in the Fraser Eagle fleet are built to the latest T9 design. Pictured while undertaking rail replacement services at Preston, S324JNW shows the livery style used by the company. **Bob Downham**

GRAYWAY of WIGAN

J R & M Gray, 237 Manchester Road, Wigan, WN2 2EA

HEK86G	Bedford J2SZ10	Plaxton Embassy	C20F	1968	Eavesway, Ashton-in-Makerfield, '74
ACH942A	Leyland Leopard PSU5C/4R	Plaxton Viewmaster IV	C57F	1980	Stubbs, Wigan, 1992
NEH103V	Volvo B58-61	Plaxton Supreme IV	C57F	1980	The Birmingham Coach Co, 1996
NEH104V	Volvo B58-61	Plaxton Supreme IV	C57F	1980	The Birmingham Coach Co, 1996
STM238W	Volvo B58-61	Plaxton Supreme IV	C57F	1981	Cass, Greasby, 1987
VAV257X	Leyland Tiger TRCTL11/3R	Plaxton Supreme V Express	C57F	1982	Rapson, Inverness, 2002
WEC263Y	Leyland Tiger TRCTL11/3R	Plaxton Paramount 3200	C53F	1982	Holmeswood Coaches, 1993
TIA9275	Volvo B10M-61	Jonckheere Jubilee	C51FT	1983	Hurst's of Wigan, 1996
GSU386	Volvo B10M-61	Jonckheere Jubilee	C51FT	1983	Yorkshire Rider, 1991
UOV721	Leyland Tiger TRCTL11/3R	Duple Caribbean	C48FT	1983	Walls of Wigan, 1999
FXI547	Scania K112CRS	Jonckheere Jubilee	C51FT	1984	Mitchell, Plean, 1990
LIL3061	Leyland Tiger TRCTL11/3RH	Plaxton Paramount 3500 II	C48FT	1984	Walls of Wigan, 1999
LIL5947	Leyland Tiger TRCTL11/3R	Plaxton Paramount 3200 II	C57F	1984	Walls of Wigan, 1999
LIL5948	Leyland Tiger TRCTL11/3RH	Plaxton Paramount 3500 II	C49FT	1985	Walls of Wigan, 1999
LIL6147	Leyland Tiger TRCTL11/3RZ	Plaxton Paramount 3200 II	C57F	1985	Walls of Wigan, 1999
RIB7856	Volvo B10M-61	Jonckheere Jubilee	C51FT	1985	Cass. Moreton, 2000
B153NKB	Leyland Tiger TRCTL11/3R	Jonckheere Jubilee P90	C47/12FT	1985	Topping, Wavertree, 1995
D836KWT	Freight Rover Sherpa	Dormobile	M16	1986	Whittaker, Penwortham, 1991
E671FSH	Mercedes-Benz 609D	Reeve Burgess Beaver	BC23F	1987	Costello, Dundee, 1993
E373FKX	Leyland Tiger TRCTL11/3ARZ	Plaxton Paramount 3200 III	C57F	1987	Walls of Wigan, 1999
LIL6149	Leyland Tiger TRCTL11/3ARZ	Plaxton Paramount 3200 III	C57F	1988	Walls of Wigan, 1999
F793FOS	Mercedes-Benz 609D	North West CS	BC26F	1988	Airey, Arkholme, 1995
F289GNB	Mercedes-Benz 609D	Made-to-Measure	C24F	1988	Walls of Wigan, 1999
G902WAY	Volvo B10M-60	Caetano Algarve	C57F	1990	Walls of Wigan, 1999
H461BEU	Volvo B10M-60	Plaxton Paramount 3200 III	C57F	1990	Walls of Wigan, 1999
H583JDB	Volvo B10M-60	Van Hool Alizée	C49FT	1991	Walls of Wigan, 1999

Following the acquisition of Walls of Wigan the Grayway fleet has seen considerable expansion. Repainting has all but seen the last Walls colour removed. Newest vehicle in the fleet is former Wallace Arnold tour coach P312VWR, shown here in Ripon while on a day excursion. *Bob Downham*

A collection of ten Leyland Tigers has been built up by Grayway with Plaxton Paramount bodywork being t
more common. The combination is seen in WEC263Y which carries the lower height 3200 model.
Bob Downham

H584JDB	Volvo B10M-60	Van Hool Alizée	C49FT	1991	Walls of Wigan, 1999
H919SWF	Mercedes-Benz 811D	Reeve Burgess Beaver	BC25F	1991	South Wales Police, 1996
J567DFU	Mercedes-Benz 410D	Autobus Classique	M13	1991	Walls of Wigan, 1999
J867JNS	Volvo B10M-60	Van Hool Alizée	C52FT	1992	Walls of Wigan, 1999
K838HUM	Volvo B10M-60	Jonckheere Deauville 45	C53F	1993	Hilton's, Newton-le-Willows, 1998
L950NWW	Volvo B10M-60	Jonckheere Deauville 45	C51FT	1993	Hilton's, Newton-le-Willows, 2001
L412CDB	Mercedes-Benz 811D	Autobus Classique Nouvelle	BC18F	1994	Walls of Wigan, 1999
M598RFS	Mercedes-Benz 814D	Plaxton Beaver	BC33F	1994	City Nippy, Middleton, 2001
M832HNS	Volvo B10M-62	Van Hool Alizée	C53F	1995	Parks of Hamilton, 1998
P312VWR	Volvo B10M-62	Van Hool Alizée	C53F	1997	Wallace Arnold, 2000

Previous registrations

ACH942A	NGP86V	LIL6149	E444MFV
B153NKB	B764VHG, TOP11N	LIL6167	BJA856Y
F793FOS	A1WHO, F48GNS	M832HNS	LSK496
FXI547	B519CBD, PR1787, B904JRP	NEH103V	PSV323, HTV17V
GSU386	A334YDT	NEH104V	MDS231V, 803HOM
H583JDB	H179DVM, SPR35, H191JNE, ESU121	RIB7856	C407URP
H584JDB	H180DVM, 5140RU	TIA9275	ONV648Y
LIL3061	B86SWX	UOV721	BJA856Y
LIL5947	B690BFV	WEC263Y	MEO200Y, 466YMG
LIL5948	C456OFL		

Depots: Brown Street, Higher Ince, Wigan and Firth Street, Wigan.

HOLMESWOOD

Holmeswood Coaches Ltd, Fallowfields, Sandy Way, Holmeswood, Rufford, L40 1UB
Bostocks Coaches Ltd, Spragg Street, Congleton, CW12 1QP
Walker Coaches, Malvern House - Old Road, Anderton, Northwich, CW9 6AG

H	LBD837P	Bristol VRT/SL3/6LXB	Eastern Coach Works	B43/31F	1975	
-	BCA126W	Leyland Tiger TRCTL11/3R	Duple Dominant II	C57F	1981	
H	OCW9X	Leyland Atlantean AN68C/1R	East Lancashire	B43/31F	1982	Blackburn Borough
H	VBV20Y	Leyland Atlantean AN68C/1R	East Lancashire	B43/31F	1983	Blackburn Borough
H	AAX300A	Leyland Tiger TRCTL11/3R	Berkhof Excellence 1000L ('95)	C55F	1984	Tellings - Golden Miller, 1992
W	JHF825	Volvo B10M-61	Duple Caribbean	C53F	1984	Park'sof Hamilton, 1986
W	184XNO	Volvo B10M-61	Duple Caribbean	C53F	1984	Globe, Barnsley, 1986
H	A914RRN	Leyland Tiger B43	Plaxton Paramount 3200	C49F	1984	Mercers, Longridge, 1984
H	RIB8747	Leyland Olympian ONTL11/2R	Eastern Coach Works	C45/27F	1984	Oare, Holywell, 1998
-w	B446WKE	Leyland Olympian ONTL11/2RSp	Eastern Coach Works	C45/28F	1984	Arriva Scotland West, 2000
H	SIL2732	Leyland Olympian ONTL11/2RSp	Eastern Coach Works	C45/26F	1985	Arriva Scotland West, 2000
-w	B874XWR	Volvo B10M-61	Plaxton Paramount 3500	C53F	1985	Wilts & Dorset, 2001
B	SIW1909	Leyland Tiger TRCTL11/3RH	Plaxton Paramount 3500	C53F	1985	Wilts & Dorset, 2001
B	LIB6438	Leyland Tiger TRCTL11/3R	Plaxton Paramount 3500 II	C53F	1986	Mayne, Manchester, 1999
B	LIB6440	Leyland Tiger TRCTL11/3R	Plaxton Paramount 3500 II	C53F	1986	Mayne, Manchester, 1999
W	C122PNV	Leyland Tiger TRCTL11/3RZ	Plaxton Paramount 3200 II Exp	BC70F	1986	Stagecoach United Counties, 2000
H	C454GKE	Leyland Olympian ONTL11/2RSp	Eastern Coach Works	C45/26F	1986	Arriva Scotland West, 2000
W	D261FUL	Leyland Olympian ONLXB/1RH	Eastern Coach Works	BC42/29F	1987	London Central, 1998
B	RAZ5172	DAF MB230DKFL615	Plaxton Paramount 3200 III	C55F	1987	Mayne, Manchester, 2001
W	CLZ8353	DAF MB230DKFL615	Plaxton Paramount 3200 III	C55F	1987	Mayne, Manchester, 2001
H	A19HWD	Leyland Tiger TRCTL11/3R	Duple 320	BC70F	1987	Bodman & Heath, Worton, 1999
W	JHF826	Dennis Javelin 10SDA	Plaxton Paramount 3200 II	C35F	1989	

Seen on a wet day in London's Aldwych, Berkhof-bodied MAN P5HWD illustrates the Excellence 1000 midi body. Since this picture was taken the index number has been transferred to a Van Hool Alizée.
Dave Heath

A selection of brightly coloured Hs decorate Holmeswood's Y42HHE, a Scania K124IB4 with Van Hool T9 Alizèe bodywork. It is seen in Rufford with a party of school children shortly after entering service.
Bob Downham

B	HOI7544	Scania K112CRB	Van Hool Alizée H	C55F	1987	LB of Hackney, 2000
H	A4HWD	Leyland Lion LDTL11/1R	Alexander RH	BC49/37F	1988	City of Nottingham, 2001
H	E941CDS	Leyland Lion LDTL11/1R	Alexander RH	BC49/37F	1988	City of Nottingham, 2001
H	JHF824	Volvo B10M-60	Jonckheere Jubilee P50	C55F	1989	Reading Buses, 2001
H	YXI7923	Volvo B10M-61	Van Hool Alizée H	C55F	1989	Shearings, 1993
H	LIB804	Leyland Tiger TRCTL11/3RZ	Plaxton Paramount 3200 III	BC70F	1989	Andrews, Groby, 2000
B	152ENM	Volvo B10M-60	Plaxton Paramount 3500 III	C53F	1989	Arriva Southern Counties, 1999
B	YSU991	Volvo B10M-60	Plaxton Paramount 3500 II	C53F	1989	
B	NIL5675	Volvo B10M-60	Plaxton Paramount 3200 III	C57F	1989	Wallace Arnold, 1993
H	YTY867	Volvo B10M-60	Plaxton Paramount 3200 II	C57F	1989	Woodstones, Kidderminster, 1995
B	629LFM	Volvo B10M-60	Plaxton Paramount 3200 III	C57F	1989	Arriva Southern Counties, 2001
H	F523UVW	Volvo B10M-60	Plaxton Paramount 3200 III	C57F	1989	Arriva Southern Counties, 2001
B	MIL9576	Dennis Javelin 12SDA1913	Plaxton Paramount 3200 II	C53F	1989	Brighton & Hove, 2000
H	UTF119	Leyland Tiger TRCL10/3ARZM	Duple 320	BC70F	1989	City of Nottingham, 2001
W	296HFM	Leyland Tiger TRCL10/3ARZM	Duple 320	BC70F	1989	City of Nottingham, 2001
W	G376NRC	Scania N113DRB	Alexander RH	B47/33F	1989	City of Nottingham, 2001
W	G378NRC	Scania N113DRB	Alexander RH	B47/33F	1989	City of Nottingham, 2001
H	F128KTV	Leyland Olympian ONCL10/2RZ	Northern Counties	B49/34F	1989	City of Nottingham, 2001
B	716GRM	Scania K113CRB	Plaxton Paramount 3500 III	C57F	1990	Lewis Meridian, Greenwich, 2001
B	G805BPG	Volvo B10M-60	Plaxton Paramount 3500 III	C49FT	1990	Airlinks, 2002
B	G809BPG	Volvo B10M-60	Plaxton Paramount 3500 III	C49FT	1990	Airlinks, 2002
H	J91JFR	Dennis Javelin 12SDA2118	Plaxton Première 320	BC70F	1991	Dunn-Line, Nottingham, 2001
W	J29LJA	Dennis Javelin 11SDA1921	Duple 320	BC68F	1991	Mayne, Manchester, 2001
H	J796CNN	Leyland Tiger TRCL10/3ARZM	Plaxton Paramount 3200 III	C57F	1991	City of Nottingham, 2001
W	H929DRJ	Scania K93CRB	Plaxton Paramount 3200 III	C55F	1991	Shearings, 1995
W	H2HWD	Scania K93CRB	Plaxton Paramount 3200 III	C55F	1991	Shearings, 1995
W	848AFM	Volvo B10M-60	Van Hool Alizée H	C53F	1989	
W	PBZ7052	Dennis Javelin 11SDA1921	Duple 320	BC68F	1991	Mayne, Manchester, 2001
B	K5HWD	Volvo B10M-60	Jonckheere Jubilee P599	C49FT	1992	Longmynd, Pontesbury, 1999
W	464HYB	Volvo B10M-60	Van Hool Alizée	C53F	1992	
W	LIB804	Scania K113CRB	Van Hool Alizée H	C53F	1992	Hardings, Redditch, 2001
B	J220XKY	Scania K93CRB	Van Hool Alizée H	C55F	1992	Pemico, South Bermondsey, 1998
H	J276NNC	Scania K93CRB	Plaxton Première 320	C53F	1992	Galloway, Mendlesham, 2001
W	J915OAY	Dennis Javelin 12SDA1929	Caetano Algarve II	C53F	1992	, Radcliffe, 2001
B	J455FSR	Volvo B10M-60	Plaxton Paramount 3500 III	C57F	1992	Stagecoach Scotland East, 2001

A pair of Ayats Bravo coaches joined the Holmeswood fleet in 2001. Pictured at Hampton Court is Y98KRJ, one of the pair. The coach is using a luggage trailer, a feature more common in other European countries.
Dave Heath

-	L548EHD	DAF SB3000DKVF601	Van Hool Alizée H	C51FT	1993	?, 2002
-	L549EHD	DAF SB3000DKVF601	Van Hool Alizée H	C51FT	1993	?, 2002
-	L550EHD	DAF SB3000DKVF601	Van Hool Alizée H	C51FT	1993	?, 2002
-	L551EHD	DAF SB3000DKVF601	Van Hool Alizée H	C51FT	1993	?, 2002
-	L552EHD	DAF SB3000DKVF601	Van Hool Alizée H	C51FT	1993	?, 2002
H	L553EHD	DAF SB3000DKVF601	Van Hool Alizée H	C51FT	1993	?, 2002
-	L554EHD	DAF SB3000DKVF601	Van Hool Alizée H	C51FT	1993	?, 2002
H	L5HWD	Dennis Javelin 10SDA2119	Berkhof Excellence 1000L	C34FT	1994	Owen, Oswestry, 2000
W	466YMG	Volvo B10M-60	Van Hool Alizée H	C49FT	1993	Castell Coaches, Trethormas, 1999
B	ESK807	Volvo B10M-60	Van Hool Alizée H	C49FT	1993	Chambers, Bures, 2000
B	IIL5133	Volvo B10M-60	Caetano Algarve II	C49FT	1993	Belle Vue, Wakefield, 2001
H	K4HWD	Dennis Javelin 12SDA2131	Plaxton Première 320	BC70F	1993	?,
B	L335PWX	Bova FLD12.270	Bova Futura	C53F	1994	Wilfreda, Adwick-le-Street, 2001
B	L388YNV	Dennis Javelin 12SDA2131	Plaxton Première 320	C57F	1994	Country Lion, Northampton, 2000
B	L6HWD	Dennis Javelin 10SDA2139	Berkhof Excellence 1000L	C39FT	1994	
W	L18HWD	Mercedes-Benz 711D	Plaxton Beaver	BC25F	1994	Hillary, Prudhoe, 1997
B	M31KAX	Mercedes-Benz 711D	Autobus Classique	C25F	1995	Roberts, Maerdy, 2000
B	ASV237	Dennis Javelin GX	Caetano Algarve	C51FT	1995	Allied, Uxbridge, 2000
H	M911OVR	Dennis Javelin GX	Neoplan Transliner	C53F	1995	Camden, West Kingsdown, 2001
H	M335KRY	Volvo B10M-60	Jonckheere Jubilee P599	C51FT	1995	Chambers, Moneymore, 1999
B	M364LFX	Scania K113CRB	Van Hool Alizée H	C48FT	1995	Dorset Travel, 2000
H	M500GSM	Scania K93CRB	Van Hool Alizée H	C55F	1995	Mayne, Buckie, 2001
H	201SC	Volvo B10M-62	Plaxton Première 350	C49FT	1996	Redwing, Camberwell, 2000
H	N91WVC	Scania K113TRB	Van Hool Astrobel	C57/17CT	1996	Harry Shaw, Coventry, 1999
B	N368TJT	Scania K113CRB	Van Hool Alizée HE	C44FT	1996	?
H	N78CVP	Volvo B10M-62	Jonckheere Deauville 45	C53F	1996	Kerry Tours, Killarney, 2001
H	N547SJF	Volvo B10M-62	Jonckheere Deauville 45	C53F	1996	Clarke of London, 1999
B	N910DWJ	Dennis Javelin 10SDA2163	Berkhof Excellence 1000 L	C39FT	1996	Buddens, Romsey, 1998
B	N897KFA	Dennis Javelin GX	Plaxton Première 350	C49FT	1996	Happy Days, Woodseaves, 2000
B	N899KFA	Dennis Javelin GX	Plaxton Première 350	C53F	1996	Happy Days, Woodseaves, 2000
B	N443WUX	Dennis Javelin 12SDA2155	Plaxton Première 320	C57FT	1996	Longmynd, Pontesbury, 1999
B	5AAX	Volvo B10M-60	Berkhof Excellence 1000 LD	C57FT	1997	?
B	P50HWD	Dennis Javelin GX	Plaxton Première 350	C49FT	1997	Dunn-Line, Nottingham, 2000
W	P4HWD	Dennis Javelin 12SDA2131	Plaxton Première 320	C53F	1997	Dunn-Line, Nottingham, 2001
H	P2HWD	MAN 11.220 HOCL - R	Caetano Algarve II	C35F	1997	

Previous registrations:

5AAX		K4HWD	L491JFU
152ENM	G802BPG, ESK807, G881RRN	K5HWD	K870ANT, K2TGE, K240EUX
184XNO	B359DWF	L5HWD	L3SLT, L320CVM
201SC		L6HWD	
296HFM	JLS457V	L18HWD	L584RWJ
464HYB	J206NNC	L388YNV	A8CLN
466YMG	LSK473, KSK948, L141AHS	LIB804	J835JNP
629LFM	F452PSL, NXI9007, F572UPB	LIB6438	C348YBA
716GRM	H808RWJ, 686CXV, H582DMY	LIB6440	C426YBA
848AFM	F338SMD	MIL9576	
A4HWD	E160YGB, VLT166, E889CDS	NIL5675	F447DUG
A19HWD	E179WDV	P4HWD	P745GNU
A20HWD	C256FHJ, A4HWD, 201SC	P5HWD	P263YGG
AAX300A	A257VWO	R6HWD	R427
ASV237	N784ORY	R7BOS	R448FWT
		P50HWD	P744GNU
CLZ8353	D640WNU	PBZ7052	
D261FUL	D261FUL, 2CLT	RAZ5172	D634WNU
E941CDS	E162YGB, 32CLT	RIB8747	A105FPL
ESK807	K816HUM	S618KUT	3353RU
HOI7544	E125BRG, TTC86, A15LBH, E969LRR	SIL2732	G452GKE
H2HWD	H927DRJ	SIW1909	F909UPR
IIL5133	K588VBC	TJI4927	F725ENE
JHF824	F755OJH	UTF119	F791JTV
JHF825	A731HFP	YSU991	KCA
JHF826	F906LAP, MIL9576	YTY867	
J276NNC	J276NNC, 1754PP	YXI7923	

Depots: Fallowfields, Sandy Way, Holmeswood, Cowling Brow, Chorley; Spragg Street, Congleton; Old Road, Northwich and Derby Road, Southport

HULME HALL

Hulme Hall Coaches Ltd, 75 Hulme Hall Road, Cheadle Hulme, Stockport SK8 6LA

WTU468W	Bristol VRT/SL3/6LXB	Eastern Coach Works	B43/31F	1980	Arriva Cymru, 2000
YMB500W	Bristol VRT/SL3/6LXB	Eastern Coach Works	B43/31F	1981	Arriva Cymru, 2000
PFC514W	Bristol VRT/SL3/6LXB	Eastern Coach Works	B43/27D	1981	Oxford Bus Company, 1993
PFC515W	Bristol VRT/SL3/6LXB	Eastern Coach Works	B43/27D	1981	Oxford Bus Company, 1993
MEF823W	Bristol VRT/SL3/6LXB	Eastern Coach Works	B43/31F	1981	Arriva North East, 1999
DPX685W	Bristol VRT/SL3/6LXB	Eastern Coach Works	B43/31F	1981	Southern Vectis, 2001
VEX291X	Bristol VRT/SL3/6LXB	Eastern Coach Works	BC41/25F	1981	GHA Coaches, New Broughton,1999
VUA472X	Bristol VRT/SL3/6LXB	Eastern Coach Works	B43/31F	1981	West Riding, 1994
VJI6694	Leyland National NL116AL11/2R	East Lancashire Greenway	BC49F	1982	Stagecoach Ribble, 1999
SIB2014	Volvo B10M-61	Plaxton Paramount 3500 II	C49FT	1986	National Holidays, 1998
515VTB	Volvo B10M-61	Plaxton Paramount 3500 III	C53F	1988	National Holidays, 1999
OTK802	Volvo B10M-61	Plaxton Paramount 3500 III	C49FT	1988	National Holidays, 1998
VJI6850	Iveco TurboDaily 59.10	Mellor	BC29F	1993	Wood & Woodbridge, Benton, 2001

Previous registrations:

515VTB	E574UHS, PXI7915	VJI6694	FCA9X, 292CLT, WPC316X
OTK802	E578UHS, PJI8916	VJI6850	L321BOD
SIB2014	C106AFX		

Depot:- Lower Bent Farm, Stanley Road, Cheadle Hulme

Hulme Hall's principal work is the provision of school services employing eight Bristol VR as its main type. Pictured at the depot is former Crosville WTU468W which latterly operated with Arriva Cymru. *Cliff Beeton*

JP TRAVEL

City Nippy - JP Executive Travel - Hail & Ride

P V Walsh, Cromer Garage, John Lee Fold, Middleton, Rochdale, M24 2LR

Reg	Chassis	Body	Seating	Year	History
C752OCN	MCW Metrobus DR102/55	MCW	B46/31F	1986	Go-Ahead Northern, 2000
D683MHS	MCW Metrobus DR102/52	MCW	B45/33F	1986	Chester, Walkden, 2000
D337VBB	Mercedes-Benz 307D	Mercedes-Benz	M12	1987	
E218WBG	Leyland Olympian ONCL10/1RZ	Alexander RH	B45/30F	1988	Arriva North West, 2001
E222WBG	Leyland Olympian ONCL10/1RZ	Alexander RH	B45/30F	1988	Arriva North West, 2001
F245YTJ	Leyland Olympian ONCL10/1RZ	Alexander RH	B45/30F	1988	Arriva North West, 2001
w F678YOG	MCW MetroRider MF150/113	MCW	B21F	1988	Arriva North West, 2001
F674XMS	Mercedes-Benz 811D	Alexander AM	B29F	1989	Avondale, Greenock, 2001
HDZ5468	Renault S75	Wright NimBus	B31F	1990	Attain, Birmingham, 2001
G889TJA	Mercedes-Benz 709D	Phoenix	B29F	1990	
G34TGW	Dennis Dart 8.5SDL3003	Carlyle Dartline	BC28F	1990	Stagecoach Devon, 2001
G35TGW	Dennis Dart 8.5SDL3003	Carlyle Dartline	BC28F	1990	Stagecoach Devon, 2001
G36TGW	Dennis Dart 8.5SDL3003	Carlyle Dartline	BC28F	1990	Stagecoach Devon, 2001
G37TGW	Dennis Dart 8.5SDL3003	Carlyle Dartline	BC28F	1990	Stagecoach Devon, 2001
H147CBU	Mercedes-Benz 709D	Phoenix	B29F	1991	
H691FNB	Mercedes-Benz 709D	Phoenix	B29F	1991	
J375GKH	Dennis Dart 8.5SDL3010	Plaxton Pointer	B24F	1991	London United, 2002
J376GKH	Dennis Dart 8.5SDL3010	Plaxton Pointer	B24F	1991	London United, 2002
J377GKH	Dennis Dart 8.5SDL3010	Plaxton Pointer	B24F	1991	London United, 2002
J378GKH	Dennis Dart 8.5SDL3010	Plaxton Pointer	B24F	1991	London United, 2002
K84UND	Mercedes-Benz 609D	Made-to-Measure	B21F	1992	
K123AJA	Mercedes-Benz 709D	Wright NimBus	B27F	1993	
L196DVM	Mercedes-Benz 709D	Wright NimBus	B27F	1993	

Six double-deck buses are now employed by J P Travel following the introduction of the type on Manchester services. Seen on a homeward leg is East Lancashire Lolyne-bodied Volvo B7TL X2JPT. As shown in this early evening view, the vehicle is fitted with high-back seating. *Bill Potter*

Now the oldest of the double-deck buses is Metrobus C752OCN. The fleet livery is all-silver relieved by coloured splashes of vinyl the same as those used to make up the fleetname. *Richard Godfrey*

L708LKY	Mercedes-Benz 811D	Wright NimBus	B29F	1993	Mercedes-Benz demonstrator, 1996
M2JPT	Mercedes-Benz 709D	Marshall C19	B27F	1994	
M598RFS	Mercedes-Benz 814D	Plaxton Beaver	BC33F	1994	Fairline, Glasgow, 2001
P876PWW	Dennis Dart SLF	Plaxton Pointer	N29F	1997	Valet Parking, Luton Airport, 1999
P878PWW	Dennis Dart SLF	Plaxton Pointer	N29F	1997	Valet Parking, Luton Airport, 1999
P6JPT	Mercedes-Benz 811D	Plaxton Beaver	B31F	1997	
P8JPT	Mercedes-Benz 811D	Plaxton Beaver	B31F	1997	
S3JPT	Mercedes-Benz Vario O814	Plaxton Beaver 2	B31F	1998	
V82EVU	Optare Solo M920	Optare	N37F	1999	
V689FPB	Optare Solo M920	Optare	N37F	1999	
V3JPT	Optare Solo M920	Optare	N37F	1999	
V4JPT	Optare Solo M920	Optare	N37F	1999	
W5JPT	Optare Solo M920	Optare	N37F	2000	
W6JPT	Optare Solo M920	Optare	N37F	2000	
W7JPT	Optare Solo M920	Optare	N37F	2000	
X2JPT	Volvo B7TL	East Lancashire Lolyne	NC47/29F	2000	
Y2JPT	Dennis Dart SLF	Plaxton Pointer MPD	N29F	2001	
Y3JPT	Dennis Dart SLF	Plaxton Pointer MPD	N29F	2001	

Previous registrations:
V82EVU   V2JPT

JIM STONES COACHES

J B Stones, The Bus Garage, Hope Carr Way, Leigh, WN7 3DE

A499MHG	Leyland-DAB Tiger Cub	Leyland	B43F	1984	Leyland demonstrator, 1986
B10JYM	Leyland Tiger TRCTL11/3LZ	East Lancashire Spryte (1998)	B53F	1985	MoD, 1996 (37KC41)
B11JYM	Leyland Tiger TRCTL11/3RZ	East Lancashire Spryte (1998)	B53F	1986	MoD Police, 1998 (69KE46)
B14JYM	Leyland Tiger TRCTL11/3LZM	Plaxton Derwent	B54F	1987	MoD, 2001 (64KG98)
B16TYG	Leyland Tiger TRCTL11/3LZM	Plaxton Derwent	B54F	1989	MoD, 1996 (03KJ36)
BUS1T	Dennis Dart SLF	Plaxton Pointer MPD	N29F	1999	
B1BUS	Dennis Dart SLF	Plaxton Pointer MPD	N29F	1999	
M1BUS	Dennis Dart SLF	Plaxton Pointer MPD	N29F	1999	
BUS1S	Dennis Dart SLF	Plaxton Pointer MPD	N28F	2000	
B1JYM	Dennis Dart SLF	Plaxton Pointer MPD	N28F	2000	
J5BUS	Dennis Dart SLF	Plaxton Pointer MPD	N28F	2000	
T1KET	Dennis Dart SLF	Plaxton Pointer MPD	N28F	2000	
H1JYM	Dennis Dart SLF	Plaxton Pointer 2	N36F	2000	
BUS51T	Dennis Dart SLF	Plaxton Pointer 2	N37F	2001	
JB51BUS	Dennis Dart SLF	Plaxton Pointer MPD	N29F	2002	
BUS1N	Dennis Dart SLF	Plaxton Pointer MPD	N29F	2002	

Previous registrations:

A499MHG	A499MHG, BUS1T	B11JYM	C529GVU

2002 sees Jim Stones Coaches celebrate their 35th anniversary. The fleet was mostly Mercedes minibuses but is now just three types, with only the four Tigers, used only on contracts, not to low-floor specification. The Darts all carry interesting index marks to which much thought had been given. Partly preserved is the remaining Leyland-DAB Tiger Cub considered at one time to be the potential successor to the Bristol LH. A499MHG is seen at rest. *Jim Stones Coaches*

KEN ROUTLEDGE

K J Routledge, 1A St Helens Street, Cockermouth, Cumbria, CA13 9HX

J712BAO	Mercedes-Benz 811D	Autobus Classique	C33F	1991
P884CHH	Mercedes-Benz 711D	Crest	BC24F	1996
R484YVV	Mercedes-Benz 412D	Onyx	M16	1997
R776PRM	Ford Transit VE6	Ford	M8	1997
S193UAO	Ford Transit VE6	Crest	M12	1998
S299JRM	Mercedes-Benz Vario O814	Autobus Nouvelle 2	C33F	1998
V674DHH	Mercedes-Benz Vario O814	Autobus Nouvelle 2	C33F	1999
V138EAO	Mercedes-Benz Vario O814	Plaxton Cheetah	C29F	2000
X983SHH	Mercedes-Benz Vario O814	Plaxton Cheetah	C29F	2000
X984SHH	Mercedes-Benz Vario O814	Autobus Nouvelle	C16F	2000
Y432WHH	Mercedes-Benz Vario O814	Crest	C24F	2001

nibus operator, Ken Routledge, added a pair of Autobus Nouvelle 3 coaches in recent years. This model is
sed on the Mercedes-Benz Vario, though only the three-pronged star indicates the chassis make from this
ew. *Bob Downham*

KIRKBY LONSDALE COACHES HIRE

S J & J M Sutton, Twenty Acres, Moor End, Hutton Roof, Carnforth, LA6 2PF

w	B909BGA	Mercedes-Benz L608D	PMT Hanbridge	BC21F	1984	Cunningham, Carlisle, 1993
	RBZ4221	DAF MB230DKFL615	Duple 340	C53F	1986	Janeway, Stockport, 2001
	TAZ5285	Mercedes-Benz 609D	PMT Burslem	BC26F	1988	Smith, Ledbury, 1994
	GIL2781	DAF MB230DKFL615	Caetano Algarve	C53F	1988	Dawson, Chesterfield, 2001
	TAZ5284	Mercedes-Benz 609D	Scott/Olympic	BC24F	1988	Tidbury, St Helens, 1998
	H407BVR	Mercedes-Benz 609D	Reeve Burgess Beaver	B20F	1990	Arriva Cymru, 2000
	H85PTG	Mercedes-Benz 811D	Optare StarRider	B33F	1991	Silverwing, Bristol, 1999
	K487BCY	DAF MB230DKFL615	Caetano Algarve	C57F	1992	Reliant, Ibstock, 2002
	RIL1026	Mercedes-Benz 814D	Crystals	BC33F	1994	Courtney, Bracknell, 1999
	M465RVO	Volkswagen Transporter	Kirkham	M8	1995	private owner, 1997
	N657AEO	Mercedes-Benz 609D	Onyx	B24F	1996	
	R633EYS	Mercedes-Benz Sprinter 614D	Onyx	BC24F	1997	Stewart, Inverinian, 2001
	S445JTP	Mercedes-Benz Vario O810	Plaxton Beaver 2	B32F	1998	Tillingbourne, Cranleigh, 2001
	S446JTP	Mercedes-Benz Vario O810	Plaxton Beaver 2	B32F	1998	Tillingbourne, Cranleigh, 2001
	W361SNN	Mercedes-Benz Vario O814	Frank Guy	B24F	2000	
	PO51BXU	Renault Master	Rohill Harrier	B16FL	2002	

Previous registrations:

GIL2781	E167KNH	RIL1026	L89EWO
KAZ4127	(retention)	TAZ5284	F259VCS
RBZ4221	D615SJX, WSV491, D672FYJ	TAZ5285	E430YLG

With a fleet dominated by Mercedes-Benz, Kirkby Lonsdale Coach Hire operates tendered services in northern Lancashire and southern Cumbria. Vario W361SNN is seen in Bowness in March 2002. *Mark Doggett*

LAKELAND COACHES

J Lakeland, Smithy Row, Hurst Green, Clitheroe, BB7 9QA

K833HUM	Volvo B10M-60	Jonckheere Deauville 45L	C50F	1993	Wallace Arnold, 1997
FDZ362	Volvo B10M-60	Van Hool Alizée H	C48FT	1993	Wallace Arnold, 1997
ESU926	Volvo B10M-62	Van Hool Alizée HE	C53F	1996	Park's of Hamilton, 1999
N955DWJ	Volvo B10M-62	Plaxton Première 350	C53F	1996	
P226YGG	Volvo B10M-62	Van Hool Alizée	C53F	1997	Park's of Hamilton, 2000
P962SFR	Mercedes-Benz 814D	Plaxton Beaver	BC32F	1996	
R672NFR	Scania L113CRL	East Lancashire European	N49F	1997	
T486CCK	Volvo B10M-62	Plaxton Excalibur	C49F	1999	
T487CCK	Mercedes-Benz Vario O814	Plaxton Cheetah	C29F	1999	
T436EBD	Mercedes-Benz Vario O814	Plaxton Beaver 2	B31F	1999	
W349CCK	Mercedes-Benz Vario O814	Plaxton Cheetah	C33F	2000	
V389SVV	Mercedes-Benz Vario O814	Plaxton Beaver 2	B31F	2000	
X685REC	DAF DE02GSSB220	East Lancashire Myllennium	NC46F	2000	

Previous registrations:

ESU926	HSK649, N516PYS	P226YGG	KSK977
FDZ362	K801HUM, WA3399, K619KWT		

Year 2000, the end of the last Millennium, saw the arrival with Lakeland of East Lancashire Myllennium X635REC, based on a DAF SB220 chassis and plies the road between Skipton in North Yorkshire and Preston where it was seen in September 2001, though the Lancashire County contract has now been expired.
Richard Godfrey

LANCASHIRE UNITED

Lancashire United, Prospect Park, Broughton Way, Starbeck, Harrogate, HG2 7NY

Part of the Blazefield Group

57	M457UUR	Mercedes-Benz 811D	Reeve Burgess Beaver	B31F	1994	Sovereign, 2001
59	M459UUR	Mercedes-Benz 811D	Reeve Burgess Beaver	B31F	1994	Sovereign, 2001
60	M460UUR	Mercedes-Benz 811D	Reeve Burgess Beaver	B31F	1994	Sovereign, 2001
61	M461UUR	Mercedes-Benz 811D	Reeve Burgess Beaver	B31F	1994	Sovereign, 2001
68	R668LFV	Mercedes-Benz Vario O814	Plaxton Beaver 2	B27F	1997	Stagecoach Lancashire, 2001
69	R669LFV	Mercedes-Benz Vario O814	Plaxton Beaver 2	B27F	1997	Stagecoach Lancashire, 2001
71	R671LFV	Mercedes-Benz Vario O814	Plaxton Beaver 2	B27F	1997	Stagecoach Lancashire, 2001
79	H79CFV	Mercedes-Benz 811D	Alexander AM	B31F	1991	Stagecoach Lancashire, 2001

176-180   Dennis Lance SLF 11SDA3201   Berkhof 2000   N35F   1996   Stagecoach Lancashire, 2001

176w	N176LCK	177w	N177LCK	178w	N178LCK	179w	N179LCK	180w	N180LCK

181-196   Dennis Lance 11SDA3101   Alexander PS   B45F   1992   Stagecoach Lancashire, 2001

181	J101WSC	185	J105WSC	189	J109WSC	193	J113WSC	195	J115WSC
184	J104WSC	188	J108WSC	192	J112WSC	194	J114WSC	196	J116WSC

201-215   Volvo B6LE   Alexander ALX200   N36F   1997   Stagecoach Lancashire, 2001

201	P336JND	207	P342JND	211	P346JND	213	P348JND	215	P341JND
204	P339JND	210	P345JND	212	P347JND				

296	G296KWY	Leyland Lynx LX112L10ZR1R	Leyland Lynx	B49F	1989	Sovereign, 2001
297	G297KWY	Leyland Lynx LX112L10ZR1R	Leyland Lynx	B49F	1989	Sovereign, 2001
298	G298KWY	Leyland Lynx LX112L10ZR1R	Leyland Lynx	B49F	1989	Sovereign, 2001
299	G299KWY	Leyland Lynx LX112L10ZR1R	Leyland Lynx	BC49F	1989	Harrogate & District, 2001

428-441   Volvo B10M-55   Alexander PS   BC48F   1994-95   Stagecoach Lancashire, 2001

428	M782PRS	432	M232TBV	434	M234TBV	438	M795PRS	440	M797PRS
429	M783PRS	433	M233TBV	437	M794PRS	439	M796PRS	441	M798PRS
431	M231TBV								

The minibus fleet acquired in 2001 has seen much change during the first year with all the 709s being withdrawn. Four replacements at Blackburn are Reeve Burgess Beavers from Sovereign represented by 59 M459UUR seen leaving Blackburn bus station for Feniscowles. *Mark Doggett*

New vehicles for the fleet include Volvo B10BLEs with Wrightbus Renown bodywork with a batch that is currently being delivered, providing additional buses for Bolton. Seen in Blackburn with lettering for the *Hyndburn Circular* is 1094, PO51MUW. *Richard Godfrey*

451-455

		Volvo B10B		Wright Endurance		BC49F	1996	Yorkshire Coastliner, 2002	
451	N451NWY	452	N452NWY	453	N453NWY	454	N454NWY	455	N455NWY

464	K740DAO	Volvo B10M-55	Alexander PS	B48F	1993	Stagecoach Lancashire, 2001
660	E60WDT	Leyland Lynx LX112TL11ZR1	Leyland Lynx	BC49F	1988	Stagecoach Lancashire, 2001
661	E61WDT	Leyland Lynx LX112TL11ZR1	Leyland Lynx	BC49F	1988	Stagecoach Lancashire, 2001
684	F167SMT	Leyland Lynx LX112L10ZR1S	Leyland Lynx	B49F	1989	Stagecoach Lancashire, 2001
685	F171SMT	Leyland Lynx LX112L10ZR1S	Leyland Lynx	B49F	1989	Stagecoach Lancashire, 2001
691	E87KGV	Leyland Lynx LX112L10ZR1R	Leyland Lynx	B52F	1988	Stagecoach Lancashire, 2001
695	E113RBO	Leyland Lynx LX112TL11ZR1	Leyland Lynx	B48F	1987	Stagecoach Lancashire, 2001
696	E114SDW	Leyland Lynx LX112TL11ZR1	Leyland Lynx	B48F	1987	Stagecoach Lancashire, 2001
698	F74DCW	Leyland Lynx LX2R11C15Z4R	Leyland Lynx 2	B45F	1989	Stagecoach Lancashire, 2001
701	W701BFV	Dennis Dart SLF	Plaxton Pointer MPD	N31F	2000	Stagecoach Lancashire, 2001
702	W702BFV	Dennis Dart SLF	Plaxton Pointer MPD	N31F	2000	Stagecoach Lancashire, 2001

1073-1111

		Volvo B10BLE		Wrightbus Renown		NC44F	2001-02		
1073	Y173HRN	1082	PO51MTU	1090	PO51MUE	1098	PN02HVY	1105	PN02
1074	Y174HRN	1083	PO51MTV	1091	PO51MUP	1099	PN02HVX	1106	PN02
1076	Y176HRN	1084	PO51MTX	1092	PO51MUU	1100	PN02HVZ	1107	PN02
1077	Y177HRN	1085	PO51MTY	1093	PO51MUV	1101	PN02	1108	PN02
1078	Y178HRN	1086	PO51MTZ	1094	PO51MUW	1102	PN02	1109	PN02
1079	PO51MTE	1087	PO51MUA	1095	PO51MUY	1103	PN02	1110	PN02
1080	PO51MTF	1088	PO51MUB	1096	PO51MVA	1104	PN02	1111	PN02
1081	PO51MTK	1089	PO51MUC	1097	PN02HVV				

The fleet of Bristol VRs, Atlanteans and Metrobuses have been replaced by more modern Olympians and Lynx from other Blazefield fleets. Seven Northern Counties-boded Olympians from Sovereign are shared between Bolton and Blackburn. Allocated to the latter 2941, H141GGS, is seen heading west out of Burnley. *Richard Godfrey*

1303-1312	Volvo Citybus B10M-50	Alexander RV	B47/37F	1989	Stagecoach Lancashire, 2001

1303	F103XCW	1305	F105XCW	1307	F107XCW	1309	F109XCW	1311	F111XCW
1304	F104XCW	1306	F106XCW	1308	F108XCW	1310	F110XCW	1312	F112XCW

2103	JFR3W	Leyland Olympian ONLXB/1R*	Eastern Coach Works	B45/32F	1981	Stagecoach Lancashire, 2001
2114	OFV14X	Leyland Olympian ONLXB/1R*	Eastern Coach Works	B45/32F	1982	Stagecoach Lancashire, 2001
2118	OFV18X	Leyland Olympian ONLXB/1R*	Eastern Coach Works	B45/32F	1982	Stagecoach Lancashire, 2001
2124w	SCK224X	Leyland Olympian ONLXB/1R*	Eastern Coach Works	B45/32F	1983	Stagecoach Lancashire, 2001
2127	VRN827Y	Leyland Olympian ONLXB/1R*	Eastern Coach Works	B45/32F	1983	Stagecoach Lancashire, 2001
2142	A142MRN	Leyland Olympian ONLXB/1R	Eastern Coach Works	B45/32F	1984	Stagecoach Lancashire, 2001
2143	A143MRN	Leyland Olympian ONLXB/1R	Eastern Coach Works	B45/32F	1984	Stagecoach Lancashire, 2001
2145w	A145OFR	Leyland Olympian ONLXB/1R	Eastern Coach Works	B45/32F	1984	Stagecoach Lancashire, 2001
2152	B152TRN	Leyland Olympian ONLXB/1R	Eastern Coach Works	B45/32F	1984	Stagecoach Lancashire, 2001

2156-2178	Leyland Olympian ONLXB/1R	Eastern Coach Works	BC41/26F	1984-85	Stagecoach Lancashire, 2001

2156	A156OFR	2157	A157OFR	2159w	A159OFR	2173	C173ECK	2178	C178ECK

2250	H650VVV	Leyland Olympian ON2R56G13Z4 Alexander RL	B51/34F	1990	Huntingdon & District, 2001
2251	H651VVV	Leyland Olympian ON2R56G13Z4 Alexander RL	B51/34F	1990	Huntingdon & District, 2001

2939-2952	Leyland Olympian ON2R50C13Z4 Northern Counties Palatine	B47/30F	1991	Sovereign, 2002

2939	H139GGS	2941	H141GGS	2944	H144GGS	2947	H147GGS	2951	H151GGS
2940	H140GGS	2942	H142GGS	2946	H146GGS	2949	H149GGS	2952	H152GGS

2981	A581HDB	Leyland Olympian ONLXCT/1R	Northern Counties	B43/30F	1983	Stagecoach Lancashire, 2001
2982	A582HDB	Leyland Olympian ONLXCT/1R	Northern Counties	B43/30F	1983	Stagecoach Lancashire, 2001
2983	A583HDB	Leyland Olympian ONLXCT/1R	Northern Counties	B43/30F	1983	Stagecoach Lancashire, 2001

Ancillary vehicles

157	L157BFV	Dennis Javelin 11SDL2133	Plaxton Interurban	TV	1993	Stagecoach Lancashire, 2001
417	H417FGS	Mercedes-Benz 811D	Reeve Burgess Beaver	TV	1991	Harrogate & District, 2001

Allocations:-

Blackburn (George Street)

Mercedes-Benz	57	59	60	61	79			
Dart	701	702						
Volvo B6	201	204	207	210	211	212	213	215
Lynx	684	691						
Volvo B10M	432	433	434					
Volvo B10B	451	452	453	454	455			
Volvo B10BLE	1073	1074	1076	1077	1078	1079	1080	1081
	1082	1083	1084	1085	1086	1087	1088	1089
	1090	1091	1092	1093	1094	1095		
Olympian	2103	2114	2118	2127	2142	2143	2152	2156
	2157	2173	2178	2941	2942	2982	2983	

Bolton (Goodwin Street)

Mercedes-Benz	68	69	71					
Lance	181	184	185	188	189	192	193	194
	195	196						
Lynx	296	297	298	299	660	661	685	696
	698							
Volvo B10M	428	429	431	437	438	439	440	441
	464							
Volvo B10BLE	1096	1097	1098	1099	1100			
Volvo Citybus	1303	1304	1305	1306	1307	1308	1309	1310
	1311	1312						
Olympian	2250	2251	2939	2940	2944	2946	2947	2949
	2951	2952						

Unallocated

Lance	176	177	178	179	180			
Volvo B10BLE	1101	1102	1103	1104	1105	1106	1107	1108
	1109	1110	1111					
Lynx	695							
Olympian	2124	2145	2159	2981				

Ribble operated the initial pair of Mini Pointer Darts within the Stagecoach group and these were based at the Clitheroe depot until it was closed in April 2002. The buses are used on village services to the north of Blackburn. Now repainted into its new colours, 701, W701BFV carries the motif of the Quality Partnership that funds the service.
Bob Downham

M & M COACHES

Accrington Buses - M & M Coaches

M & M Coaches, Newark Street, Accrington, BB5 0BT

WDZ6975	Mercedes-Benz L608D	PMT	B20F	1986	Western Buses, 1999
C410VVN	Mercedes-Benz L608D	Reeve Burgess	B20F	1986	Darwen Mini Coaches, 2001
D528RCK	Mercedes-Benz L608D	Reeve Burgess	B20F	1986	Stagecoach North West, 2000
D103TTJ	Renault -Dodge S56	Northern Counties	B22F	1986	Welco, Newcastle, 2000
D44UAO	Mercedes-Benz L608D	Reeve Burgess	B20F	1987	Stagecoach North West, 2000
D45UAO	Mercedes-Benz L608D	Reeve Burgess	B20F	1987	Stagecoach North West, 2000
E103JNH	Renault -Dodge S56	Alexander AM	B23F	1987	Arvonia, Llanrug, 2000
E423AFT	Mercedes-Benz 709D	Reeve Burgess	B20F	1988	Stagecoach Busways, 2000
E424AFT	Mercedes-Benz 709D	Reeve Burgess	B20F	1988	Stagecoach Busways, 2000
E430AFT	Mercedes-Benz 709D	Reeve Burgess	B20F	1988	Stagecoach Busways, 2000
E415EPE	Renault -Dodge S56	Northern Counties	B29F	1988	Kinnaird, East Lothian, 1998
E702UEM	Renault -Dodge S56	Alexander AM	B23F	1988	Bull, Smithybridge, 1995
E328WYS	Renault -Dodge S56	Alexander AM	B23F	1988	Clydeside Buses, 1997
F73FKK	Iveco Daily 49-10	Robin Hood City Nippy	B23F	1990	Ramsey, Clayton-le-Moors, 1999
H196JVT	Mercedes-Benz 814D	Wright NimBus	B33F	1990	Arriva Midlands North, 2001
XJI7908	Mercedes-Benz 811D	Alexander Sprint	B31F	1990	Chiltern Queens, 2000
J227JJR	Renault S75	Plaxton Beaver	B28F	1991	MK Metro, 2001
K342PJR	Renault S75	Plaxton Beaver	B31F	1991	MK Metro, 1999
X3MMC	Mercedes-Benz Vario O814	Mellor	B29F	2000	

Previous registrations:

WDZ6975	C594SHC	XJI7908	?

Stopping in Whalley bus station, WDZ6975 of M&M Coaches illustrates the styling of the first generation of Mercedes minibuses supplied to the National Bus Company fleets. In the vogue of the time this PMT body was a conversion of the L608D. Though the oldest vehicle in the fleet it was in excellent condition when pictured. *Bob Downham*

M R TRAVEL

Mr M Royds, 8 Scotts Industrial Park, Fishwick Street, Rochdale, OL16 5ND

KPJ286W	Leyland Atlantean AN68D/1R	Roe	B43/20F	1981	Finglands, 2000
SND437X	Leyland Atlantean AN68D/1R	Northern Counties	B43/32F	1981	Evans, Prenton, 2000
SND440X	Leyland Atlantean AN68D/1R	Northern Counties	B43/32F	1981	Evans, Prenton, 2000
ANA538Y	Leyland Atlantean AN68D/1R	Northern Counties	B43/32F	1981	Finglands, 2000
E687UNE	Leyland Tiger TRCTL11/3RZ	Plaxton Paramount 3200 III	C53F	1988	Horseman, Reading, 1999
E694UNE	Leyland Tiger TRCTL11/3RZ	Plaxton Paramount 3200 III	C53F	1988	Horseman, Reading, 1999
K509RJX	DAF SB3000DKVF601	Van Hool Alizée H	C51FT	1993	Moxon, Oldcoates, 2001
P459EFL	Marshall Minibus	Marshall MM	N26F	1997	Harwood, Birkenhead, 2001
R809WJA	Dennis Dart SLF	UVG Urbanstar	N40F	1998	Universal, Chadderton, 2000
T73JBA	Dennis Dart SLF	Plaxton Pointer MPD	N29F	1999	Mistral, 2000
T78JBA	Dennis Dart SLF	Plaxton Pointer MPD	N29F	1999	Mistral, 2001
T79JBA	Dennis Dart SLF	Plaxton Pointer MPD	N29F	1999	Mistral, 2001
V944DNB	Dennis Dart SLF	Plaxton Pointer MPD	N29F	2000	Mistral, 2001
X169GAW	Ford Transit VE6	Ford	M8	2001	
Y500MRT	Optare Solo M850	Optare	N29F	2001	

A new operator for this edition is M R Travel of Rochdale who operate local services from the town alongside school contracts. For its local services low floor Mini Pointer Darts are used represented here by V944DNB, the latest arrival. *Richard Godfrey*

MANCHESTER INTERNATIONAL AIRPORT

Manchester Airport plc, Manchester International Airport, Ringway, Manchester, M22 5PA

H199ENC	Mercedes-Benz 709D	Reeve Burgess Beaver	B20F	1990
H201ENC	Mercedes-Benz 709D	Reeve Burgess Beaver	B20F	1990
K125TCP	DAF SB220LC550	Ikarus Citibus	B26DL	1993
K126TCP	DAF SB220LC550	Ikarus Citibus	B26DL	1993
K127TCP	DAF SB220LC550	Ikarus Citibus	B26DL	1993
K977JWW	Optare MetroRider MR03	Optare	B23F	1993
K978JWW	Optare MetroRider MR03	Optare	B23F	1993
M958VWY	Optare MetroRider MR03	Optare	B23F	1995
M359OBU	Dennis Dart 9SDL3053	Plaxton Pointer	B29F	1994
M360OBU	Dennis Dart 9SDL3053	Plaxton Pointer	B29F	1994
M361OBU	Dennis Dart 9SDL3053	Plaxton Pointer	B29F	1994
M362OBU	Dennis Dart 9SDL3053	Plaxton Pointer	B29F	1994
N962WJA	Dennis Dart 9SDL3053	Marshall C36	B27F	1995
N963WJA	Dennis Dart 9SDL3053	Marshall C36	B27F	1995
N964WJA	Dennis Dart 9SDL3053	Marshall C36	B27F	1995
N599XRJ	Dennis Dart 9SDL3053	Marshall C36	B25F	1995
N601XRJ	Dennis Dart 9SDL3053	Marshall C36	B25F	1995
N602XRJ	Dennis Dart 9SDL3053	Marshall C36	B25F	1995
T522JCA	Mercedes-Benz Vario O814	Balmoral	C29F	1999
T284PVM	Dennis Dart SLF	Plaxton Pointer 2	N34F	1999
Y191KNB	Dennis Dart SLF	Alexander ALX200	N25F	2001
Y192KNB	Dennis Dart SLF	Alexander ALX200	N25F	2001
Y193KNB	Dennis Dart SLF	Alexander ALX200	N25F	2001

Manchester International Airport operate a fleet of buses on the links between the terminals and car parks, and air side between the terminals and aircraft parked on the central stands that do not have direct walkways. Buses confined to the air side do not carry index numbers. Pictured at rest is Dennis Dart N962WJA which is fitted with a Marshall C36 body. *Cliff Beeton*

Y194KNB	Dennis Dart SLF	Alexander ALX200	N25F	2001	
Y195KNB	Dennis Dart SLF	Alexander ALX200	N25F	2001	
Y196KNB	Dennis Dart SLF	Alexander ALX200	N25F	2001	
Y431PBD	Dennis Dart SLF	East Lancashire Spryte	N27F	2001	Carminder Livery
Y432PBD	Dennis Dart SLF	East Lancashire Spryte	N27F	2001	Carminder Livery

Air side buses

N1	NHH358W	Leyland National 2 NL116AL11/3R		B30T	1981
N2	NHH359W	Leyland National 2 NL116AL11/3R		B30T	1981
N3	Q580GRJ	Leyland National 2 NL116AL11/3R		B30T	1981
N4	un-registered	Leyland National 2 NL116AL11/3R		B30T	1981
N5	un-registered	Leyland National 2 NL116AL11/3R		B30T	1981
N6	un-registered	Leyland National 2 NL116AL11/3R		B30T	1981
N7	un-registered	Leyland National 2 NL116AL11/3R		B30T	1981
N8	un-registered	Leyland National 2 NL116AL11/3R		B30T	1981
1	un-registered	Neoplan N9022	Neoplan	B10D	1994
2	un-registered	Neoplan N9022	Neoplan	B10D	1994
1	un-registered	Dennis Dart SLF	East Lancashire Flyte	N29F	1998
2	un-registered	Dennis Dart SLF	East Lancashire Flyte	N29F	1998
3	un-registered	Dennis Dart SLF	East Lancashire Flyte	N29F	1998
4	un-registered	Dennis Dart SLF	East Lancashire Flyte	N29F	1998
5	un-registered	Dennis Dart SLF	East Lancashire Flyte	N27F	1998

Note: Numbered vehicles operate air side at Manchester International Airport.
Depot: Melbourne Avenue, Manchester Airport

MANCHESTER METROLINK

Serco Metrolink, Metrolink House, Queens Road, Manchester, M8 0RY

1001-1026   GEC Alsthom   Firema   86-seat   1991-92

1001	1005	1009	1012	1015	1018	1021	1024
1002	1006	1010	1013	1016	1019	1022	1025
1003	1007	1011	1014	1017	1020	1023	1026
1004	1008						

2001-2008   GEC Alsthom   Firema   86-seat   1999

| 2001 | 2002 | 2003 | 2004 | 2005 | 2006 | 2007 | 2008 |

| | Boeing Vertol | | ?-seat | 1975 | San Francisco, 2002 |
| | Boeing Vertol | | ?-seat | 1975 | San Francisco, 2002 |

Livery: Ivory and turquoise

Named trams:
1002 Manchester Arndale Voyager; 1003 The Robert Owen; 1005 Greater Altrincham Enterprise; 1007 The Guiness Record Breaker; 1009 Co-operative Insurance; 1010 Manchester Champion; 1014 Manchester 2000; 1015 Sparky; 1016 Signal Express; 1017 Rosie; 1019 The Eric Black; 1024 The John Greenwood; 1025 Christie Metro Challenger.

MAYNE

A Mayne and Son Ltd, Ashton New Road, Clayton, Manchester M11 4PD
Mayne Coaches Ltd, The Coach Station, Battersby Lane, Warrington WA2 7ET

1	P101HNC	Scania N113DRB	East Lancashire Cityzen	B45/31F	1996	
2	P102HNC	Scania N113DRB	East Lancashire Cityzen	B45/31F	1996	
3	P103HNC	Scania N113DRB	East Lancashire Cityzen	B45/31F	1996	
4	P104HNC	Scania N113DRB	East Lancashire Cityzen	B45/31F	1996	
8	R108YBA	Scania N113DRB	East Lancashire Cityzen	B45/33F	1997	
9	R109YBA	Scania N113DRB	East Lancashire Cityzen	B45/33F	1997	
10	M210NDB	Scania N113DRB	East Lancashire	B45/31F	1995	
11	M211NDB	Scania N113DRB	East Lancashire	B45/31F	1995	
12	F112HNC	Scania N113DRB	Northern Counties	B47/32F	1989	
13	F113HNC	Scania N113DRB	Northern Counties	BC47/30F	1989	
14	L114DNA	Scania N113DRB	East Lancashire	B47/31F	1993	
15	G115SBA	Scania N113DRB	Northern Counties	B47/32F	1989	
16	G116SBA	Scania N113DRB	Northern Counties	B47/32F	1989	
17	G117SBA	Scania N113DRB	Northern Counties	B47/32F	1989	
18	X118ABA	Scania N113DRB	East Lancashire Cityzen	BC47/31F	2000	
19	X119ABA	Scania N113DRB	East Lancashire Cityzen	BC47/31F	2000	
	E701EFG	Scania N112DRB	East Lancashire	B47/33F	1988	Brighton & Hove, 2002
	E704EFG	Scania N112DRB	East Lancashire	B47/33F	1988	Brighton & Hove, 2002
	E705EFG	Scania N112DRB	East Lancashire	B47/33F	1988	Brighton & Hove, 2002
	E706EFG	Scania N112DRB	East Lancashire	B47/33F	1988	Brighton & Hove, 2002
	E707EFG	Scania N112DRB	East Lancashire	B47/33F	1988	Brighton & Hove, 2002
	E709EFG	Scania N112DRB	East Lancashire	B47/33F	1988	Brighton & Hove, 2002
	F711LFG	Scania N112DRB	East Lancashire	B47/33F	1988	Brighton & Hove, 2002
24	R24YNC	Dennis Dart SLF	Marshall Capital	N39F	1997	

1999 saw the arrival of the first low-floor double-decks for Mayne in the form of Dennis Tridents with East Lancashire Lolyne bodywork. The batch is represented by 27, V127DJA, pictured turning from Oldham Street in Manchester. *Richard Godfrey*

As well as its commercial and tendered operations, Mayne provide coaching services. Pictured while on a day excursion to Fleetwood market and Freeport in the summer of 2001, 65, T65JDB is one of five Irizar InterCentury coaches now used. Currently the Irizar product is only supplied to the UK market on Scania chassis, though elsewhere in Europe the body is supplied on other makes. *J C Walton*

25-29		Dennis Trident		East Lancashire Lolyne		N51/30F	1999		
25	V125DJA	26	V126DJA	27	V127DJA	28	V128DJA	29	V129DJA

42	M42ONF	Scania L113CRL	Northern Counties Paladin	B51F	1994	
43	M113RNK	Scania L113CRL	Northern Counties Paladin	B51F	1994	Scania demonstrator, 1995

45-49		Dennis Dart SLF		Marshall Capital		N37F	1998		
45	R45CDB	46	R46CDB	47	R47CDB	48	R48CDB	49	R49CDB

50	403BGO	Leyland Tiger TRCTLXCT/3RZ	Plaxton Paramount 3200	C55F	1985	
52	PIL7752	DAF MB230DKFL615	Plaxton Paramount 3200 III	C55F	1987	Trent, 1998
56	SIL3856	Bova FLD 12-280	Bova Futura Club	C55F	1996	
57	S57TNA	Bova FHD 12-340	Bova Futura	C49FT	1998	
58	T58JDB	Bova FHD 12-340	Bova Futura	C49FT	1999	
60	RIL8160	Volvo B10M-61	Plaxton Paramount 3500 III	C40FT	1992	Arriva Fox County, 1999
62	NIB4162	Leyland Leopard PSU5C/4R	Plaxton Supreme IV	C57F	1982	
63	S63TNA	Scania L94IB	Irizar InterCentury 12.32	C55F	1998	
64	T64JDB	Scania L94IB	Irizar InterCentury 12.32	C55F	1999	
65	T65JDB	Scania L94IB	Irizar InterCentury 12.32	C55F	1999	
	02	Scania L94IB	Irizar InterCentury 12.32	C55F	2002	
67	N67YVR	Dennis Javelin 12SDA2155	UVG UniStar	C57F	1996	
68	N68YVR	Dennis Javelin 12SDA2155	UVG UniStar	C57F	1996	
71	RAZ5171	DAF MB230LB615	Plaxton Paramount 3200 III	C55F	1988	Trent, 1997
73	NIL9773	DAF MB230DKFL615	Plaxton Paramount 3200 III	C55F	1987	Trent, 1997
74	NIL9774	DAF MB230DKFL615	Plaxton Paramount 3200 III	C55F	1987	Trent, 1997
75	TKU540	Volvo B1 0M-62	Plaxton Première 320	C55F	1997	
76	EUK978	Volvo B10M-62	Plaxton Première 320	C55F	1997	
77	LIB6437	Leyland Tiger TRCTLXCT/3RZ	Plaxton Paramount 3500 II	C53F	1986	
81	W81JBN	Volvo B7R	Plaxton Prima	C53F	2000	
82	W82JBN	Volvo B7R	Plaxton Prima	C53F	2000	
83	W83JBN	Volvo B7R	Plaxton Prima	C53F	2000	

Maynes Coaches Ltd (Warrington allocation)

5	IAZ4775	Leyland Fleetline FE30AGR	Northern Counties	B43/32F	1980	Barry Cooper, 1995
6	IAZ4776	Leyland Fleetline FE30AGR	Northern Counties	B43/32F	1980	Barry Cooper, 1995
4	GND505N	Daimler Fleetline CRG6LXB	Northern Counties	B43/32F	1974	Greater Manchester, 1988
6	NIL8256	Leyland Atlantean AN68A/1R	Northern Counties	B43/32F	1982	GMS Buses, Stockport, 1996
8	NIL8258	Leyland Atlantean AN68A/1R	Northern Counties	B43/32F	1981	GMS Buses, Stockport, 1996
10	C110UBC	Scania N112DRB	East Lancashire	B46/33F	1988	Brighton & Hove, 2001
11	C111UBC	Scania N112DRB	East Lancashire	B46/33F	1988	Brighton & Hove, 2001
12	C112UBC	Scania N112DRB	East Lancashire	B46/33F	1988	Brighton & Hove, 2001
13	C113UBC	Scania N112DRB	East Lancashire	B46/33F	1988	Brighton & Hove, 2001
19	UOL337	Volvo B10M-62	Plaxton Première 320	C57FT	1998	
20	YPL764	Volvo B10M-62	Plaxton Première 320	C57FT	1998	
21	906GAU	Volvo B10M-62	Plaxton Première 320	C55F	1997	
22	289BUA	Volvo B10M-62	Plaxton Première 320	C55F	1997	
23	T223JND	Scania L94IB	Irizar InterCentury 12.32	C55F	1999	
24	T224JND	Scania L94IB	Irizar InterCentury 12.32	C55F	1999	
25	W425JBN	Volvo B10M-62	Plaxton Première 320	C55F	2000	
26	W426JBN	Volvo B10M-62	Plaxton Première 320	C55F	2000	
27	W427JBN	Volvo B7R	Plaxton Prima	C53F	2000	
28	W428JBN	Volvo B7R	Plaxton Prima	C53F	2000	
36	BVR100T	Leyland Fleetline FE30AGR	Northern Counties	B43/32F	1979	Barry Cooper, 1996
37	KDB137V	Leyland Fleetline FE30AGR	Northern Counties	B43/32F	1980	Barry Cooper, 1996
63	NMX643	Leyland Leopard PSU3F/5R	Plaxton Supreme IV	C53F	1980	
65	MJI5765	Leyland Leopard PSU5C/4R	Plaxton Supreme IV	C57F	1982	
66	UCE665	Leyland Leopard PSU4A/4R	Plaxton Supreme IV (1982)	C53F	1968	Midland Red, 1982
69	SSV269	Leyland Tiger TRCTL11/3R	Plaxton Paramount 3500 Exp	C55F	1983	
79	LIB6439	Leyland Tiger TRCTLXCT/3RZ	Plaxton Paramount 3200 II	C57F	1986	
	A101DPB	Dennis Falcon HC	W Stringer Vanguard (1987)	BC49F	1983	Wycombe Bus, 1991
	OED201	Leyland Tiger TRCTL11/3R	Plaxton Paramount 3200 II	C53F	1985	

Previous registrations:

289BUA	P122JNF	NIL8258	SND425X
403BGO	B350RNA	NIL9773	D637WNU
906GAU	P121JNF	NIL9774	D643WNU
EUK978	P76JND	NMX643	HDB355V
IAZ4775	MNC487W	OED201	B424RNA
IAZ4776	MNC488W	PIL7752	D639WNU
LIB6437	C347YBA	RAZ5171	E644DAU
LIB6439	B349RNA	RIL8160	J247MFP
		SIL3856	N56CNF
MJI5765	SNC365X	SSV269	ANA368Y
NIB4162	SNC362X	UCE665	WHA236H, SNC355X
		UOL337	B425RNA
NIL8256	SND483X	YPL764	R120CNE

The majority of the bus fleet have been sourced from Scania with 74% of the Clayton-based double-decks of that make. Seen working route 217 is 16, G116SBA, which has Northern Counties bodywork.
Richard Godfrey

MOUNTAIN GOAT

Mountain Goat Holidays and Tours, 10 Victoria Street, Windermere, LA23 1AD

M20MGH	Renault Master T35D	CSM	M15	1995	private owner, 1998
M6OAT	Renault Master T35D	Dobson	M16	1996	
N829REC	Renault Master T35D	Dobson	M16	1996	
N103YHH	Renault Master T35D	Cymric	M16	1996	
N554SOA	Renault Master T35D	Jubilee	M16	1996	
T85HFV	Renault Master T35D	CSM	M16	1999	
M60ATS	Renault Master	Dobson	M16	2000	
M6MGH	Renault Master	CSM	M16	2001	
M10MGH	Renault Master	Crest	M16	2002	
M8MGH	Renault Master	Crest	M16	2002	

Previous registration

M20MGH	M185OBU	T85HFV	YAZ7315
G60ATS	W644CCK		

Depot: Chestnut Road Garage, Windermere

Mountain Goat operate a fleet of Renault minibuses on the roads and passes of English Lakeland. Four of the latest version of the Renault Master have now been placed in service represented by M60ATS.
David Longbottom

NORTHERN BLUE

Travelspeed Ltd, F West End Business Park, Blackburn Road, Oswaldtwistle, BB5 4WE
Viscount Central Coaches Ltd, 6 Dean Mill, Plumb Street, Burnley, BB11 2AG

2	RJI6862	Leyland National 10351B/1R	East Lancashire Greenway (94)	B41F	1979	Arriva The Shires, 2001
5	V725AGD	Leyland National NL116HLXCT/1R		B52F	1985	Arriva Scotland West, 1999
7	SIB1287	Leyland National 10351B/1R	East Lancashire Greenway (92)	B41F	1979	Arriva North East, 2001
39	H139UUA	Optare MetroRider MR03	Optare	B26F	1990	London Central, 2000
40	H140UUA	Optare MetroRider MR03	Optare	B26F	1990	London Central, 2000
55	G155NRC	Renault-Dodge S56	Reeve Burgess	B25F	1989	City of Nottingham, 1999
57	G157NRC	Renault-Dodge S56	Reeve Burgess	B25F	1989	City of Nottingham, 1999
75	G575PRM	Mercedes-Benz 709D	Alexander Sprint	B23F	1990	MK Metro. Burnley, 2000
77	K75XCW	Optare MetroRider MR03	Optare	B29F	1993	Burnley & Pendle, 2001
79	L179LHG	Optare MetroRider MR17	Optare	B29F	1994	Lancashire United, 2001
84	H840UUA	Optare MetroRider MR03	Optare	B25F	1990	Arriva North East, 2002
87	H887UUA	Optare MetroRider MR03	Optare	B25F	1990	Arriva North East, 2002
90	L190DDW	Optare MetroRider MR15	Optare	B31F	1994	Cardiff Bus, 2000
91	L191DDW	Optare MetroRider MR15	Optare	B31F	1994	Cardiff Bus, 2000
94	G94ERP	Mercedes-Benz 709D	Dormobile Routemaker	B29F	1989	MK Metro, Burnley, 2000
96	G96ERP	Mercedes-Benz 709D	Dormobile Routemaker	B29F	1989	MK Metro, Burnley, 2000
99	G99NBD	Mercedes-Benz 709D	Dormobile Routemaker	B29F	1989	MK Metro, Burnley, 2000
105	EJR105W	Leyland Atlantean AN68A/2R	Alexander AL	B49/37F	1981	Stagecoach Busways, 1999
107	B107UAT	Dennis Dominator DDA904	Alexander AL	B49/32F	1984	Stagecoach Transit, 2000
112	C112CAT	Dennis Dominator DDA1007	East Lancashire	B45/30F	1985	Stagecoach Transit, 2000
124	C124CAT	Dennis Dominator DDA1007	East Lancashire	B45/30F	1985	Stagecoach Transit, 2000
125	C125CAT	Dennis Dominator DDA1006	East Lancashire	B45/30F	1985	Stagecoach Transit, 2000
129	C129CAT	Dennis Dominator DDA1006	East Lancashire	B45/30F	1985	Stagecoach Transit, 2000
138	AVK138V	Leyland Atlantean AN68A/2R	Alexander AL	B49/37F	1980	Stagecoach Busways, 1999

Northern Blue operate mostly in the Burnley area from their base in Oswaldtwistle. Pictured while operating route 88 is East Lancashire-bodied Dennis Dominator 112, C112CAT, and one of five Dominators acquired from Stagecoach in 2000. *Richard Godfrey*

As well as the Dominators, nine other double-decks carry the blue and cream livery. Number 105, EJR105W, is one of four Atlantean new to Busways that feature Alexander bodywork with panoramic windows in their 10-metre overall length. Tyne and Wear, the PTE owners of Busways, had stuck to the domed roof rather than opt for the more popular peaked alternative. *Bob Downham*

145	B45NDX	Leyland Olympian ONLXB/1RV	East Lancashire	B40/33F	1985	Arriva North East, 2001
150	AVK150V	Leyland Atlantean AN68A/2R	Alexander AL	B49/37F	1980	Stagecoach Busways, 1999
152	G452FVX	Dennis Condor DDA1702	Duple Metsec	B63/44F	1989	New World First Bus, HK, 2001
158	AVK158V	Leyland Atlantean AN68A/2R	Alexander AL	B49/37F	1980	Stagecoach Busways, 1999
179	A679HNB	Leyland Atlantean AN68D/1R	Northern Counties	B43/32F	1983	Burnley & Pendle, 2001
180	AUP380W	Leyland Atlantean AN68B/1R	Roe	B43/30F	1980	Go-Ahead Northern, 1999
231	GOG231W	MCW Metrobus DR104/8	MCW	B43/30F	1981	MK Metro, Burnley, 2001
302	J2HMT	Toyota Coaster HDB30R	Caetano Optimo II	C21F	1992	Mil-Ken, Kentford, 2000
305	R508RCH	Iveco EuroRider 391.12.29	Beulas Stergo E	C55F	1997	Glenn Coaches, Port Glasgow, 2001
307	XSU907	Volvo B10M-60	Ikarus Blue Danube	C49FT	1991	Goode, West Bromwich, 2000
308	XSU908	Volvo C10M-70	Ramseier & Jenzer	C49FT	1985	Burnley & Pendle, 1997
309	XSU909	Volvo B10M-61	Jonckheere Jubilee P50	C51FT	1986	Burnley & Pendle, 1997
311	HXI311	Volvo B10M-61	Jonckheere Jubilee P50	C51FT	1986	Burnley & Pendle, 1997
326	DCZ2326	Volvo B10M-61	Caetano Algarve	C49FT	1987	Blackburn, 2000
349	LIJ749	Volvo B10M-61	Caetano Algarve	C49FT	1988	Blackburn, 2000
354	K454VVR	Volvo B10M-60	Van Hool Alizée HE	C49FT	1993	Shearings, 2000
355	K455VVR	Volvo B10M-60	Van Hool Alizée HE	C49FT	1993	Shearings, 2000
397	M797NFJ	Volvo B10M-62	Van Hool Alizée HE	C49FT	1995	Rapsons, 2001

Previous registrations:

DCZ2326	E841EUT, MIB920, E635PFV	SIB1287	BPL483T
G452FVX	EJ1293 (HK)	XSU907	J889NFD, B10MGC, J173WUK
HXI311	E508KNV	XSU908	C661KDS
LIJ749	F870TNH	XSU909	D111BNV
JI6862	MCA677T		

PILKINGTON

R M & J Pilkington, 135 Blackburn Road, Accrington, BB5 0AA

12	PIL7012	Leyland National 11351A/1R		B49F	1978	Arriva North West, 1998
13	PIL7013	Leyland National 2 NL116L11/1R		B52F	1980	Arriva North West, 1998
14	PIB7014	Leyland National 10351B/1R		B44F	1979	North Western, 1996
17	PIL6617	Leyland National 11351A/1R		B49F	1979	Brewers, 1998
23	PIB5823	Leyland National 11351A/1R		B49F	1978	Stagecoach East Midland, 1997
34	PIB6434	Leyland National 10351B/1R		B44F	1978	Stagecoach Midland Red, 1997
36	PIL9536	Leyland National 2 NL116AL11/1R		B48F	1981	Stagecoach Western Buses, 1999
41	PIL5941	Leyland National 2 NL106AL11/1R		B44F	1981	Arriva North West, 1998
46	PIL9546	Leyland National 2 NL106AL11/1R		B44F	1981	Arriva North West, 1998
51	PIB9051	Leyland National 2 NL116L11/1R		B49F	1980	Cherry, Bootle, 1998
52	PIB5952	Leyland National 11351A/1R		B49F	1979	Thamesway, 1995
55	PIL2755	Leyland National 2 NL106HLXB/1R		B41F	1980	Stagecoach Western Buses, 1999
56	PIB7256	Leyland National 2 10351A/1R		B44F	1979	Glyn Williams, Crosskeys, 1997
60	PIL8560	Leyland National 2 NL116HLXB/1R		B52F	1982	Stagecoach North West, 1999
62	PIL9562	Leyland National 10351A/2R(Volvo)		B44F	1979	Arriva North West, 1999
67	PIB6667	Leyland National 11351/1R		B52F	1973	Cooper, Dukinfield, 1995
76	PIB8076	Leyland National 11351A/1R		B49F	1977	MTL (Merseybus), 1995
82	PIB9482	Leyland National 11351A/1R		B49F	1977	Glyn Williams, Crosskeys, 1997
125	PIB1125	Leyland Leopard PSU3B/4R	Duple Dominant IV (1981)	C51F	1975	Barry Raybould, Walsall, 1996
301	PIB8301	Bedford YLQ	Duple Dominant II	C45F	1978	Bond, Willington, 1992
514	TJI7514	Leyland Tiger TRCTL11/2R	Eastern Coach Works B51	BC49F	1982	Hellyers, Fareham, 1998
	RDZ4278	Leyland National 11351/1R (Volvo)		B49F	1980	Blue Bird, Middleton, 2001
	WJI3506	Leyland National 11351A/1R		B49F	1975	Arriva North West, 2000
	PIB3488	Leyland National 10351A/2R		B39F	1977	Frank Thorpe, Wembley, 2000
	OJD899R	Leyland National 10351A/2R		B38F	1977	Frank Thorpe, Wembley, 2000
	PIB5507	Leyland National 10351A/2R		B37F	1977	Frank Thorpe, Wembley, 2000
	PIB6945	Leyland National 10351A/2R		B39F	1979	Frank Thorpe, Wembley, 2000
	RJI6861	Leyland National 10351B/1R (Gardner) E Lancs Greenway		B41F	1977	Arriva The Shires, 2001

An interesting frontal arrangement has been applied to Lynx F722LRG, one of a pair added to the predominantly Leyland National fleet. Pilkington are also marketing their services as Accrington Buses, reflecting the administrative and dominant district within the borough. *Richard Godfrey*

The latest arrival with Pilkingtons is a Dennis Dart previously owned by Devon County Council and operated on their behalf by Stagecoach. Wright Handy-bus bodywork is fitted as seen in this view at Accrington bus station. Bob Downham

IIL4821	Leyland 10351/1R/SC(6HLX)	East Lancs Greenway (1993)	B41F	1974	Arriva The Shires, 2001
IIL4822	Leyland 10351/1R/SC(6HLX)	East Lancs Greenway (1993)	B41F	1976	Arriva The Shires, 2001
VBG82V	Leyland National NL116L11/1R		B49F	1980	Bluebird, Middleton, 2001
A132FDC	Leyland National NL116AHLXCT/1R		B47F	1983	GHA, New Broughton, 2000
D32MWN	Leyland Lynx LX112TL112R1	Leyland	B51F	1987	Citybus, Liverpool, 2001
F722LRG	Leyland Lynx LX1126LXCT2R1S	Leyland	B51F	1989	City Nippy, Middleton, 2001
PIL4921	DAF SB220LC550	Optare Delta	B30D	1989	Airport Parking, Gatwick, 2001
PIL6726	DAF SB220LC550	Optare Delta	B30D	1989	Airport Parking, Gatwick, 2001
PIL8380	DAF SB220LC550	Optare Delta	B30D	1989	Airport Parking, Gatwick, 2001
PIL8381	DAF SB220LC550	Optare Delta	B30D	1989	Airport Parking, Gatwick, 2001
F514TPA	DAF SB220LC550	Optare Delta	B30D	1989	Airport Parking, Gatwick, 2001
F516TPA	DAF SB220LC550	Optare Delta	B30D	1989	Airport Parking, Gatwick, 2001
F517TPA	DAF SB220LC550	Optare Delta	B30D	1989	Airport Parking, Gatwick, 2001
F332FWW	DAF SB220LC550	Optare Delta	B49F	1989	UK North, Manchester, 2001
PIB9189	Dennis Dart 8.5SDL3020	Wright Handy-bus	B28FL	1993	Devon CC, 2001

Previous registrations:

IIL4821	XPD299N	PIL2755	GSO8V, KRS542V
IIL4822	LPB180P	PIL4921	F477FUA
PIB1125	KDB672P, SND88X, PIB5073	PIL5941	LFR869X
PIB3488	OJD896R	PIL6617	OEP794
PIB5507	AYR335T	PIL6726	F478FUA
PIB5823	VKU73S	PIL7012	GMB386T
PIB5952	BNO669T, PIB5513	PIL7013	AFM2W
PIB6434	WFR392V	PIL8380	F333FWW
PIB6667	MAN14A, CNB432M	PIL8381	F515TPA
PIB6945	AYR337T	PIL8560	WAO398Y
PIB7014	MCA675T	PIL9536	JTF971W
PIB7256	YDW401T	PIL9546	LFR867X
PIB8076	XCW956R	PIL9562	BYW402V
PIB8301	APT891S	RDZ4278	JOX481P
PIB9051	VBG95V	RJI6861	HMA569T
PIB9189	L547CDV	TJI7514	TPC111X
PIB9482	CBV790S	WJI3506	UHG749R

Depot: Argyle Street

PRESTON BUS

Preston Bus Ltd, 221 Deepdale Road, Preston, PR1 6NY

1-10 — Optare MetroRider MR37 — Optare — B25F — 1994-95

1	M401TCK	3	M403TCK	5	M405TCK	7	M407TCK	9	M409TCK
2	M402TCK	4	M404TCK	6	M406TCK	8	M408TCK	10	M410TCK

11-16 — Optare MetroRider MR37 — Optare — B25F — 1996

11	P411TFR	13	P413TFR	14	P414TFR	15	P415TFR	16	P416TFR
12	P412TFR								

17-40 — Optare MetroRider MR17 — Optare — B29F — 1995-98

17	R417RCW	22	N422GBV	27	N427GBV	32	R432NFR	37	R437NFR
18	R418RCW	23	N423GBV	28	N428GBV	33	R433NFR	38	R438RCW
19	R419RCW	24	N424GBV	29	N429GBV	34	R434NFR	39	R439RCW
20	N420GBV	25	N425GBV	30	N430GBV	35	R435NFR	40	R440RCW
21	N421GBV	26	N426GBV	31	N431GBV	36	R436NFR		

41	J967CGK	Optare MetroRider MR03	Optare		B26F	1991	Blackburn, 2001
42	J969CGK	Optare MetroRider MR03	Optare		B26F	1991	Blackburn, 2001

51-58 — Optare Solo M850 — Optare — N29F — 2001-02

51	PE51YHF	53	PE51YHH	55	PE51YHK	57	PE51YHM	58	PE51YHN
52	PE51YHG	54	PE51YHJ	56	PE51YHL				

Preston retain just one coach to supplement their commercial and tendered services. This is a Duple-bodied Leyland Tiger fitted with the express version of the 320 body which incorporates such features as wide, electrically operated entrance doors, fare collection equipment and destination box. Lettered as Preston Coach and numbered 309, PRN909 is seen on an excursion to Fleetwood. *J C Walton*

Preston Bus have chosen the Dennis Trident to meet their low-floor double-deck needs and, like almost all of the UK, have purchased the 2-axle model. East Lancashire Lolyne bodywork is fitted to 191, V191EBV, seen here lettered for route 35. *Richard Godfrey*

01	H101BFR	Leyland Olympian ON2R50C13Z4	Northern Counties Palatine	B47/30F	1991	
02	H102BFR	Leyland Olympian ON2R50C13Z4	Northern Counties Palatine	B47/30F	1991	
03	H103BFR	Leyland Olympian ON2R50C13Z4	Northern Counties Palatine	B47/30F	1991	
04	H104BFR	Leyland Olympian ON2R50C13Z4	Northern Counties Palatine	B47/30F	1991	
06	J976PRW	Leyland Olympian ON2R50C13Z4	Leyland	B47/31F	1991	

07-114

		Leyland Olympian ON2R50C13Z4 Leyland		B47/31F*	1991-92	*107/14 are BC43/29F

07	J107KCW	109	J109KCW	112	J112KCW	113	J113KCW	114	J114KCW
08	J108KCW	110	J110KCW						

32	F32AHG	Leyland Olympian ONCL10/2RZ	Northern Counties	B51/34F	1989
33	A33MRN	Leyland Olympian ONTL11/2R	Eastern Coach Works	B47/25F	1984
34	G34OCK	Leyland Olympian ONCL10/1RZ	Eastern Coach Works	BC43/29F	1990
35	G35OCK	Leyland Olympian ONCL10/1RZ	Eastern Coach Works	BC43/29F	1990
36	G36OCK	Leyland Olympian ONCL10/1RZ	Eastern Coach Works	B47/31F	1990
37	G37OCK	Leyland Olympian ONCL10/1RZ	Eastern Coach Works	B47/31F	1990
2	UHG142V	Leyland Atlantean AN68A/2R	Alexander AL	B49/36F	1980
3	UHG143V	Leyland Atlantean AN68A/2R	Alexander AL	B49/36F	1980
2	GBV152W	Leyland Atlantean AN68B/2R	East Lancashire	B50/36F	1981
6	GBV156W	Leyland Atlantean AN68B/2R	East Lancashire	B50/36F	1981
8	OBV158X	Leyland Atlantean AN68C/2R	East Lancashire	B50/36F	1982
9	OBV159X	Leyland Atlantean AN68C/2R	East Lancashire	B50/36F	1982
5	OBV165X	Leyland Atlantean AN68C/2R	East Lancashire	B50/36F	1982

Fleet numbers recommenced at 101 in 1991 when Leyland Olympian H101BFR was delivered. Fitted with Northern Counties Palatine bodywork it is seen heading north from the town for the district of Fulwood. *Richard Godfrey*

168-177

		Leyland Atlantean AN68D/2R		East Lancashire		B50/36F	1982-83		
168	URN168Y	172	URN172Y	174	DRN174Y	176	DRN176Y	177	DRN177Y
170	URN170Y	173	DRN173Y	175	DRN175Y				

182-199

		Dennis Trident		East Lancashire Pyoneer		N45/30F	1999-2001		
182	X182RRN	186	X186RRN	190	V190EBV	194	V194EBV	197	X197RRN
183	X183RRN	187	X187RRN	191	V191EBV	195	V195EBV	198	X198RRN
184	X184RRN	188	X188RRN	192	V192EBV	196	V196EBV	199	X199RRN
185	X185RRN	189	X189RRN	193	V193EBV				

210	F210YHG	Leyland Lynx LX112L10ZR1R	Leyland		B47F	1989	
211	F211YHG	Leyland Lynx LX112L10ZR1R	Leyland		B47F	1989	
212	F212YHG	Leyland Lynx LX112L10ZR1R	Leyland		BC45F	1989	
213	F213YHG	Leyland Lynx LX112L10ZR1R	Leyland		BC45F	1989	

214-218

		Leyland Lynx LX2R11C15Z4R	Leyland			BC45F	1989		
214	G214KRN	215	G215KRN	216	G216KRN	217	G217KRN	218	G218KRN

223-229

		Leyland Lynx LX2R11C15Z4R	Leyland			BC45F	1990-91		
223	H23YBV	226	H26YBV	227	H27YBV	228	H28YBV	229	H29YBV
224	H24YBV								

309	PRN909	Leyland Tiger TRBTL11/2RP	Duple 320		C51F	1987

Previous Registrations:

PRN909   D40AFV

ROBINSONS

O&C Holdsworth Ltd, Park Garage, Great Harwood, Blackburn, BB6 7SP

243	J243LFR	DAF MB230LT615	Van Hool Alizée H	C49FT	1992
243	J244LFR	DAF MB230LT615	Van Hool Alizée H	C49FT	1992
244	J245LFR	DAF MB230LT615	Van Hool Alizée H	C49FT	1992
246	J246LFR	DAF MB230LT615	Van Hool Alizée H	C49FT	1992
247	J247LFR	DAF MB230LT615	Van Hool Alizée H	C49FT	1992
248	L248JBV	Volvo B10M-62	Jonckheere Deauville 45	C48FT	1994
249	L249JBV	Volvo B10M-62	Jonckheere Deauville 45	C48FT	1994
250	L250JBV	Volvo B10M-62	Jonckheere Deauville 45	C48FT	1994
251	N251KFR	Volvo B10M-62	Plaxton Première 350	C49FT	1996
252	N252KFR	Volvo B10M-62	Plaxton Première 350	C49FT	1996
253	N253KFR	Volvo B10M-62	Plaxton Première 350	C49FT	1996
254	N254KFR	Volvo B10M-62	Plaxton Première 350	C49FT	1996
255	P255YFR	Volvo B10M-62	Plaxton Première 350	C49FT	1997
256	P256YFR	Volvo B10M-62	Plaxton Première 350	C49FT	1997
257	P257YFR	Volvo B10M-62	Plaxton Première 350	C49FT	1997
258	S258JFR	Volvo B10M-62	Plaxton Excalibur	C49FT	1998
259	S259JFR	Volvo B10M-62	Plaxton Excalibur	C49FT	1998
260	S260JFR	Volvo B10M-62	Plaxton Excalibur	C49FT	1998
261	W261GBV	Scania L94IB	Irizar Century 12.35	C49FT	2000
262	W262GBV	Scania L94IB	Irizar Century 12.35	C49FT	2000
263	W263GBV	Scania L94IB	Irizar Century 12.35	C49FT	2000
264	W264GBV	Scania L94IB	Irizar Century 12.35	C49FT	2000

Robinsons retain great respect in north west England for their tour programme which uses a fleet of coaches purchased new for the work. Picking up passengers in Stockport before heading for Italy, number 253, N253KFR illustrates the use of the letter 'R' in the fleetname on a new livery replacing the long-established green and black. *Cliff Beeton*

ROBINSON'S

P R Elliott, Station Road Garage, Appleby-in-Westmorland, CA16 6TX

CHA460K	Leyland Leopard PSU3B/4R	Plaxton Panorama	C47F	1971	Midland Red, 1981
4761TR	DAF MB200DKTL600	Plaxton Supreme IV	C57F	1980	Harris Bus, West Thurrock, 1991
NUS333Y	Bedford YNT	Wright TT	B53F	1983	Go-Goodwin, Stockport, 1991
A745DRM	Volkswagen Transporter	Devon Conversions	M10	1984	private owner, 1990
9884TR	DAF MB200DKFL600	LAG Galaxy	C51F	1985	
F842EHH	Ford Transit VE6	Mellor	M16	1988	Swallow, Sheffield, 1989
990ENR	Volvo B10M-61	Van Hool Alizée H	C53F	1988	Excelsior, Bournemouth, 1991
R357URM	LDV Convoy	LDV	M16	1998	
3937TR	LDV Convoy	LDV	M16	2000	

Previous registrations:

3927TR	From new	9884TR	From new
990ENR	E303OPR, XEL55S, E406SEL	4761TR	NEV773V, SIB2632

Straying far from its idyllic Cumbrian base, Robinson's fleet is represented by its LAG Galaxy 9884TR seen seen at rest in Park Lane, London. The windscreen label indicates the party had journeyed south for a football match with England hosting Bulgaria. *Dave Heath*

ROSSENDALE

Rossendale - Ellen Smith - Coachways

Rossendale Transport Ltd; Ellen Smith (Tours) Ltd,
35 Bacup Road, Rawtenstall, BB4 7NG

11	L911ECW	Optare MetroRider MR09	Optare			B23F	1993	
12	L912ECW	Optare MetroRider MR09	Optare			B23F	1993	
13	L813KCW	Optare MetroRider MR31	Optare			B25F	1994	
14	L814KCW	Optare MetroRider MR31	Optare			B25F	1994	
15	P915XUG	Optare MetroRider MR31	Optare			B23F	1997	
16	P916XUG	Optare MetroRider MR31	Optare			B23F	1997	

17-26 Dennis Dart 8.5SDL3003 Carlyle Dartline B25F 1990 Metroline, 1997-98

17	H117MOB	19	H119MOB	21	H621MOM	23	H110MOB	25	H115MOB
18	H611MOM	20	H620MOM	22	H108MOB	24	H113MOB	26	H116MOB

29	M529RHG	Volvo Olympian YN2RV18Z4	Alexander Royale	B43/29F	1994
30	M530RHG	Volvo Olympian YN2RV18Z4	Alexander Royale	B43/29F	1994

34-38 Leyland Olympian ON2R50C13Z4* Leyland B47/51F 1989 London United, 1999
*34 is ONCL10/1RZ

34	G304UYT	35	G307UYT	36	G312UYT	37	G313UYT	38	G314UYT

In 1999 Rossendale acquired five all-Leyland Olympians from London United. This batch had been assembled at Lillyhall, in the factory built for National production. Seen in Rawtenstall carrying its new identity, 35, G307UYK was fitted with a Cummins engine when new. *Richard Godfrey*

In the early 1990s, Rossendale embarked on a programme to re-body Leyland Leopards with bus bodies. These well-respected chassis continue to provide sterling service and in its later guise, 71, PJI9171, was pictured in Burnley in March 2002. Rossendale's heritage can be traced to the merger of Haslingden and Rawtenstall municipal transport undertakings in 1968. The company also operate the Ellen Smith coach business which boasts seven integral Bova Futura models. *Richard Godfrey*

39-50

						Leyland Olympian ONLXB/1RH	Eastern Coach Works	B42/30F	1986	London Central, 1998

39	C39CHM	41	C34CHM	44	C84CHM	46	C96CHM	49	C89CHM
40	C40CHM	43	C93CHM	45	C85CHM	48	C88CHM	50	C90CHM

No	Reg	Chassis	Body			
54	J584CUB	Optare MetroRider MR07	Optare	BC25F	1992	Parking Express, Sunbury, 1999
57	J587CUB	Optare MetroRider MR07	Optare	BC25F	1992	Parking Express, Sunbury, 1999
58	J588CUB	Optare MetroRider MR07	Optare	BC25F	1992	Parking Express, Sunbury, 1999
59	J589CUB	Optare MetroRider MR07	Optare	BC25F	1992	Parking Express, Sunbury, 1999
66	G728JJC	Volvo B10M-55	Plaxton Derwent 2	BC53F	1989	Go-Goodwin, Eccles, 1999
67	G727JJC	Volvo B10M-55	Plaxton Derwent 2	BC53F	1989	Go-Goodwin, Eccles, 1999
68	F338VSD	Volvo B10M-56	Duple 300	B53F	1988	Hutchison, Overtown, 1997
69	F339VSD	Volvo B10M-56	Duple 300	B53F	1988	Hutchison, Overtown, 1997
70	PJI9170	Leyland Leopard PSU4D/2R	East Lancashire EL2000 (1993)	B47F	1977	National Welsh, 1989
71	PJI9171	Leyland Leopard PSU4D/2R	East Lancashire EL2000 (1993)	B47F	1977	National Welsh, 1989
72	PJI9172	Volvo B10M-61	Duple Dominant	B53F	1987	Alexander, Milngavie, 1997
73	PJI9173	Volvo B10M-61	East Lancashire EL2000 (1992)	B51F	1981	Alexander, Milngavie, 1997
74	PJI9174	Leyland Tiger TRCTL11/3R	East Lancashire EL2000 (1993)	B53F	1981	Alexander, Milngavie, 1997
75	PJI9175	Leyland Leopard PSU3E/4R	East Lancashire EL2000 (1993)	BC49F	1980	Blue Bus, Horwich, 1993
76	PJI9176	Leyland Leopard PSU3E/4R	East Lancashire EL2000 (1992)	B51F	1977	South Lancs, St Helens, 1993
77	PJI9177	Leyland Leopard PSU3C/4R	East Lancashire EL2000 (1992)	B51F	1977	Ellen Smith, Rochdale, 1991
78	PJI9178	Leyland Leopard PSU3E/4R	East Lancashire EL2000 (1992)	B51F	1979	Ribble, 1987
79	PJI9179	Leyland Leopard PSU3E/4R	East Lancashire EL2000 (1992)	B51F	1980	Barry Cooper, Stockton Heath, 1980

80-91

						Dennis Dart 8.5SDL3003	Carlyle Dartline	B25F	1990	Metroline, 1997-98

80	H118MOB	83	H109MOB	86	H114MOB	88	H128MOB	90	H130MOB
81	H102MOB	84	H120MOB	87	H127MOB	89	H129MOB	91	H131MOB
82	H104MOB	85	H112MOB						

No	Reg	Chassis	Body			
101	H101VFV	Dennis Dart 9.0SDL3002	Duple/Carlyle Dartline	B36F	1990	
102	H102VFV	Dennis Dart 9.0SDL3002	Duple/Carlyle Dartline	B36F	1990	
103	H103VFV	Dennis Dart 9.0SDL3002	Duple/Carlyle Dartline	B36F	1990	
104	H104CHG	Dennis Dart 9.0SDL3002	Reeve Burgess Pointer	B35F	1991	
105	H105CHG	Dennis Dart 9.0SDL3002	Reeve Burgess Pointer	B35F	1991	

Latest arrivals for the service bus fleet are six Dennis Darts bodied locally by East Lancashire using the Spryte design. First to arrive was 135, PO51WEC, seen here in Rochdale bus station. *Easyrider* names have been adopted by Rossendale for low-floor units while *Handyrider* is applied to other single-decks.
Mark Doggett

106-113

									Dennis Dart SLF	East Lancashire Spryte	N28F	1996-97

106	N106LCK	108	N108LCK	110	N110LCK	112	P212DCK	113	P213DCK
107	N107LCK	109	N109LCK	111	P211DCK				

114-123

Dennis Dart SLF — Plaxton Pointer SPD — N40F — 1998

114	S114KRN	116	S116KRN	118	S118KRN	120	S120KRN	122	S122KRN
115	S115KRN	117	S117KRN	119	S119KRN	121	S121KRN	123	S123KRN

126	L26FNE	Dennis Dart 9.8SDL3035	Marshall C37	B40F	1994	Mayne, Manchester, 1998
127	L27FNE	Dennis Dart 9.8SDL3035	Marshall C37	B40F	1994	Mayne, Manchester, 1998
128	K28XBA	Dennis Dart 9.8SDL3012	Marshall C27	B40F	1992	Mayne, Manchester, 1998
29	K29XBA	Dennis Dart 9.8SDL3012	Marshall C27	B40F	1993	Mayne, Manchester, 1998
31	X131JCW	Dennis Dart SLF	Plaxton Pointer SPD	N40F	2000	
32	X132JCW	Dennis Dart SLF	Plaxton Pointer SPD	N40F	2000	
33	X133JCW	Dennis Dart SLF	Plaxton Pointer SPD	N40F	2000	
34	X134JCW	Dennis Dart SLF	Plaxton Pointer SPD	N40F	2000	

135-140

Dennis Dart SLF — East Lancashire Spryte — N28F — 2001-02

135	PO51WEC	137	PF51KMO	138	PF51KMU	139	PF51KMV	140	PF51KMX
136	PF51KMM								

177-186

Leyland Lynx LX2R11C15Z4S — Leyland Lynx 2 — B51F* — 1991 — Lothian Buses, 2000 *varies

177	H177OSG	179	H179OSG	181	H181OSG	183	H183OSG	185	H185OSG
178	H178OSG	180	H180OSG	182	H182OSG	184	H184OSG	186	H186OSG

94	G994VWV	Leyland Lynx LX112L10ZR1R	Leyland Lynx	B47F	1990	Brighton & Hove, 2001
96	G996VWV	Leyland Lynx LX112L10ZR1R	Leyland Lynx	B47F	1990	Brighton & Hove, 2001
98	G915UPP	Mercedes-Benz 709D	Reeve Burgess Beaver	B23F	1989	Harrogate & District, 2000
99	N352BKK	Mercedes-Benz 709D	Plaxton Beaver	BC16FL	1995	Arriva Midlands North, 2000

In 1998 four Dennis Darts with Marshall C37 bodywork were acquired from Mayne of Manchester. Pictured in Burnley, 129, K29XBA illustrates the design which has evolved from the original Duple Dartline. *Dave Heath*

300	N300EST	Dennis Javelin 12SDA2159	Plaxton Première 350	C48FT	1995	
303	OIB5403	Leyland Tiger TRCTL11/3RZ	Plaxton Paramount 3200 II	C53F	1985	Ellen Smith, Rochdale, 1991
311	P211RWR	DAF DE33WSSB3000	Ikarus Blue Danube	C55F	1997	North Kent Express, 2001
320	RJI8720	Volvo B10M-61	Van Hool Alizée H	C53F	1989	Shearings, 1993
322	RJI8722	Volvo B10M-61	Van Hool Alizée H	C53F	1987	Clarkson, South Elmsall, 1993
341	T341NBV	Bova FHD 12.340	Bova Futura	C49FT	1999	
342	T342NBV	Bova FHD 12.340	Bova Futura	C49FT	1999	
343	T343NBV	Bova FHD 12.340	Bova Futura	C49FT	1999	
344	T344NBV	Bova FHD 12.340	Bova Futura	C49FT	1999	
345	W445CFR	Bova FHD 12.370	Bova Futura	C49FT	2000	
346	W446CFR	Bova FHD 12.370	Bova Futura	C49FT	2000	
347	M347MCY	Dennis Javelin 12SDA2134	Berkhof Excellence 1000L	C50FT	1994	Diamond-Glantawe, Morriston, 1998
348	M348MCY	Dennis Javelin 12SDA2134	Berkhof Excellence 1000L	C50FT	1994	Diamond-Glantawe, Morriston, 1998
352	R252KWY	Bova FHD 12.370	Bova Futura	C49FT	1998	Associated, Harlow, 2001
382	VOY182X	Leyland Tiger TRCTL11/2R	Plaxton Viewmaster IV Express	C53F	1981	Border Buses, Burnley, 1996
501	R570ANB	Volkswagen Caravelle	Volkswagen	M8	1998	
502	T231JNC	Volkswagen Caravelle	Volkswagen	M8	1999	
503	T232JNC	Volkswagen Caravelle	Volkswagen	M8	1999	

Previous Registrations:

G727JJC	G900MNS, WSV553	PJI9175	WCK139V
G728JJC	G899MNS, WSV550	PJI9176	VAJ784S
OIB5403	B887WRJ	PJI9177	UGG369R
PJI9170	PHB362R	PJI9178	WCK123V
PJI9171	PHB363R	PJI9179	GRF268V
PJI9172	D376RHS	RJI8720	F763ENE
PJI9173	NCS117W	RJI8722	D561MVR, MIW2422, D709NYG
PJI9174	BSG551W		

Named Vehicles:- 115 *Valley Tripper,* 116 *Valley Shopper,* 117 *Valley Wanderer,* 118 *Valley Traveller,* 119 *Valley Venturer,* 120 *Valley Rover,* 121 *Valley Commuter,* 122 *Valley Explorer,* 123 *Valley Rambler*

Allocations: Rochdale (Mandale Park) and Buxton outstation: 54/8, 66/7, 70/2-8, 80-91, 101-13, 231/2, 300-82, 570, 98 Rawtenstall (Bacup Road) and Burnley outstation - remainder

SHEARINGS

Shearings Ltd, Miry Lane, Wigan WN3 4AG

101-116 Volvo B10M-62 Van Hool T9 Alizée C46FT 1999

101	T101JBA	105	T105JBA	108	T108JBA	111	T197JBA	114	T114JBA
102	T102JBA	106	T106JBA	109	T109JBA	112	T112JBA	115	T115JBA
103	T103JBA	107	T107JBA	110	T110JBA	113	T113JBA	116	T116JBA
104	T104JBA								

117-122 Volvo B10M-62 Jonckheere Mistral 50 C46FT 1999

117	T117JBA	119	T119JBA	120	T120JBA	121	T198JBA	122	T122JBA
118	T118JBA								

123-132 Volvo B10M-62 Jonckheere Mistral 50 C50F 1999

123	T199JBA	125	T125JBA	127	T127JBA	129	T129JBA	131	T131JBA
124	T124JBA	126	T126JBA	128	T128JBA	130	T130JBA	132	T132JBA

201-220 Volvo B10M-62 Van Hool T9 Alizée C46FT 2000

201	W201JBN	205	W282JBN	209	W209JBN	213	W213JBN	217	W217JBN
202	W202JBN	206	W283JBN	210	W284JBN	214	W214JBN	218	W218JBN
203	W203JBN	207	W207JBN	211	W211JBN	215	W215JBN	219	W219JBN
204	W204JBN	208	W208JBN	212	W212JBN	216	W216JBN	220	W285JBN

221-230 Volvo B10M-62 Plaxton Panther C50F 2000

221	W221JBN	223	W223JBN	225	W287JBN	227	W227JBN	229	W229JBN
222	W286JBN	224	W224JBN	226	W226JBN	228	W228JBN	230	W288JBN

301-315 Volvo B10M-62 Van Hool T9 Alizée C46FT 2001

301	Y301KBN	304	Y304KBN	307	Y307KBN	310	Y387KBN	313	Y313KBN
302	Y302KBN	305	Y305KBN	308	Y308KBN	311	Y311KBN	314	Y314KBN
303	Y303KBN	306	Y306KBN	309	Y309KBN	312	Y312KBN	315	Y315KBN

316-321 Volvo B10M-62 Jonckheere Mistral 50 C46FT 2001

316	Y388KBN	318	Y389KBN	319	Y319KBN	320	Y391KBN	321	Y392KBN
317	Y317KBN								

401-433 Volvo B12M Van Hool T9 Alizée C46FT 2002

401	MV02UMA	407	MV02UMH	415	MV02UMS	422	MV02ULM	428	MV02ULT
402	MV02UMB	408	MV02UMJ	416	MV02UMT	423	MV02ULN	429	MV02ULU
403	MV02UMC	409	MV02UMK	417	MV02UMU	424	MV02ULO	430	MV02ULW
404	MV02UMD	410	MV02UML	418	MV02UMW	425	MV02ULP	431	MV02ULX
405	MV02UME	412	MV02UMM	419	MV02UMX	426	MV02ULR	432	MV02ULY
406	MV02UMF	413	MV02UMO	420	MV02ULK	427	MV02ULS	433	MV02ULZ
407	MV02UMG	414	MV02UMR	421	MV02ULL				

601-615 Volvo B10M-62 Jonckheere Deauville 45 C53F 1995

601	M601ORJ	604	M604ORJ	607	M607ORJ	610	M610ORJ	613	M613ORJ
602	M602ORJ	605	M605ORJ	608	M608ORJ	611	M611ORJ	614	M614ORJ
603	M603ORJ	606	M606ORJ	609	M609ORJ	612	M612ORJ	615	M615ORJ

677-681 Volvo B10M-62 Van Hool Alizée HE C46FT 1995

677	M677KVU	678	M678KVU	679	M679KVU	680	M680KVU	681	M681KVU

Shearings is claimed to be Europe's largest coach holiday operator and for 2002 has taken delivery of thirty-three new Volvo B12M coaches, the first major order for the model. The whole batch carry Van Hool T9 Alizée bodywork with 46-seats for continental work. The new B12M is based on the TX platform featuring a 12.1 litre Volvo DH12 engine. Pictured during the official hand-over at Haigh Hall, 404, MV02UMD also shows the latest livery application. *Volvo Bus*

701-720   Volvo B10M-62   Van Hool Alizée HE   C46FT   1996

701	N701UVR	705	N705UVR	709	N709UVR	713	N713UVR	717	N717UVR
702	N702UVR	706	N706UVR	710	N710UVR	714	N714UVR	718	N718UVR
703	N703UVR	707	N707UVR	711	N711UVR	715	N715UVR	719	N719UVR
704	N704UVR	708	N708UVR	712	N712UVR	716	N716UVR	720	N720UVR

721-735   Volvo B10M-62   Jonckheere Deauville 45   C46FT   1996

721	N721UVR	724	N724UVR	727	N727UVR	730	N730UVR	733	N733UVR
722	N722UVR	725	N725UVR	728	N728UVR	731	N731UVR	734	N734UVR
723	N723UVR	726	N726UVR	729	N729UVR	732	N732UVR	735	N735UVR

801-35   Volvo B10M-62   Van Hool Alizée HE   C46FT   1997

801	P801GBA	808	P808GBA	815	P815GBA	822	P822GBA	829	P829GBA
802	P802GBA	809	P809GBA	816	P816GBA	823	P823GBA	830	P830GBA
803	P803GBA	810	P810GBA	817	P817GBA	824	P824GBA	831	P831GBA
804	P804GBA	811	P811GBA	818	P818GBA	825	P825GBA	832	P832GBA
805	P805GBA	812	P812GBA	819	P819GBA	826	P826GBA	833	P833GBA
806	P806GBA	813	P813GBA	820	P820GBA	827	P827GBA	834	P834GBA
807	P807GBA	814	P814GBA	821	P821GBA	828	P828GBA	835	P835GBA

836	P305VWR	Volvo B10M-62		Van Hool Alizée HE		C46FT	1997	Wallace Arnold, 2001
837	P306VWR	Volvo B10M-62		Van Hool Alizée HE		C46FT	1997	Wallace Arnold, 2001

901-915   Volvo B10M-62   Van Hool T9 Alizée   C46FT   1998

901	R901YBA	904	R904YBA	907	R907YBA	910	R910YBA	913	R913YBA
902	R902YBA	905	R905YBA	908	R908YBA	911	R991ANB	914	R914YBA
903	R903YBA	906	R906YBA	909	R909YBA	912	R912YBA	915	R915YBA

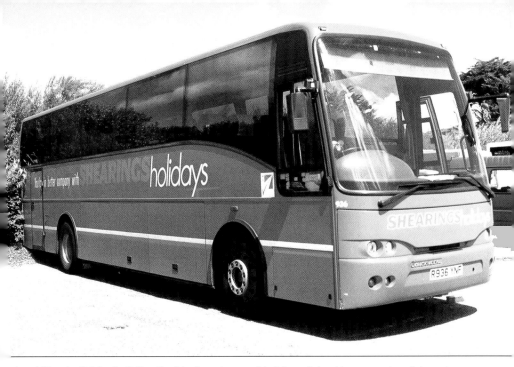

In addition to Belgian-built Van Hool bodywork several batches of Jonckheere coachwork have been supplied to Shearings and these, too, are built in Belgium. Mistral styling is seen in this view of 936, R936YNF from the 1998 batch of coaches allocated to British tours. It is seen in Newquay during the 2001 season. *J C Walton*

916-934

									Volvo B10M-62		Plaxton Excalibur		C50F		1998

916	R916YBA	920	R920YBA	924	R924YBA	928	R928YBA	932	R932YBA
917	R917YBA	921	R921YBA	925	R925YBA	929	R929YBA	933	R933YBA
918	R918YBA	922	R922YBA	926	R926YBA	930	R930YBA	934	R934YBA
919	R919YBA	923	R923YBA	927	R927YBA	931	R931YBA		

935-954

Volvo B10M-62   Jonckheere Mistral 50   C50F   1998

935	R935YNF	939	R939YNF	943	R943YNF	947	R947YNF	951	R951YNF
936	R936YNF	940	R940YNF	944	R944YNF	948	R948YNF	952	R952YNF
937	R937YNF	941	R941YNF	945	R945YNF	949	R949YNF	953	R953YNF
938	R938YNF	942	R942YNF	946	R946YNF	950	R950YNF	954	R954YNF

Crew transporters

W652RCA	Ford Tourneo GLX	Ford	M8	2000
W672RCA	Ford Tourneo GLX	Ford	M8	2000
W715RCA	Ford Tourneo GLX	Ford	M8	2000
W738RCA	Ford Tourneo GLX	Ford	M8	2000
W743RCA	Ford Tourneo GLX	Ford	M8	2000
Y266KCA	Ford Tourneo GLX	Ford	M8	2001
Y289KCA	Ford Tourneo GLX	Ford	M8	2001
Y309KCA	Ford Tourneo GLX	Ford	M8	2001
Y356KCA	Ford Tourneo GLX	Ford	M8	2001
Y431KCA	Ford Tourneo GLX	Ford	M8	2001
DK02GCU	Ford Tourneo GLX	Ford	M8	2002
DK02GDF	Ford Tourneo GLX	Ford	M8	2002
DK02GNY	Ford Tourneo GLX	Ford	M8	2002
DK02GJU	Ford Tourneo GLX	Ford	M8	2002
DK02GMV	Ford Tourneo GLX	Ford	M8	2002

Previous Registrations:

305VWR	P305VWR, 7243WA		P306VWR	P306VWR, 7820WA

SIM'S TRAVEL

William Sim & Son, Hunholme Garage, Boot, Holmrock, Eskdale, CA19 1TF

Reg	Chassis	Body	Seating	Year	History
F130AEL	Volvo B10M-60	Plaxton Paramount 3200 III	C57F	1989	Excelsior, Bournemouth, 1995
219DLV	DAF MB230LB615	Caetano Algarve H-NDH	C53F	1989	Abbeyways, Halifax, 1991
WXI5865	Van Hool T815H	Van Hool Alizée H	C49F	1990	Peter Carol, Bristol, 1994
A15TVL	Volvo B10M-60	Van Hool Alizée H	C49FT	1992	Shearings, 1999
A16TVL	Volvo B10M-60	Van Hool Alizée H	C49FT	1992	Brown, Edinburgh, 2000
N298VRM	Mercedes-Benz 609D	Onyx	C21F	1995	
N256THO	Volvo B10M-62	Plaxton Première 320	C49FT	1996	Excelsior, Bournemouth, 1998
P505GHH	Mercedes-Benz 814D	Autobus Classique Nouvelle	BC33F	1997	
R853WRM	Ford Tourneo	Ford	M8	1997	
R296PTF	Volvo B10M-62	Berkhof Axial	C49FT	1998	Group Travel, Stourbridge, 2001
T953JAO	Mercedes Benz 410D	Autobus	BC16F	1999	
X287TAO	Mercedes Benz Sprint 410D	Autobus	BC16F	2001	

Previous registrations:

219DLV	F234RJX	F130AEL	F458WFX, A18EXC
A15TVL	J242NNC	N256THO	XEL31
A16TVL	HSK658, L648AYS	WXI5865	G731XHY

Sim's Travel are based in the attractive Eskdale valley famed for its narrow-gauge railway and the near-b nuclear power plant. Seen at the opposite side of England however, in Barnard Castle, is Plaxton Premiè 320 N256THO. *J C Walton*

The Lancashire, Cumbria and Manchester Bus Handbook

SOUTH LANCS TRAVEL

South Lancs Travel - Green Triangle - B & D Coaches

Green Triangle Buses Ltd; 22/23 Chanters Ind Est, Arley Way, Atherton,
Manchester, M46 9BP

1	T11SLT	Dennis Dart SLF	Plaxton Pointer MPD	N28F	1999	
2	V22SLT	Dennis Dart SLF	Plaxton Pointer MPD	N28F	1999	
3	V33SLT	Dennis Dart SLF	Plaxton Pointer MPD	N28F	1999	
4	W44SLT	Dennis Dart SLF	Plaxton Pointer MPD	N28F	2000	
5	W55SLT	Dennis Dart SLF	Plaxton Pointer MPD	N28F	2000	
6	Y66SLT	Dennis Dart SLF	Plaxton Pointer MPD	N28F	2001	
7	Y77SLT	Dennis Dart SLF	Plaxton Pointer MPD	N28F	2001	
8	M88SLT	Dennis Dart SLF	Transbus Pointer MPD	N29F	2002	
9	M99SLT	Dennis Dart SLF	Transbus Pointer MPD	N29F	2002	
10	H101EKR	Iveco Daily 49.10	Phoenix	B23F	1991	Stagecoach South (EK), 1997
14	F914XWY	Mercedes-Benz 811D	Optare StarRider	B26F	1988	London Central, 1998
17	P417HVR	Iveco TurboDaily 59.12	Mellor Solo	B27F	1997	
19	W19SLT	Mercedes-Benz Vario O814	Plaxton Beaver 2	B27F	2000	
20	W20SLT	Mercedes-Benz Vario O814	Plaxton Beaver 2	B27F	2000	
21	G121PGT	Mercedes-Benz 811D	Alexander AM	B28F	1990	HMB Services, Gateshead, 1998
22	K2SLT	Mercedes-Benz 709D	Plaxton Beaver	B31F	1993	Arriva North West, 2001
23	K3SLT	Mercedes-Benz 709D	Plaxton Beaver	B31F	1993	Arriva North West, 2001
24	P248KND	Iveco TurboDaily 59.12	Mellor Solo	B27F	1996	
27	J627KCU	Dennis Dart 9.8SDL3017	Wright Handy-bus	B40F	1991	Go-Northern, 2000
35	J635KCU	Dennis Dart 9.8SDL3017	Wright Handy-bus	B40F	1991	Go-Northern, 2000
38	J638KCU	Dennis Dart 9.8SDL3017	Wright Handy-bus	B40F	1991	Go-Northern, 2000
48	R948AMB	Mercedes-Benz Vario O814	Plaxton Beaver 2	B31F	1998	

South Lancs Travel operate four Dennis Javelins with Duple bus bodywork, the 300 model being the bus version of th 320/340 coach frame. New to Bebbs of Lantwit Fardre and latterly with Eastbourne, 115, G25HDW is seen leaving central Wigan for Atherton, now a district within the Metropolitan Borough of Wigan. *Richard Godfrey*

Since its formation, South Lancs Travel has been taking delivery of Mini Pointer Darts, the latest arrivals being produced at the Transbus assembly line in Falkirk latterly known as Alexanders and where all Transbus single-deck bus assembly now takes place. The only standard floor Dart in the fleet is numbered 74. K374RTY was new to the Go-Ahead group and has a Wright Handy-bus body. *Richard Godfrey*

49	R949AMB	Mercedes-Benz Vario O814	Plaxton Beaver 2	B31F	1998	
53	L653MYG	Mercedes-Benz 711D	Plaxton Beaver	B27F	1993	Gibson Direct, Renfrew, 2001
57	L657MYG	Mercedes-Benz 711D	Plaxton Beaver	B27F	1993	Gibson Direct, Renfrew, 2001
58	N258DUR	Mercedes-Benz 709D	Plaxton Beaver	B27F	1995	Pete's Travel, West Bromwich, 1999
61	R661GCA	Mercedes-Benz Vario O814	Plaxton Beaver 2	B31F	1998	
65	R165ESG	Mercedes-Benz Vario O810	Plaxton Beaver 2	B29F	1997	G Bell, Silksworth, 1999
66	R166ESG	Mercedes-Benz Vario O810	Plaxton Beaver 2	B29F	1997	G Bell, Silksworth, 1999
67	M167LNC	Mercedes-Benz 709D	Alexander AM	B23F	1994	Arriva North West, 2002
68	M166LNC	Mercedes-Benz 709D	Alexander AM	B23F	1994	Arriva North West, 2002
74	K374RTY	Dennis Dart 9.8SDL3017	Wright Handy-bus	B40F	1993	Go-Northern, 2000
96	N796XRA	Mercedes-Benz 709D	Plaxton Beaver	B23F	1995	
99	R399CVR	Iveco TurboDaily 59.12	Mellor Solo	B29F	1998	
111	G911RPN	Dennis Javelin 11SDL1914	Duple 300	B55F	1989	Eastbourne Buses, 1999
112	G621CPS	Dennis Javelin 11SDL1914	Duple 300	B55F	1990	Leask, Lerwick, 1999
114	G914RPN	Dennis Javelin 11SDL1914	Duple 300	B55F	1990	Eastbourne Buses, 1999
115	G25HDW	Dennis Javelin 11SDL1914	Duple 300	B55F	1990	Eastbourne Buses, 1999
159	G59RND	Leyland Tiger TR2R62C16Z4	Alexander Q	B55F	1989	Border Buses, Burnley, 1999
161	G61RND	Leyland Tiger TR2R62C16Z4	Alexander Q	B55F	1989	Border Buses, Burnley, 1999
162	G62SMC	Leyland Tiger TRCTL11/2RP	Duple 300	B55F	1988	Arriva The Shires, 2000
163	G63SMC	Leyland Tiger TRCTL11/2RP	Duple 300	B55F	1988	Arriva The Shires, 2000
164	G61SMC	Leyland Tiger TRCTL11/2RP	Duple 300	B55F	1988	Arriva The Shires, 2000
173	TIL1173	Volvo Citybus B10M-50	East Lancashire	B45/35F	1991	Tillingbourne, Cranleigh, 2000
178	H678GPF	Volvo Citybus B10M-50	East Lancashire	B45/35F	1990	Tillingbourne, Cranleigh, 2000
192	G492XWS	Leyland Tiger TRCTL11/3LZM	Plaxton Derwent II	B54F	1989	MoD (03KJ25), 1998
466	AFB597V	Bristol LH6L	Eastern Coach Works	B43F	1980	Arriva North West, 1998

Previous registrations:

K3SLT	K455EDT, 30938, K455EDT	TIL1173	H673GPF

STAGECOACH

...in Cumbria ...in Lancaster ...in Lancashire

Stagecoach (North West) Ltd, 2/F Broadacre House,
16-20 Lowther Street, Carlisle, CA3 8DA

1-15		Mercedes-Benz 709D		Alexander Sprint		B23F	1995		
1	N201UHH	4	N204UHH	7	N207UHH	10	N210UHH	13	N213UHH
2	N202UHH	5	N205UHH	8	N208UHH	11	N211UHH	14	N214UHH
3	N203UHH	6	N206UHH	9	N209UHH	12	N212UHH	15	N215UHH

16-33		Mercedes-Benz 709D		Alexander Sprint		B23F	1996		
16	N116YHH	20	N120YHH	24	N124YHH	28	N128YRM	31	N131YRM
17	N117YHH	21	N121YHH	25	N125YHH	29	N129YRM	32	N132YRM
18	N118YHH	22	N122YHH	26	N126YRM	30	N130YRM	33	N133YRM
19	N119YHH	23	N123YHH	27	N127YRM				

36	R36LSO	Mercedes-Benz Vario O810	Plaxton Beaver 2	B27F	1997	Stagecoach Western Buses, 2000

47	E47CHH	Mercedes-Benz 709D	Alexander Sprint	B25F	1988
48	E48CHH	Mercedes-Benz 709D	Alexander Sprint	B25F	1988
49	E49CHH	Mercedes-Benz 709D	Alexander Sprint	B25F	1988
50	E50CHH	Mercedes-Benz 709D	Alexander Sprint	B25F	1988

54-70		Mercedes-Benz 709D		Alexander Sprint		B23F*	1990-91	55-70 Magicbus, 1990-91	
								*57-9/61-4 are B25F	
54	G178PAO	58	G268TSL	61	G263TSL	64	G266TSL	67	G295TSL
55	G299TSL	59	G269TSL	62	G264TSL	65	G297TSL	68	G294TSL
56	G300TSL	60	G296TSL	63	G265TSL	66	G298TSL	70	G293TSL
57	G267TSL								

71-78		Mercedes-Benz 709D		Alexander Sprint		B25F	1993		
	K871GHH	73	K873GHH	75	K875GHH	77	K877GHH	78	K878GHH
	K872GHH	74	K874GHH	76	K876GHH				

79-86		Mercedes-Benz 709D		Alexander Sprint		B25F	1993		
	K626UFR	81	K622UFR	83	K121XHG	85	L123DRN	86	K113XHG
	K623UFR	82	K114XHG	84	L126DRN				

	N327XRP	Mercedes-Benz 709D	Alexander Sprint	BC23F	1996
	N328XRP	Mercedes-Benz 709D	Alexander Sprint	BC23F	1996
	N329XRP	Mercedes-Benz 709D	Alexander Sprint	BC23F	1996

90-96		Mercedes-Benz Vario O814		Alexander ALX100		B29F	1998		
	S190RAO	92	S192RAO	94	S194RAO	95	S195RAO	96	S196RAO
	S191RAO	93	S193RAO						

	N645VSS	Mercedes-Benz 709D	Alexander Sprint	B25F	1996	Stagecoach Manchester, 1998
	N646VSS	Mercedes-Benz 709D	Alexander Sprint	B25F	1996	Stagecoach Manchester, 1998
	A102DAO	Leyland Tiger TRCTL11/2R	Duple Laser	C50F	1984	

104	K563GSA	Volvo B10M-60	Plaxton Premiére Interurban	BC51F	1993	Stagecoach Fife, 2001
105	P977UBV	Volvo B10M-62	Plaxton Premiére Interurban	BC51F	1996	
	P978UBV	Volvo B10M-62	Plaxton Premiére Interurban	BC51F	1996	
	P979UBV	Volvo B10M-62	Plaxton Premiére Interurban	BC51F	1996	

Stagecoach in Lancashire names are applied to buses based at Chorley, Preston and its outstation Fleetwood. Seen in Blackburn is Volvo B6 303, M743PRS, one of many of the type with high-back seating. It seen on rural service 124 from Chorley. *Mark Doggett*

108-114		Volvo B10M-62		Plaxton Premiére Interurban	BC51F	1997	
108	P108DCW	**8110**	P110DCW	**112**	P112DCW	**113**	P113DCW	**8114**	P114DCW
109	P109DCW						

111	VRR447	Leyland Tiger TRCTL11/3RH	Plaxton Paramount 3500 II	C48FT	1985	Hampshire Bus, 1988
114	PSU787	Leyland Tiger TRCTL11/3RZ	Duple Caribbean 2	C49FT	1986	East Midland, 1995
120	J120AHH	Volvo B10M-60	Plaxton Expressliner	C46FT	1991	
121	J121AHH	Volvo B10M-60	Plaxton Expressliner	C46FT	1991	
123	S269KHG	Volvo B10M-62	Jonckheere Modulo	BC51F	1998	
124	S270KHG	Volvo B10M-62	Jonckheere Modulo	BC51F	1998	
130	N130VAO	Volvo B10M-62	Plaxton Expressliner 2	C46FT	1995	
131	N131VAO	Volvo B10M-62	Plaxton Expressliner 2	C46FT	1995	
132	N132VAO	Volvo B10M-62	Plaxton Expressliner 2	C46FT	1995	
133	S133KRM	Volvo B10M-62	Jonckheere Mistral 50	C44FT	1998	
134	S134KRM	Volvo B10M-62	Jonckheere Mistral 50	C44FT	1998	
135	F135SPX	Dennis Javelin 11SDL1914	Duple 300	B63F	1989	
136	F136SPX	Dennis Javelin 11SDL1914	Duple 300	B63F	1989	
137	F137SPX	Dennis Javelin 11SDL1914	Duple 300	B63F	1989	
143	L143BFV	Dennis Javelin 11SDL2129	Plaxton Premiére Interurban	BC47F	1993	
152	L152BFV	Dennis Javelin 11SDL2133	Plaxton Premiére Interurban	BC47F	1993	
154	L154BFV	Dennis Javelin 11SDL2133	Plaxton Premiére Interurban	BC47F	1993	
156	PCK335	Leyland Tiger TRCTL11/3RH	Duple Laser 2	C53F	1985	
159	LJY145	Volvo B10M-61	Plaxton Paramount 3500 III	C48FT	1987	
160	YDG616	Volvo B10M-61	Plaxton Paramount 3500 III	C48FT	1987	
8160	L160CCW	Dennis Javelin 11SDL2133	Plaxton Premiére Interurban	BC47F	1993	
8161	L161CCW	Dennis Javelin 11SDL2133	Plaxton Premiére Interurban	BC47F	1993	
161	JPU817	Volvo B10M-61	Plaxton Paramount 3500 III	C53F	1987	Wallace Arnold, 1990
163	RIL5084	Volvo B10M-60	Plaxton Paramount 3500 III	C48FT	1990	Stagecoach Oxford, 1999
164	OIW5804	Volvo B10M-61	Van Hool Alizée	C53F	1983	Arriva (Heysham Travel), 2000
165	VKB708	Volvo B10M-61	Van Hool Alizée	C53F	1985	Arriva (Heysham Travel), 2000

The Lancashire, Cumbria and Manchester Bus Handbook

200-206 — Mercedes-Benz 709D, Alexander Sprint, B25F, 1996, Stagecoach Cambus, 1999

200	N614VSS	202	N617VSS	204	N641VSS	205	N613VSS	206	N616VSS
201	N615VSS	203	N619VSS						

Fleet	Reg	Chassis	Body	Layout	Year	Source
215	EKA215Y	Leyland Tiger TRCTL11/2R	Duple Dominant IV Express	C49F	1982	Arriva (Heysham Travel), 2000
220	EKA220Y	Leyland Tiger TRCTL11/2R	Duple Dominant IV Express	C49F	1982	Arriva (Heysham Travel), 2000
237	L237CCW	Volvo B6-9.9M	Alexander Dash	BC40F	1993	
243	L243SDY	Volvo Olympian YN2RV18Z4	Northern Counties Palatine	BC43/25F	1993	
244	L244SDY	Volvo Olympian YN2RV18Z4	Northern Counties Palatine	BC43/25F	1993	
245	L245SDY	Volvo Olympian YN2RV18Z4	Northern Counties Palatine	BC43/25F	1993	
252	L252CCK	Volvo B6-9.9M	Alexander Dash	BC40F	1993	
255	L255CCK	Volvo B6-9.9M	Alexander Dash	BC40F	1993	
256	L256CCK	Volvo B6-9.9M	Alexander Dash	BC40F	1993	
258	L658MSF	Volvo B6-9.9M	Alexander Dash	BC40F	1993	Fife Scottish, 1994
262	L662MSF	Volvo B6-9.9M	Alexander Dash	BC40F	1993	Fife Scottish, 1994
265	L665MSF	Volvo B6-9.9M	Alexander Dash	BC40F	1993	Fife Scottish, 1994
270	L270LHH	Volvo B6-9.9M	Alexander Dash	B40F	1993	
8284	L271LHH	Volvo B6-9.9M	Alexander Dash	B40F	1993	
8285	L272LHH	Volvo B6-9.9M	Alexander Dash	B40F	1993	
286	L273LHH	Volvo B6-9.9M	Alexander Dash	B40F	1993	
287	L274LHH	Volvo B6-9.9M	Alexander Dash	B40F	1993	

275-283 — Volvo B6-9.9M, Alexander Dash, B40F, 1993

275	L275JAO	277	L277JAO	281	L281JAO	282	L282JAO	8283	L283JAO
276	L276JAO	278	L278JAO							

Fleet	Reg	Chassis	Body	Layout	Year	Source
283	M460VHE	Volvo B6-9.9M	Alexander Dash	B40F	1993	Manchester, 1997
284	M733BSJ	Volvo B6-9.9M	Alexander Dash	BC40F	1994	Stagecoach Western Buses, 2000
285	M734BSJ	Volvo B6-9.9M	Alexander Dash	BC40F	1994	Stagecoach Western Buses, 2000

302-310 — Volvo B6-9.9M, Alexander Dash, BC40F, 1994, Stagecoach Manchester, 1999

302	M742PRS	304	M744PRS	306	M746PRS	8308	M748PRS	310	M750PRS
303	M743PRS	305	M745PRS	8307	M847PRS	309	M749PRS		

311-321 — Volvo B6-9.9M, Alexander Dash, B40F, 1994, Stagecoach Manchester, 1999

311	M461VHE	314	M454VHE	316	M456VHE	318	M458VHE	320	M741PRS
313	M846HDF	315	M455VHE	317	M457VHE	319	M459VHE	321	M462VHE

Fleet	Reg	Chassis	Body	Layout	Year	Source
22	H622ACK	Volvo B10M-55	Alexander PS	B51F	1991	Burnley & Pendle, 1997
23	H623ACK	Volvo B10M-55	Alexander PS	B51F	1991	Burnley & Pendle, 1997
24	J24MCW	Volvo B10M-50	East Lancashire EL2000	B45F	1992	Burnley & Pendle, 1997
25	J25MCW	Volvo B10M-50	East Lancashire EL2000	B45F	1992	Burnley & Pendle, 1997
27	FAO427V	Bristol VRT/SL3/6LXB	Eastern Coach Works	B43/31F	1980	
40	M230TBV	Volvo B10M-55	Alexander PS	BC48F	1995	
41	KRM431W	Bristol VRT/SL3/6LXB	Eastern Coach Works	B43/31F	1980	
45	KRM435W	Bristol VRT/SL3/6LXB	Eastern Coach Works	B43/31F	1980	
435	M235TBV	Volvo B10M-55	Alexander PS	BC48F	1995	
6	M236TBV	Volvo B10M-55	Alexander PS	BC48F	1995	
9	K449YCW	Optare MetroRider MR01	Optare	B31F	1992	
0	K450YCW	Optare MetroRider MR01	Optare	B31F	1992	
1	M451VCW	Volvo B10M-55	Alexander PS	BC48F	1995	
2	M452VCW	Volvo B10M-55	Alexander PS	BC48F	1995	
4	M454VCW	Volvo B10M-55	Alexander PS	BC48F	1995	

55-463 — Volvo B10M-55, Alexander PS, B48F, 1995

5	M455VCW	457	M457VCW	458	M458VCW	459	M459VCW	463	M463VCW
6	M456VCW								

5-472 — Volvo B10M-55, Alexander PS, B49F, 1996

	P127XCN	467	P129XCN	469	P131XCN	471	P133XCN	472	P134XCN
	P128XCN	468	P130XCN	470	P132XCN				

3-478 — Volvo B10M-55, Alexander PS, B49F, 1997

	R473MCW	475	R475MCW	476	R476MCW	477	R477MCW	478	R478MCW
	R474MCW								

527	H617ACK	Volvo B10M-55	Alexander PS	B51F	1991	Stagecoach Western, 2002
528	H618ACK	Volvo B10M-55	Alexander PS	B51F	1991	Stagecoach Western, 2002
529	H619ACK	Volvo B10M-55	Alexander PS	B51F	1991	Stagecoach Western, 2002

540-547   Volvo B10M-55   Alexander PS   B49F   1997   Stagecoach Western, 2002

| 540 | P540ESA | 542 | P542ESA | 544 | P544ESA | 546 | P546ESA | 547 | P547ESA |
| 541 | P541ESA | 543 | P543ESA | 545 | P545ESA | | | | |

8546	N648VSS	Mercedes-Benz 709D	Alexander Sprint	B25F	1996	Manchester, 1998
8547	N647VSS	Mercedes-Benz 709D	Alexander Sprint	B25F	1996	Manchester, 1998
565	G665PHH	Mercedes-Benz 709D	Alexander Sprint	B23F	1990	
566	G566PRM	Mercedes-Benz 709D	Alexander Sprint	B23F	1990	
567	G567PRM	Mercedes-Benz 709D	Alexander Sprint	BC25F	1990	
570	G570PRM	Mercedes-Benz 709D	Alexander Sprint	BC25F	1990	
571	G571PRM	Mercedes-Benz 709D	Alexander Sprint	BC25F	1990	
580	G180PAO	Mercedes-Benz 709D	Alexander Sprint	B23F	1990	Magicbus, 1990
590	G190PAO	Mercedes-Benz 709D	Alexander Sprint	B23F	1990	
592	G192PAO	Mercedes-Benz 709D	Alexander Sprint	B23F	1990	

595-624   Mercedes-Benz 709D   Alexander Sprint   B25F   1993

595	K115XHG	600	K120XHG	608	L128DRN	613	K613UFR	618	K618UFR
596	K116XHG	602	L122DRN	610	K610UFR	614	K614UFR	619	K619UFR
597	K117XHG	604	K124XHG	611	K611UFR	615	K615UFR	620	K620UFR
598	K118XHG	605	L125DRN	612	K612UFR	616	K616UFR	8624	K624UFR
599	L119DRN	607	L127DRN						

624	CKC624X	Leyland Tiger TRCTL11/2R	Duple Dominant IV Express	C49F	1982	Arriva, Heysham Travel, 2000
625	K625UFR	Mercedes-Benz 709D	Alexander Sprint	B25F	1993	Ribble, 1998
626	CKC626X	Leyland Tiger TRCTL11/2R	Duple Dominant IV Express	C49F	1982	Arriva, Heysham Travel, 2000

629-637   Mercedes-Benz 709D   Alexander Sprint   B25F   1993

| 629 | L629BFV | 631 | L631BFV | 633 | L633BFV | 635 | L635BFV | 637 | K112XHG |
| 630 | L630BFV | 632 | L632BFV | 634 | L634BFV | 636 | L636BFV | | |

638	N519BJA	Mercedes-Benz 709D	Alexander Sprint	B25F	1996	
639	N520BJA	Mercedes-Benz 709D	Alexander Sprint	B25F	1996	
641	N452VOD	Mercedes-Benz 709D	Alexander Sprint	B25F	1996	
644	N455VOD	Mercedes-Benz 709D	Alexander Sprint	B25F	1996	
645	WAO645Y	Leyland Tiger TRCTL11/2R	Alexander TE	BC47F	1983	

649-658   Mercedes-Benz 709D   Alexander Sprint   B25F   1996   649-52 Manchester, 1998

| 649 | N649VSS | 651 | N651VSS | 8652 | N461VOD | 654 | N463VOD | 657 | N466VOD |
| 650 | N650VSS | 652 | N652VSS | 653 | N462VOD | 656 | N465VOD | 658 | N467VOD |

660-667   Mercedes-Benz 709D   Alexander Sprint   B25F   1996

| 660 | N201LFV | 662 | N194LFV | 664 | N196LFV | 666 | N198LFV | 667 | N199LFV |
| 661 | N202LFV | 663 | N195LFV | 665 | N197LFV | | | | |

| 670 | R670LFV | Mercedes-Benz Vario O814 | Plaxton Beaver 2 | B27F | 1997 | |
| 672 | R672LFV | Mercedes-Benz Vario O814 | Plaxton Beaver 2 | B27F | 1997 | |

673-681   Optare Solo M850   Optare   N24F   2001

| 673 | PO51WLF | 675 | PO51WLH | 677 | PO51WLK | 679 | PO51WLN | 681 | PO51WLR |
| 674 | PO51WLG | 676 | PO51WLJ | 678 | PO51WLL | 680 | PO51WLP | | |

North West, along with South Midlands, are the two Stagecoach fleets to receive Optare Solo minibuses. Several are based at Fleetwood and carry route branding for local service F4 and work along-side Mercedes-Benz minibuses. Seen in Poulton-le-Fylde is 654, N463VOD. *Bill Potter*

99-788		Volvo B10M-55		Alexander PS		B49F*	1992-93	*772-788 are BC48F

99	K699ERM	717	K717DAO	735	K735DAO	754	K754DAO	771	K771DAO
00	K700DAO	718	K718DAO	736	K736DAO	755	K755DAO	772	K772DAO
01	K701DAO	719	K719DAO	737	K737DAO	756	K756DAO	773	K773DAO
02	K702DAO	720	K720DAO	738	K738DAO	757	K757DAO	774	K774DAO
03	K703DAO	721	K721DAO	739	K739DAO	758	K758DAO	775	K775DAO
04	K704ERM	722	K722DAO	741	K741DAO	759	K759DAO	776	K776DAO
05	K705DAO	723	K723DAO	742	K742DAO	760	K760DAO	777	K777DAO
06	K706DAO	724	K724DAO	743	K743DAO	761	K761DAO	778	K778DAO
07	K707DAO	725	K725DAO	744	K744DAO	762	K762DAO	779	K779DAO
08	K708DAO	726	K726DAO	745	K745DAO	763	K763DAO	780	K780DAO
09	K709DAO	727	K727DAO	746	K746DAO	764	K764DAO	781	K781DAO
10	K710DAO	728	K728DAO	748	K748DAO	765	K765DAO	783	K783DAO
11	K711DAO	729	K729DAO	749	K749DAO	766	K766DAO	784	K784DAO
12	K712DAO	730	K730DAO	750	K750DAO	767	K767DAO	785	K785DAO
13	K713DAO	731	K731DAO	751	K751DAO	768	K768DAO	786	K786DAO
14	K714DAO	732	K732DAO	752	K752DAO	769	K769DAO	787	K787DAO
15	K715DAO	733	K733DAO	753	K753DAO	770	K770DAO	788	K788DAO
16	K716DAO	734	K734DAO						

	N789VRM	Volvo B10M-55	Alexander PS	BC48F	1995
	N790VRM	Volvo B10M-55	Alexander PS	BC48F	1995
	R791PAO	Volvo B10M-62	Plaxton Premiére Interurban	BC51F	1997
	R792PAO	Volvo B10M-62	Plaxton Premiére Interurban	BC51F	1997
	R793URM	Volvo B10M-55	Alexander PS	B49F	1998
	R794URM	Volvo B10M-55	Alexander PS	B49F	1998
	R795URM	Volvo B10M-55	Alexander PS	B49F	1998
	S796KRM	Volvo B10M-62	Jonckheere Modulo	BC51F	1998
	S797KRM	Volvo B10M-62	Jonckheere Modulo	BC51F	1998
	S798KRM	Volvo B10M-62	Jonckheere Modulo	BC51F	1998
	S799KRM	Volvo B10M-62	Jonckheere Modulo	BC51F	1998

Jonckheere Modulo express buses are used by Cumberland for the *Cumbrian Connexion* and, along with one of the MAN buses , carry a special livery for these routes. Seen at the Rheged is 799, S799KRM. Local names have been applied to the buses allocated this service. Here we see Bassenthwaite Lake, while 798 is River Derwent and 814 Great Nell Fell. *Richard Godfrey*

801-809

MAN 18.220 HOCL - R   Alexander ALX300   N42F   1999-2000

801	V801DFV	803	V803DFV	805	X805SRM	807	V807DFV	809	V809DFV
802	V802DFV	804	V804DFV	806	V806DFV	808	V808DFV		

811-827

MAN 18.220 HOCL - R   Alexander ALX300   N42F   1999-2000

811	V811DFV	815	X815SRM	819	X819SRM	822	X822SRM	825	X825SRM
812	V812DFV	816	X816SRM	820	X721NSE	823	X823SRM	826	X826SRM
813	X813SRM	817	X817SRM	821	X821SRM	824	X824SRM	827	X827SRM
814	X814SRM	818	X818SRM						

875-888

Mercedes-Benz 709D   Alexander Sprint   B25F   1993   Stagecoach South East, 2002

875	K875ODY	878	K878ODY	883	L883SDY	885	L885SDY	887	L887SDY
876	K876ODY	881	L881SDY	884	L884SDY	886	L886SDY	888	L188SDY
877	K877ODY	882	L882SDY						

900	B900WRN	Leyland Tiger TRCTL11/1R	Duple Dominant	B49F	1984	Ribble, 1997
935	CUL179V	Leyland Titan TNLXB2RRSp	Park Royal	B44/26D	1980	Stagecoach Scotland West, 2001
944	GYE254W	Leyland Titan TNLXB2RR	Leyland	B44/29D	1981	Stagecoach Western Buses, 2000
946	GYE281W	Leyland Titan TNLXB2RR	Leyland	B44/29D	1981	Stagecoach Western Buses, 2000
947	OHV684Y	Leyland Titan TNLXB2RR	Leyland	B44/29D	1983	Stagecoach Western Buses, 2000
951	OHV739Y	Leyland Titan TNLXB2RR	Leyland	B44/29F	1983	Stagecoach Devon, 2002
952	OHV729Y	Leyland Titan TNLXB2RR	Leyland	B44/29F	1983	Stagecoach Devon, 2002
954	OHV728Y	Leyland Titan TNLXB2RR	Leyland	B44/29F	1983	Stagecoach Scotland West, 2001
955	KYV340X	Leyland Titan TNLXB2RR	Leyland	B44/26F	1981	Stagecoach Scotland East, 2002
956	KYV311X	Leyland Titan TNLXB2RR	Leyland	B44/26F	1981	Stagecoach Scotland East, 2002
958	OHV809Y	Leyland Titan TNLXB2RR	Leyland	B44/29F	1983	Stagecoach Western Buses, 2000
965	WYV56T	Leyland Titan TNLXB2RRSp	Park Royal	B44/26D	1979	Stagecoach Western Buses, 2000
973	B91WUV	Leyland Titan TNLXB2RR	Leyland	O44/29F	1984	Stagecoach Western, 2001
974	B100WUV	Leyland Titan TNLXB2RR	Leyland	O44/29F	1984	Stagecoach Bluebird, 2001
975	B110WUV	Leyland Titan TNLXB2RR	Leyland	O44/29F	1984	Stagecoach Bluebird, 2001
976	KYV512X	Leyland Titan TNLXB2RR	Leyland	O44/29F	1981	Stagecoach London, 2001
982	A855SUL	Leyland Titan TNLXB2RR	Leyland	B44/29F	1983	Stagecoach Scotland West, 2001

A recent three-way exchange of buses in Lancaster, Newcastle and Glasgow has seen the departure of Olympians from Lancaster replaced by Alexander PSs from Glasgow. One of the first into service was 540, P540ESA which is seen near the new bus station while working route 2 from Lancaster University to Heysham Towers. *Bob Downham*

| 001 | URM801Y | Leyland Olympian ONLXB/1R | Eastern Coach Works | BC45/30F | 1982 |
| 002 | URM802Y | Leyland Olympian ONLXB/1R | Eastern Coach Works | B45/32F | 1982 |

003-1011
Leyland Olympian ONLXB/2RZ Alexander RL   B51/36F   1988

| 003 | F803FAO | 1005 | F805FAO | 1007 | F807FAO | 1009 | F809FAO | 1011 | F811FAO |
| 004 | F804FAO | 1006 | F806FAO | 1008 | F808FAO | 1010 | F810FAO | | |

012-1019
Leyland Olympian ON2R56G13Z4 Alexander RL   B51/34F   1990

| 012 | H112SAO | 1014 | H114SAO | 1016 | H116SAO | 1018 | H118SAO | 1019 | H119SAO |
| 013 | H113SAO | 1015 | H115SAO | 1017 | H117SAO | | | | |

020-1027
Leyland Olympian ON2R56G13Z4 Alexander RL   BC47/27F 1991

| 020 | J120AAO | 1022 | J122AAO | 1024 | J124XHH | 1026 | J126XHH | 1027 | J127XHH |
| 021 | J121AAO | 1023 | J123XHH | 1025 | J125XHH | | | | |

028-1035
Leyland Olympian ON2R50G13Z4 Alexander RL   BC43/27F 1992

| 028 | K128DAO | 1030 | K130DAO | 1032 | K132DAO | 1034 | K134DAO | 1035 | K135DAO |
| 029 | K129DAO | 1031 | K131DAO | 1033 | K133DAO | | | | |

030	C382SAO	Leyland Olympian ONLXB/1RV	Alexander RL	B47/30F	1986	Bluebird, 1991
031	C383SAO	Leyland Olympian ONLXB/1RV	Alexander RL	B47/30F	1986	Bluebird, 1991
032	D384XAO	Leyland Olympian ONLXB/1RV	Alexander RL	B47/30F	1987	Bluebird, 1991
033	D380XRS	Leyland Olympian ONLXB/1RV	Alexander RL	B47/30F	1987	Bluebird, 1992
034	D381XRS	Leyland Olympian ONLXB/1RV	Alexander RL	B47/30F	1987	Bluebird, 1992
0	G520LWU	Volvo B10M-60	Plaxton Paramount 3500 III	C49FT	1990	Cambus (Premier), 1997
0	R120VFR	Volvo B10M-62	Jonckheere Mistral 50	C46FT	1998	
1	S905JHG	Volvo B10M-62	Jonckheere Mistral 50	C46FT	1998	
2	L126NAO	Volvo B10M-62	Plaxton Expressliner 2	C46FT	1994	
4	M406BFG	Volvo B10M-62	Plaxton Premiére 350	C51FT	1995	Stagecoach Bluebird, 2000
5	L125NAO	Volvo B10M-62	Plaxton Expressliner 2	C46FT	1994	
6	S906JHG	Volvo B10M-62	Jonckheere Mistral 50	C46FT	1998	
7	L127NAO	Volvo B10M-62	Plaxton Expressliner 2	C46FT	1994	
8	N128VAO	Volvo B10M-62	Plaxton Expressliner 2	C46FT	1994	
9	N129VAO	Volvo B10M-62	Plaxton Expressliner 2	C46FT	1994	
0	J702CWT	Volvo B10M-60	Plaxton Premiére 350	C48FT	1992	Stagecoach Midland Red, 2000
1	N447XVA	Volvo B10M-62	Plaxton Expressliner 2	C49FT	1995	Stagecoach East, 2001
4	E131ORP	Volvo B10M-61	Plaxton Paramount 3200 III	C53F	1988	Stagecoach United Counties, 2000
2	E132ORP	Volvo B10M-61	Plaxton Paramount 3200 III	C53F	1988	Stagecoach United Counties, 2000

1133	E133ORP	Volvo B10M-61	Plaxton Paramount 3200 III	C53F	1988	Stagecoach United Counties, 2000
1134	E134ORP	Volvo B10M-61	Plaxton Paramount 3200 III	C53F	1988	Stagecoach United Counties, 1999
1135	E135ORP	Volvo B10M-61	Plaxton Paramount 3200 III	C53F	1988	Stagecoach United Counties, 2000
1136	VLT104	Volvo B10M-60	Plaxton Expressliner	C53F	1990	Stagecoach Scotland West, 2001
1137	IIL3507	Volvo B10M-60	Plaxton Paramount 3500 III	C51F	1989	Stagecoach Scotland West, 2001
1151	B151WRN	Leyland Tiger TRCTL11/2RH	Duple Laser 2	C49F	1985	
1153w	B153WRN	Leyland Tiger TRCTL11/2RH	Duple Laser 2	C53F	1985	
1155	B43MAO	Leyland Tiger TRCTL11/3RH	Duple Laser 2	C53F	1985	
1162	WLT980	Volvo B10M-61	Plaxton Paramount 3500 II	C48F	1986	
1164	M164SCK	Volvo B10M-62	Plaxton Expressliner 2	C46FT	1994	
1165	M165SCK	Volvo B10M-62	Plaxton Expressliner 2	C46FT	1994	
1528	N885AVV	Mercedes-Benz 709D	Alexander Sprint	B25F	1996	Stagecoach Manchester, 1998
2017	B117TVU	Leyland Olympian ONLXB/1R	Northern Counties	O43/30F	1985	Stagecoach Manchester, 1999
2024	DBV24W	Bristol VRT/SL3/6LXB	Eastern Coach Works	B43/31F	1980	
2100	DBV100W	Leyland Olympian B45.02	Eastern Coach Works	B45/33F	1980	
2102	JFR2W	Leyland Olympian ONLXB/1R	Eastern Coach Works	O45/32F	1981	
2116	OFV16X	Leyland Olympian ONLXB/1R	Eastern Coach Works	B45/32F	1982	
2117	OFV17X	Leyland Olympian ONLXB/1R	Eastern Coach Works	B45/32F	1982	
2129	VRN829Y	Leyland Olympian ONLXBT/1R	Eastern Coach Works	O45/32F	1982	
2134	DBV134Y	Leyland Olympian ONLXB/1R	Eastern Coach Works	B45/32F	1983	
2138	A138MRN	Leyland Olympian ONLXB/1R	Eastern Coach Works	B45/32F	1984	
2145	A545HAC	Leyland Olympian ONLXB/1R	Eastern Coach Works	O45/32F	1984	Stagecoach Midland Red, 2000
2170	C170ECK	Leyland Olympian ONLXB/1R	Eastern Coach Works	BC42/30F	1985	
2174	C174ECK	Leyland Olympian ONLXB/1R	Eastern Coach Works	BC42/30F	1985	
2175	C175ECK	Leyland Olympian ONLXB/1R	Eastern Coach Works	BC42/30F	1985	
2176	C176ECK	Leyland Olympian ONLXB/1R	Eastern Coach Works	BC42/30F	1985	
2177	C177ECK	Leyland Olympian ONLXB/1R	Eastern Coach Works	BC42/30F	1986	
2179	C179ECK	Leyland Olympian ONLXB/1R	Eastern Coach Works	BC41/26F	1985	
2187	G187JHG	Leyland Olympian ON2R56G16Z4 Alexander RL		BC51/31F	1989	
2188	G188JHG	Leyland Olympian ON2R56G16Z4 Alexander RL		BC51/31F	1989	
2190	CUB72Y	Leyland Olympian ONLXB/1R	Roe	B47/29F	1983	Stagecoach Western, 2001
2193	H193WFR	Leyland Olympian ON2R56G16Z4 Alexander RL		B47/30F	1990	
2195	H195WFR	Leyland Olympian ON2R56G16Z4 Alexander RL		B47/30F	1990	
2196	H196WFR	Leyland Olympian ON2R56G16Z4 Alexander RL		B47/30F	1990	

2198-2210

Leyland Olympian ON2R56G13Z4 Alexander RL — BC43/27F* 1991 — *2204-6/10 are BC47/27F

2198	J198HFR	2202	J202HFR	2205	J205HFR	2207	J207HFR	2209	J209HFR
2199	J199HFR	2203	J203HFR	2206	J206HFR	2208	J208HFR	2210	J210HFR
2201	J201HFR	2204	J204HFR						

2216-2223

Leyland Olympian ONLXB/1R — Alexander RL — B45/32F 1984-85 — Highland Scottish, 1991

2216	B892UAS	2217	B893UAS	2219	B895UAS	2220	B896UAS	2223	B899UAS

2224-2235

Volvo Olympian YN2RV18Z4 — Northern Counties Palatine — B49/33F 1996

2224	P224VCK	2227	P227VCK	2230	P230VCK	2232	P232VCK	2234	P234VCK
2225	P225VCK	2228	P228VCK	2231	P231VCK	2233	P233VCK	2235	P235VCK
2226	P226VCK	2229	P229VCK						

2236-2245

Volvo Olympian YN2RV18Z4 — Alexander RL — B45/27F 1996

2236	P260VPN	2238	P262VPN	2240	P270VPN	2242	P272VPN	2244	P274VPN
2237	P261VPN	2239	P263VPN	2241	P271VPN	2243	P273VPN	2245	P275VPN

2246-2268

Volvo Olympian — Alexander RL — B51/36F 1997

2246	R246NBV	2251	R251NBV	2256	R256NBV	2261	R261NBV	2265	R265NBV
2247	R247NBV	2252	R252NBV	2257	R257NBV	2262	R262NBV	2266	R266NBV
2248	R248NBV	2253	R253NBV	2258	R258NBV	2263	R263NBV	2267	R267NBV
2249	R249NBV	2254	R254NBV	2259	R259NBV	2264	R264NBV	2268	R268NBV
2250	R250NBV	2255	R255NBV	2260	R260NBV				

2269	S903JHG	Volvo Olympian	Alexander RL	BC43/27F	1998
2270	S904JHG	Volvo Olympian	Alexander RL	BC43/27F	1998

2271-2285

Volvo Olympian YN2RC16V3 — Alexander RL — B47/32F 1996 — Stagecoach Manchester, 1999

2271	N325NPN	2274	N328NPN	2277	N331NPN	2280	N335NPN	2283	N338NPN
2272	N326NPN	2275	N329NPN	2278	N332NPN	2281	N336NPN	2284	N339NPN
2273	N327NPN	2276	N330NPN	2279	N334NPN	2282	N337NPN	2285	N340NPN

2296	F296DRJ	Leyland Olympian ONLXB/1RZ	Northern Counties	B43/30F	1988	Stagecoach Manchester, 2001

New arrivals for the 2002 *Lakeland Experience* season are further Leyland Titans that are being converted to open-top and repainted green. These ply route 599 between Grasmere and Bowness. Ready for another load for 'walkers' is 2145, A545HAC transferred to Lakeland duties from Midland Red. *David Longbottom*

2297	F297DRJ	Leyland Olympian ONLXB/1RZ	Northern Counties	B43/30F	1988	Stagecoach Manchester, 2001
3213	C213CBU	Leyland Olympian ONLXB/1R	Northern Counties	BC43/26F	1986	Stagecoach Manchester, 2001

Ancillary vehicles

T260	RBZ5459	Dodge Commando G13	Wadham Stinger Vanguard	TV	1985	MoD, 1999 (C973KWL)
T261	F344ECK	Dodge Commando G13	Wadham Stinger Vanguard	TV	1989	MoD, 2000 (93KF72)
T262	D375DCK	Dodge Commando G13	Reeve Burgess	TV	1987	MoD, 2000 (80KF50)
3002	RUT842	Dodge Commando G13	Wadham Stringer Vanguard	TV	1987	MoD, 2000 (94KF00)
3003	VLF578	Dodge Commando G13	Wadham Stringer Vanguard	TV	1987	MoD, 2000 (93KF81)
3004	SHH124M	Leyland Leopard PSU3/3R	Alexander AY	TV	1974	Ribble, 1997
3005	RIL5085	Dodge Commando G13	Wadham Stinger Vanguard	TV	1985	MoD, 2000 (31KC17)
3006	D513XAO	Dodge Commando G13	Wadham Stringer Vanguard	TV	1986	MoD, 1999 (80KF60)
3007	A247GAO	Dodge Commando G13	Reeve Burgess	TV	1984	MoD, 1999 (30KB44)
3008	EGB53T	Leyland Leopard PSU3E/3R	Alexander AYS	TV	1978	
3009	GSU859T	Leyland Leopard PSU3E/3R	Alexander AYS	TV	1979	Stagecoach Manchester, 2001

Previous Registrations

		PCK335	B156WRN
B43MAO	B155WRN, PCK335	PSU787	C495LJV
C382SAO	C473SSO, GSO3V		
C383SAO	C474SSO, GSO4V	RIL5084	G545LWU, 9258VC
D384XAO	D375XRS, GSO5V	SHH124M	SCS355M, TCK841
		VKB708	B483UNB
IIL3507	F410DUG	VLT104	G386PNV
JPU817	D207LWX	VRR447	B180RLJ
K449YCW	K300LCT		
K450YCW	K200LCT		
LJY145	D205LWX	WLT980	C105DWR
OIW5804	LYS513Y, 86WEH, WCN643Y	YDG616	D206LWX

Note: Full details of vehicle allocations to depots and outstations are provided each year in the Stagecoach Bus Handbook. Please see page 2 for more information.

STAGECOACH

... in Manchester

Greater Manchester Buses (South) Ltd, Hyde Road, Ardwick, Manchester, M12 6JS

101-159   MAN 18.220 HOCL - R   Alexander ALX300   N42F   1998

101	S101TRJ	116	S116TRJ	128	S128TRJ	139	S139TRJ	149	S149TRJ
102	S102TRJ	117	S117TRJ	129	S129TRJ	140	S140TRJ	150	S150TRJ
103	S103TRJ	118	S118TRJ	130	S130TRJ	141	S141TRJ	151	S151TRJ
104	S104TRJ	119	S119TRJ	131	S131TRJ	142	S142TRJ	152	S152TRJ
105	S105TRJ	120	S120TRJ	132	S132TRJ	143	S143TRJ	153	S153TRJ
106	S106TRJ	121	S121TRJ	133	S133TRJ	144	S144TRJ	154	S154TRJ
107	S107TRJ	122	S122TRJ	134	S134TRJ	145	S145TRJ	156	S156TRJ
108	S108TRJ	124	S124TRJ	135	S135TRJ	146	S146TRJ	157	S157TRJ
113	S113TRJ	125	S125TRJ	136	S136TRJ	147	S147TRJ	158	S158TRJ
114	S114TRJ	126	S126TRJ	137	S137TRJ	148	S148TRJ	159	S159TRJ
115	S115TRJ	127	S127TRJ	138	S138TRJ				

160-213   MAN 18.220 HOCL - R   Alexander ALX300   N42F   1999

160	T160MVM	165	T165MVM	173	T173MVM	182	T182MVM	187	T187MVM
161	T161MVM	166	T166MVM	178	T178MVM	183	T183MVM	188	T188MVM
162	T162MVM	167	T167MVM	179	T179MVM	184	T184MVM	189	T189MVM
163	T163MVM	168	T168MVM	180	T180MVM	185	T185MVM	212	T212TND
164	T164MVM	169	T169MVM	181	T181MVM	186	T186MVM	213	T213TND

216-246   MAN 18.220 HOCL - R   Alexander ALX300   N42F   2000

216	X216BNE	223	X223BNE	229	X229BNE	235	X235BNE	241	X241ATD
217	X217BNE	224	X224BNE	231	X231BNE	236	X236BNE	242	X242ATD
218	X218BNE	226	X226BNE	232	X232BNE	237	X237BNE	243	X243ATD
219	X219BNE	227	X227BNE	233	X233BNE	238	X238BNE	244	X244ATD
221	X221BNE	228	X228BNE	234	X234BNE	239	X239BNE	246	X246ATD

Stagecoach in Manchester has the largest fleet of MAN buses within the group, and all have Alexander ALX300 bodywork. Seen in the bus station at Wythenshawe is 166, T166MVM. Stagecoach have joined with Manchester International Airport in proving transport for staff and passengers aimed at reducing car traffic at the airport. As a result several vehicles carry additional lettering. *Mark Doggett*

Minibus operations in Stockport are based at the Charles Street depot. Seen at the stop in Wythenshawe Hospital while heading back to the town is 416, N416WVR. *Mark Doggett*

351-368

						Dennis Dart		Plaxton Pointer		B37D	1997

351	R701YWC	355	R705YWC	359	R709YWC	363	R713YWC	366	R716YWC
352	R702YWC	356	R706YWC	360	R710YWC	364	R714YWC	367	R717YWC
353	R703YWC	357	R707YWC	361	R711YWC	365	R715YWC	368	R718YWC
354	R704YWC	358	R708YWC	362	R712YWC				

401-429

Mercedes-Benz 811D   Alexander Sprint   B31F   1995-96

401	N401WVR	407	N407WVR	413	N413WVR	419	N419WVR	425	N425WVR
402	N402WVR	408	N408WVR	414	N414WVR	420	N420WVR	426	N426WVR
403	N403WVR	409	N409WVR	415	N415WVR	421	N421WVR	427	N427WVR
404	N404WVR	410	N410WVR	416	N416WVR	422	N422WVR	428	N428WVR
405	N405WVR	411	N411WVR	417	N417WVR	423	N423WVR	429	N429WVR
406	N406WVR	412	N412WVR	418	N418WVR	424	N424WVR		

432	M634FJF	Mercedes-Benz 811D	Marshall	B13F	1997	Glossopdale, Dukinfield, 1999
433	N746YVR	Mercedes-Benz 711D	Marshall C19	B27F	1995	Glossopdale, Dukinfield, 1999
434	N748YVR	Mercedes-Benz 711D	Marshall C19	B27F	1995	Glossopdale, Dukinfield, 1999

516-527

Mercedes-Benz 709D   Alexander Sprint   B25F   1996

516	N660VSS	520	N664VSS	522	N879AVV	524	N881AVV	526	N883AVV
519	N663VSS	521	N665VSS	523	N880AVV	525	N882AVV	527	N884AVV

530-566

Mercedes-Benz Vario O814   Plaxton Beaver 2   B27F   1997

530	P530PNE	537	P537PNE	544	P544PNE	551	P551PNE	559	P559PNE
531	P531PNE	538	P538PNE	545	P545PNE	552	P552PNE	562	P562PNE
532	P532PNE	539	P539PNE	546	P546PNE	553	P553PNE	563	P563PNE
533	P533PNE	540	P540PNE	547	P547PNE	554	P554PNE	564	P564PNE
534	P534PNE	541	P541PNE	548	P548PNE	556	P556PNE	565	P565PNE
535	P535PNE	542	P542PNE	549	P549PNE	557	P557PNE	566	P566PNE
536	P536PNE	543	P543PNE	550	P550PNE	558	P558PNE		

It is a long way from operations in the heat and dust of Kenya to Manchester. Magically the sun was shining when Dennis Dragon 686, M686TDB was pictured in Parrs Wood in the blue and yellow *Magic Bus* livery. This operation competes with a low-floor Stagecoach service that uses a different pricing system. *Cliff Beeton*

567	R276CBU	Mercedes-Benz Vario O814	Plaxton Beaver 2	B31F	1998	Glossopdale, Dukinfield, 1999	
568	R277CBU	Mercedes-Benz Vario O814	Plaxton Beaver 2	B31F	1998	Glossopdale, Dukinfield, 1999	
569	R446YNF	Mercedes-Benz Vario O814	Plaxton Beaver 2	B31F	1997	Glossopdale, Dukinfield, 1999	
570	R447YNF	Mercedes-Benz Vario O814	Plaxton Beaver 2	B31F	1997	Glossopdale, Dukinfield, 1999	
571	R899AVM	Mercedes-Benz Vario O814	Plaxton Beaver 2	B27F	1997	Glossopdale, Dukinfield, 1999	
572	R898AVM	Mercedes-Benz Vario O814	Plaxton Beaver 2	B27F	1997	Glossopdale, Dukinfield, 1999	
573	R901AVM	Mercedes-Benz Vario O814	Plaxton Beaver 2	B27F	1997	Glossopdale, Dukinfield, 1999	

612-624

Dennis Trident		Alexander ALX400		N51/28F	1999		
612	T612MNF	615	V615DJA	618	V618DJA	621	V621DJA	623	V623DJA
613	T613MNF	616	V616DJA	619	V619DJA	622	V622DJA	624	V624DJA
614	V614DJA	617	V617DJA	620	V620DJA				

626-647

Dennis Trident		Alexander ALX400		N51/28F	2000		
626	W626RND	631	W631RND	635	W635RND	639	W639RND	644	W644RND
627	W627RND	632	W632RND	636	W636RND	641	W641RND	645	W645RND
628	W628RND	633	W633RND	637	W637RND	642	W642RND	646	W646RND
629	W629RND	634	W634RND	638	W638RND	643	W643RND	647	W647RND

651-673

Dennis Trident		Alexander ALX400		N51/29F	1999		
651	V151DFT	656	V156DFT	661	V161DFT	665	V165DFT	670	V170DFT
652	V152DFT	657	V157DFT	662	V162DFT	667	V167DFT	671	V171DFT
653	V153DFT	658	V158DFT	663	V163DFT	668	V168DFT	672	V172DFT
654	V154DFT	659	V159DFT	664	V164DFT	669	V169DFT	673	V166DFT
655	V155DFT	660	V160DFT						

680-699

Dennis Dragon DDA1820		Duple Metsec/AVA		B51/37F	1995-96	Stagecoach Kenya, 1998-99	
680	M680TDB	684	M684TDB	688	M688TDB	692	M692TDB	696	M696TDB
681	M681TDB	685	M685TDB	689	M689TDB	693	M693TDB	697	M379TJA
682	M682TDB	686	M686TDB	690	M690TDB	694	M694TDB	698	L392LNA
683	M683TDB	687	M687TDB	691	M691TDB	695	M695TDB	699	M699TDB

716-730
Volvo Olympian • Alexander RL • B51/36F • 1996

716	P716GND	719	P719GND	722	P722GND	725	P725GND	728	P728GND
717	P717GND	720	P720GND	723	P723GND	726	P726GND	729	P729GND
718	P718GND	721	P721GND	724	P724GND	727	P727GND	730	P730GND

731-743
Volvo Olympian • Alexander RL • B51/36F • 1997 • Oxford, 1998

731	R501UWL	734	R504UWL	737	R507UWL	740	R510UWL	742	R512UWL
732	R502UWL	735	R505UWL	738	R508UWL	741	R511UWL	743	R513UWL
733	R503UWL	736	R506UWL	739	R509UWL				

744-782
Volvo Olympian • Alexander RL • B51/36F • 1998

744	R744DRJ	753	R753DRJ	761	R761DRJ	768	S768SVU	775	S775RVU
745	R745DRJ	754	R754DRJ	762	R762DRJ	769	S769RVU	776	S776RVU
746	R746DRJ	755	R755DRJ	763	R763DRJ	770	S770RVU	778	S778RVU
747	R747DRJ	756	R756DRJ	764	S764SVU	771	S771RVU	779	S779RVU
748	R748DRJ	757	R757DRJ	765	R765DRJ	772	S772RVU	780	S780RVU
749	R749DRJ	758	R758DRJ	766	S766SVU	773	S773RVU	781	S781RVU
751	R751DRJ	759	R759DRJ	767	S767SVU	774	S774RVU	782	S782RVU
752	R752DRJ	760	R760DRJ						

833	R653HCD	Volvo B10M-55	Plaxton Paladin	B48F	1998	Stagecoach East Kent, 2000
834	R674HCD	Volvo B10M-55	Plaxton Paladin	B48F	1998	Stagecoach East Kent, 2000
835	R677HCD	Volvo B10M-55	Plaxton Paladin	B48F	1998	Stagecoach East Kent, 2000

845-868
Volvo B10M-55 • Alexander PS • B49F • 1996

845	P845GND	850	P850GND	855	P855GND	860	P860GND	865	P865GND
846	P846GND	851	P851GND	856	P856GND	861	P861GND	866	P866GND
847	P847GND	852	P852GND	857	P857GND	862	P862GND	867	P867GND
848	P848GND	853	P853GND	858	P858GND	863	P863GND	868	P868GND
849	P849GND	854	P854GND	859	P859GND	864	P864GND		

875-894
Volvo B10M-55 • Northern Counties Paladin • B48F • 1997

875	P875MNE	877	P877MNE	879	P879MNE	881	P881MNE	893	P893MNE
876	P876MNE	878	P878MNE	880	P880MNE	882	P882MNE	894	P894MNE

895-984
Volvo B10M-55 • Alexander PS • B49F • 1997-98

895	R895XVM	915	R915XVM	933	R933XVM	951	R951XVM	968	R968XVM
896	R896XVM	916	R916XVM	934	R934XVM	952	R952XVM	969	R969XVM
897	R897XVM	917	R917XVM	935	R935XVM	953	R953XVM	970	R970XVM
898	R898XVM	918	R918XVM	936	R936XVM	954	R954XVM	971	R971XVM
899	R899XVM	919	R919XVM	937	R937XVM	955	R955XVM	972	R972XVM
901	R901XVM	920	R920XVM	938	R938XVM	956	R956XVM	973	R973XVM
902	R902XVM	921	R921XVM	939	R939XVM	957	R957XVM	974	R974XVM
903	R903XVM	922	R922XVM	940	R940XVM	958	R958XVM	975	R975XVM
904	R904XVM	923	R923XVM	941	R941XVM	959	R959XVM	976	R976XVM
905	R905XVM	924	R924XVM	942	R942XVM	960	R960XVM	977	R977XVM
906	R906XVM	925	R925XVM	943	R943XVM	961	R961XVM	978	R978XVM
907	R907XVM	926	R926XVM	944	R944XVM	962	R962XVM	979	R979XVM
908	R908XVM	927	R927XVM	945	R945XVM	963	R963XVM	980	R980XVM
909	R909XVM	928	R928XVM	946	R946XVM	964	R964XVM	981	R981XVM
910	R910XVM	929	R929XVM	947	R947XVM	965	R965XVM	982	R982XVM
912	R912XVM	930	R930XVM	948	R948XVM	966	R966XVM	983	R983XVM
913	R913XVM	931	R931XVM	949	R949XVM	967	R967XVM	984	R984XVM
914	R914XVM	932	R932XVM	950	R950XVM				

985-996
Volvo B10M-55 • Plaxton Paladin • B48F • 1998

985	R985XVM	988	R988XVM	991	R991XVM	993	R993XVM	995	R995XVM
986	R986XVM	989	R989XVM	992	R992XVM	994	R994XVM	996	R996XVM
987	R987XVM	990	R990XVM						

1463-1467
Scania N113DRB • Northern Counties Palatine • B47/28F • 1991 • GMS Buses, 1994

1463	H463GVM	1464	H464GVM	1465	H465GVM	1466	H466GVM	1467	H467GVM

Stagecoach Manchester are in the process of taking delivery of thirty low-height Dennis Tridents that will be employed on services for the Commonwealth Games which take place in summer 2002. Five are painted in special livery for the Queen's Golden Jubilee. The batch is allocated to Princess Road depot. Illustrated here is Alexander PS R978XVM, one of a large number brought into the fleet as many services were converted to single-deck. *Cliff Beeton*

1601-1630   Dennis Trident   Alexander ALX400   N51/28F   2002   Queen's Golden Jubilee livery

1601	ML02RWO	1607	ML02RWW	1613	ML02RWK	1619	MK02EFY	1625	ML02EGJ
1602	ML02RWU	1608	ML02RWX	1614	ML02RWN	1620	MK02EFZ	1626	ML02EGU
1603	ML02KCO	1609	ML02KCV	1615	MK02EFU	1621	MK02EGC	1627	ML02EGV
1604	ML02	1610	MK02EHC	1616	MK02EFV	1622	MK02EGD	1628	ML02EGX
1605	ML02RWV	1611	MK02EHD	1617	MK02EFW	1623	MK02EGE	1629	ML02EGY
1606	ML02KCU	1612	ML02RWJ	1618	MK02EFX	1624	MK02EGF	1630	ML02EGZ

2001-2030   Dennis Dominator DDA1003   Northern Counties   B43/32F   1985   GMS Buses, 1994

2001	B901TVR	2007	B907TVR	2013	B913TVR	2019	B919TVR	2025	B25TVU
2002	B902TVR	2008	B908TVR	2014	B914TVR	2020	B920TVR	2026	B26TVU
2003	B903TVR	2009	B909TVR	2015	B915TVR	2021	B21TVU	2027	B27TVU
2004	B904TVR	2010	B910TVR	2016	B916TVR	2022	B22TVU	2028	B28TVU
2005	B905TVR	2011	B911TVR	2017	B917TVR	2023	B23TVU	2029	B29TVU
2006	B906TVR	2012	B912TVR	2018	B918TVR	2024	B24TVU	2030	B30TVU

2031-2040   Dennis Dominator DDA2033   Northern Counties Palatine   B43/29F   1991   GMS Buses, 1994

2031	H131GVM	2033	H133GVM	2035	H135GVM	2037	H137GVM	2039	H139GVM
2032	H132GVM	2034	H134GVM	2036	H136GVM	2038	H138GVM	2040	H140GVM

3020-3025   Leyland Olympian ONLXCT/1R   Northern Counties   B43/30F   1983-84   GMS Buses, 1994

3020	A585HDB	3022	A22HNC	3023	A23HNC	3024	A24HNC	3025	A25HNC
3021	A21HNC								

3026-3035   Leyland Olympian ONLXB/1R   Northern Counties   B43/30F   1984   GMS Buses, 1994

3026	A26ORJ	3028	A28ORJ	3030	A30ORJ	3032	A32ORJ	3034	B34PJA
3027	A27ORJ	3029	A29ORJ	3031	A31ORJ	3033	A33ORJ	3035	B35PJA

The Northern Counties-bodied Olympian is the most numerous double-deck vehicle operating for Stagecoach in Manchester. Representing the type is 3080, B80PJA which was heading for the large terminus at Southern Cemetery when caught by the camera. *Richard Godfrey*

3036-3236

Leyland Olympian ONLXB/1R   Northern Counties   B43/30F*   1984-86 3198/214 are BC43/26F

GMS Buses, 1994

3036	B36PJA	3084	B84SJA	3133	B133WNB	3167	C167YBA	3197	C197YBA
3039	B39PJA	3086	B86SJA	3135	B135WNB	3169	C169YBA	3198	C198YBA
3049	B49PJA	3087	B87SJA	3137	B137WNB	3170	C170YBA	3199	C199YBA
3053	B53PJA	3088	B88SJA	3138	B138WNB	3172	C172YBA	3205	C205CBU
3055	B55PJA	3089	B89SJA	3143	B143WNB	3173	C173YBA	3207	C207CBU
3056	B56PJA	3091	B91SJA	3145	B145WNB	3174	C174YBA	3208	C208CBU
3057	B57PJA	3094	B94SJA	3146	B146XNA	3175	C175YBA	3210	C210CBU
3058	B58PJA	3095	B95SJA	3147	B147XNA	3176	C176YBA	3212	C212CBU
3060	B60PJA	3110	B110SJA	3149	B149XNA	3178	C178YBA	3214	C214CBU
3065	B65PJA	3114	B114SJA	3150	B150XNA	3179	C179YBA	3215	C215CBU
3067	B67PJA	3118	B118TVU	3153	B153XNA	3181	C181YBA	3216	C216CBU
3069	B69PJA	3119	B119TVU	3154	B154XNA	3184	C184YBA	3221	C221CBU
3070	B70PJA	3121	B121TVU	3155	B155XNA	3185	C185YBA	3224	C224CBU
3072	B72PJA	3122	B122TVU	3156	C156YBA	3191	C191YBA	3226	C226ENE
3074	B74PJA	3124	B124TVU	3158	C158YBA	3193	C193YBA	3230	C230ENE
3077	B77PJA	3125	B125TVU	3164	C164YBA	3195	C195YBA	3234	C234ENE
3080	B80PJA	3126	B126WNB	3165	C165YBA	3196	C196YBA	3236	C236EVU
3082	B82PJA	3132	B132WNB	3166	C166YBA				

3255-3277

Leyland Olympian ONLXB/1R   Northern Counties   BC43/26F   1986-87   GMS Buses, 1994

3255	C255FRJ	3268	D268JVR	3269	D269JVR	3272	D272JVR	3277	D277JVR
3260	D260JVR								

3282-3304

Leyland Olympian ONLXB/1RZ   Northern Counties   B43/30F*   1988-89   GMS Buses, 1994

*3291 is BC43/25F

3282	F282DRJ	3289	F289DRJ	3294	F294DRJ	3298	F298DRJ	3301	F301DRJ
3283	F283DRJ	3291	F291DRJ	3295	F295DRJ	3300	F300DRJ	3304	F304DRJ
3285	F285DRJ								

An exchange of vehicles has brought the two Megadekkers from Barrow to Manchester. Seen in Withington, 3401, F201FHH was returning north into the city centre. *Richard Godfrey*

3401	F201FHH	Leyland Olympian ONLXCT/3RZ	Alexander RL	BC55/41F	1989	Stagecoach North West, 2001
3402	F202FHH	Leyland Olympian ONLXCT/3RZ	Alexander RL	BC55/41F	1989	Stagecoach North West, 2001
3613	C613LFT	Leyland Olympian ONLXB/1R	Alexander RH	B45/31F	1985	Stagecoach Busways, 2000
3631	C631LFT	Leyland Olympian ONLXB/1R	Alexander RH	B45/31F	1985	Stagecoach Busways, 2000

Ancillary Vehicles

TV1	SND451X	Leyland Atlantean AN68A/1R	Northern Counties	TV	1982	GMS Buses, 1994
TV3	SND455X	Leyland Atlantean AN68A/1R	Northern Counties	TV	1982	GMS Buses, 1994
TV4	SND472X	Leyland Atlantean AN68A/1R	Northern Counties	TV	1982	GMS Buses, 1994
TV10	D431SNC	Dodge Commando G13	Wadham Stringer Vanguard	TV	1986	MoD, 2000 (80KF93)
TV12	E293PDC	Dodge Commando G13	Wadham Stringer Vanguard	TV	1987	MoD, 1998 (93KF69)
TV13	D240SNC	Dodge Commando G13	Wadham Stringer Vanguard	TV	1987	MoD, 1998 (92KF94)
TV14	D41SNE	Dodge Commando G13	Wadham Stringer Vanguard	TV	1987	MoD, 1998 (80KF70)
TV15	D56SNE	Dodge Commando G13	Wadham Stringer Vanguard	TV	1986	MoD, 1998 (80KF54)
TV16	E968CVM	Dodge Commando G13	Wadham Stringer Vanguard	TV	1987	MoD, 1998 (93KF41)
TV17	D474SNC	Dodge Commando G13	Wadham Stringer Vanguard	TV	1986	MoD, 2000 (80KF32)
TV18	E260CVR	Dodge Commando G13	Wadham Stringer Vanguard	TV	1986	MoD, 2000 (93KF86)
TV19	E269CVR	Dodge Commando G13	Wadham Stringer Vanguard	TV	1986	MoD, 2000 (80KF76)
TV20	D475SNC	Dodge Commando G13	Wadham Stringer Vanguard	TV	1986	MoD, 2000 (80KF26)
TV21	F409KOD	Mercedes-Benz 709D	Reeve Burgess Beaver	TV	1989	Stagecoach Devon, 2001

Previous Registrations:

M680TDB	KAG933E (Kenya)		M690TDB	KAG522X (Kenya)
M681TDB	KAH560B (Kenya)		M691TDB	KAG405W (Kenya)
M682TDB	KAG931E (Kenya)		M692TDB	KAG025X (Kenya
M683TDB	KAG544H (Kenya)		M693TDB	KAG601M (Kenya)
M684TDB	KAG542J (Kenya)		M694TDB	KAG470T (Kenya)
M685TDB	KAG770V (Kenya)		M695TDB	KAG544J (Kenya)
M686TDB	KAG060M (Kenya)		M696TDB	KAG264R (Kenya)
M687TDB	KAG292E (Kenya)		M379TJA	KAG602M (Kenya)
M688TDB	KAG543J (Kenya)		M699TDB	KAG472T (Kenya)
M689TDB	KAG471T (Kenya)		L392LNA	KAG932E (Kenya)

Note: Full details of vehicle allocations to depots and outstations are provided each year in the Stagecoach Bus Handbook Please see page 2 for more information.

STAINTONS

F W Stainton & Sons Ltd, Settlings Garage, 39 Burton Road, Kendal LA9 7LJ

RJI2162	Volvo B10M-61	Plaxton Paramount 3200	C57F	1985	Brooks, Kendal, 1996
LIB3769	Volvo B10M-61	Van Hool Alizée H	C49FT	1988	
A5FWS	Volvo B10M-60	Van Hool Alizée	C49FT	1990	
CAZ6835	Setra S215HD	Setra Tornado	C49FT	1992	Bebb, Llantwit Fardre, 1994
LIB3768	Volvo B10M-60	Van Hool Alizée HE	C48FT	1993	Chambers, Bures, 1996
CAZ2051	Setra S215HD	Setra Tornado	C49FT	1995	
SIB2633	Volvo B10M-62	Plaxton Excalibur	C49F	1995	Dodsworth, Broughbridge, 2001
R2SOH	Setra S250	Setra Special	C48FT	1998	
T3FWS	Setra S315 HD	Setra	C48FT	1999	
W4FWS	Setra S315 HD	Setra	C48FT	2000	
Y373UOM	Setra S315 HD	Setra	C48FT	2001	
Y374UOM	Setra S315 HD	Setra	C48FT	2001	
Y149HWE	Neoplan Euroliner N316	Neoplan Euroliner	C53F	2001	

Previous registrations:

		LIB3768	K815HUM	
		LIB3769	E327OMG	
A5FWS	G789URY	RJI2162	B634OEC	
CAZ2051	From new	SIB2633	M739YNW	
CAZ6835	J74VTG			

One wonders just how large the winning margin was as Staintons driver awaits the return of the punters at Epsom race course. A5FWS is a Volvo B10M with Van Hool Alizée bodywork that also carries Olympic Holidays titles. *Dave Heath*

TIMELINE

Timeline Travel, 31 Moor Lane, Bolton, BL1 4TA

901	R207JSF	Iveco EuroRider 391.12.35	Beulas Stergo E	C49FT	1998	Barry Raybould, Walsall, 1999
902	W902JBA	Volvo B7R	Plaxton Prima	C53F	1999	
903	W903JBA	Volvo B7R	Plaxton Prima	C53F	1999	
909	R909CAU	Volvo B10M-62	Plaxton Première 350	C53F	1997	Bus Eireann, 2001
914	P914JBC	Volvo B10M-62	Plaxton Première 350	C53F	1997	Bus Eireann, 2001
959	J259NNC	Volvo B10M-60	Plaxton Première 350	C49FT	1992	Shearings, 1999
962	L562FND	Scania K113CRB	Van Hool Alizée H	C46FT	1994	Shearings, 2000
963	L563FND	Scania K113CRB	Van Hool Alizée H	C46FT	1994	Shearings, 2000
964	L564FND	Scania K113CRB	Van Hool Alizée H	C46FT	1994	Shearings, 2000
965	L565FND	Scania K113CRB	Van Hool Alizée H	C46FT	1994	Shearings, 2000
966	J266NNC	Volvo B10M-60	Plaxton Première 350	C49FT	1992	Shearings, 1999
974	H174DVM	Volvo B10M-60	Van Hool Alizée H	C49FT	1991	Shearings, 1995

Previous Registrations:

P914JBC	97-D-7828	R909CAU	97-D-45840

Web: www.timelinetravel.co.uk

Plaxton bodywork on the rear-engined B7R coach chassis is called the Prima, though this looks outwardly similar to the Première. However, here is a Première 350 that joined the fleet in 1999 from Shearings. Numbered 959, J259NNC was waiting time in Leigh when pictured. Timeline also contols Barry Raybould Travel of Walsall in the West Midlands. *Bob Downham*

TITTERINGTON HOLIDAYS

G S I P & C Titterington, The Garage, Blencow, Penrith, , CA11 0DG

	KUM537L	Leyland Leopard PSU3B/4R	Plaxton Panorama Elite III	C49F	1973	Yeowarts, Whitehaven, 1980
w	TAO154R	Leyland Leopard PSU3C/4R	Plaxton Supreme III	C53F	1976	Holmeswood Coaches, Rufford, 1987
	368SHX	Leyland Leopard PSU3E/4R	Plaxton Supreme IV Express	C53F	1979	Brainwood High School, 1996
	188TAE	Volvo B58-61	Plaxton Supreme IV	C57F	1979	Clayton, Pudsey, 1996
	XAP956	Leyland Leopard PSU3E/4R	Plaxton Supreme IV Express	C53F	1979	West Sussex CC, 1997
	890TTE	Leyland Leopard PSU3F/4R	Plaxton Supreme IV	C49F	1981	Johnson, Hodthorpe, 1987
	AAX589A	Leyland Tiger TRCTL11/2RH	Duple Laser	C53F	1984	Stagecoach Bluebird, 2000
	212VPF	Leyland Tiger TRCTL11/3R	Duple Laser 2	C51F	1984	
	OZ4688	Volvo B10M-61	Plaxton Paramount 3500 III	C53F	1986	Clarkes of London, 1992
	CUI925	Volvo B10M-61	Plaxton Paramount 3500 III	C49FT	1986	National Travel East, 1987
	XOU692	Volvo B10M-60	Jonckheere Deauville P599	C51FT	1990	Tellings-Golden Miller, Byfleet, 1993
	L266JPY	Volvo B10M-62	Plaxton Première 320	C49F	1994	Atkinson, Ingleby Ancliffe, 2000
	M949RHH	Volvo B10M-62	Van Hool Alizée H	C49FT	1995	
	M950RHH	Volvo B10M-62	Van Hool Alizée H	C49FT	1995	
	M439ECS	Volvo B10M-62	Jonckheere Deauville 45	C53F	1995	Park's of Hamilton, 1997
	TYT653	Volvo B10M-62	Plaxton Première 350	C50F	1995	Wallace Arnold Coaches, 1997
	N214HWX	Volvo B10M-62	Plaxton Première 350	C48FT	1996	Wallace Arnold Coaches, 1998
	N354TTH	Volkswagen Transporter	Volkswagen	M7	1996	?, 1999
	T789JAO	Iveco EuroRider 391.12.35	Beulas Stergo E	C49FT	1999	
	Y962WAO	MAN 18.350 HOCL - R	Neoplan Transliner	C53F	2001	

Previous registrations:

188TAE	AFB233V	M439ECS	LSK555, KSK978
212VPF	B342GRM	OZ4688	C178LWB
368SHX	AWJ292T	TAO154R	LOT779R, XAP956
890TTE	PNW342W	TYT653	M131UWY
AAX589A	A216VWO	XAP956	BN629V
CUI925	C450CWR	XOU692	G647ONH

The latest arrival in the Titterington Holidays fleet is a MAN 18.350 with Neoplan Transliner bodywork. During the last decade there has been a steady increase in the number MAN-based coaches and further sales for bus duties are expected shortly. *Bob Downham*

THE TRAVELLERS' CHOICE

J Shaw & Son Ltd, The Coach & Travel Centre, Scotland Rd, Carnforth, LA5 9RQ

KBZ5749	Volvo B10M-61	Duple Dominant IV	C57F	1984	Brown's, Ambleside, 1994
BYP985	Neoplan N122/3	Neoplan Skyliner	C57/20CT	1986	Swallow, Rainham, 1998
XJF386	Volvo B10M-61	Plaxton Paramount 3500 III	C51FT	1988	Wallace Arnold, 1992
5129UA	Volvo B10M-61	Plaxton Paramount 3500 III	C49FT	1988	Wallace Arnold, 1992
E775WEC	Mercedes-Benz L307D	Mercedes-Benz	M15	1988	Barrow Travel, 1991
NIL9932	Mercedes-Benz 609D	Whitaker Europa	C24F	1988	
NIL9581	Mercedes-Benz 609D	Reeve Burgess Beaver	B25F	1988	Go-Ahead (OK), 1997
NIL7914	Mercedes-Benz 609D	Reeve Burgess Beaver	B25F	1988	Go-Ahead (OK), 1997
OET309	Volvo B9M	Caetano Algarve	C34FT	1988	Keir, Kenmay, 2000
F258DAG	Volkswagen LT35	Kirkham	M12L	1988	Bullock, Cheadle, 1998
YFG333	Volvo B10M-60	Duple 320	C57F	1989	Baker, Biddulph, 1995
F580OHJ	Ford Transit VE6	Ford	M12	1989	MC Travel, Melksham, 2000
G607JUG	Ford Transit VE6	Dormobile	B12FL	1990	Wakefield MBC, 1998
H251ANE	Ford Transit VE6	Deansgate	M14	1990	
824HAO	Volvo B10M-60	Van Hool Alizée H	C57F	1993	
6137RU	Volvo B10M-60	Plaxton Première 350	C49FT	1993	Go Whittle, Kidderminster, 1995
6SVK	Volvo B10M-60	Jonckheere Deauville 45	C49FT	1993	Stagecoach Oxford, 1998
XDO32	Volvo B10M-60	Jonckheere Deauville 45	C49FT	1993	Stagecoach Oxford, 1998
6682WY	Volvo B10M-60	Jonckheere Deauville 45	C49FT	1993	Stagecoach Oxford, 1998
L682GNA	Mercedes-Benz 709D	Plaxton Beaver	B27F	1994	Dennis's, Dukinfield, 2002

Since its transformtion from Shaw-Hadwin, The Travellers' Choice is now one of the largest operators in the north Lancashire area with several vehicles allocated to touring contracts. While these carry special liveries, fleet colours can be seen on Mercedes-Benz Vario X59YEC. This mini coach carries a Cymric conversion. *Bob Downham*

New to Go-Whittle as K36OUY, 6137RU is a Volvo B10M with Plaxton Première 350 bodywork. It is seen
undertaking rail replacement service on the Barrow to Preston line in February 2002. *Bob Downham*

3770RU	Volvo B10M-62	Plaxton Première 320	C51FT	1994	
7606UR	Volvo B10M-62	Plaxton Première 320	C57F	1994	
UWR294	Volvo B6M	Jockneer Ascot	C34F	1994	Chambers, Momeymore, 1999
2954XI	Volvo B10M-62	Plaxton Première 350	C49FT	1995	
OW5371	Volvo B10M-62	Plaxton Première 350	C51FT	1995	
7962IL	Volvo B10M-62	Plaxton Première 350	C49FT	1995	
LSU939	Volvo B12T	Van Hool Astrobel	C53/14CT	1995	Bakers, Weston-super-Mare, 2001
9201FH	Volvo B10M-62	Plaxton Première 350	C49FT	1996	
4150RU	Volvo B10M-62	Plaxton Première 350	C49FT	1996	
WX7622	Volvo B10M-62	Plaxton Première 350	C53F	1996	
WX9548	Volvo B10M-62	Plaxton Première 350	C49FT	1996	
N398CNB	Ford Transit VE6	Deansgate	M14	1996	
6267UA	Volvo B10M-62	Plaxton Première 350	C53F	1996	Redwing, Camberwell, 1999
UD1100	Volvo B10M-62	Plaxton Première 350	C53F	1996	Redwing, Camberwell, 1999
R791NEC	Volvo B10M-62	Jonckheere Mistral 50	C51FT	1998	
R171SUT	Volvo B10M-62	Jonckheere Mistral 50	C51FT	1998	
R954RCH	Volvo B10M-62	Jonckheere Mistral 50	C51FT	1998	Yorkshire European, 2001
R419EOS	Volvo B10M-62	Van Hool Alizée	C49FT	1998	Trathens, Plymouth, 2001
R512BUA	Mercedes-Benz Sprint 312D	Mercedes-Benz	M16	1998	
S989EEC	Volkswagen	Volkswagen	M8	1999	
T61LEC	Volvo B10M-62	Jonckheere Mistral 50	C51FT	1999	
T62LEC	Volvo B10M-62	Jonckheere Mistral 50	C51FT	1999	
T63LEC	Volvo B10M-62	Jonckheere Mistral 50	C51FT	1999	
T64LEC	Volvo B10M-62	Jonckheere Mistral 50	C51FT	1999	
W148EEC	Volvo B10M-62	Jonckheere Mistral 50	C51FT	2000	
W149EEC	Volvo B10M-62	Jonckheere Mistral 50	C51FT	2000	
W151EEC	Volvo B10M-62	Jonckheere Mistral 50	C51FT	2000	
W152EEC	Volvo B10M-62	Jonckheere Mistral 50	C51FT	2000	
X59YEC	Mercedes-Benz Vario O814	Cymric	C24F	2001	
Y2EEC	Volvo B10M-62	Jonckheere Mistral 50	C51FT	2001	
Y3EEC	Volvo B10M-62	Jonckheere Mistral 50	C51FT	2001	
Y693HEC	Volvo B12MT	Jonckheere Mistral 70	C49FT	2001	
Y724HEC	Volvo B12MT	Jonckheere Mistral 70	C49FT	2001	

Carrying the colours of Interski, The Travellers' Choice T63LEC is seen in the Italian region of Valle d'Aosta. One of four Jonckheere Mistral 50s added to the fleet in 1999 it features a continental door. *Adrian Norris*

Y984XEC	Mercedes-Benz Vario O814	Cymric	C24F	2001	
PO51BXT	Renault Master	Rohill Harrier	M16L	2002	Operated for Lancashire CC
PN02SVJ	Volvo B10M-62	Caetano Enigma	C49FT	2002	
PN02SVK	Volvo B10M-62	Caetano Enigma	C49FT	2002	
PN02SVL	Volvo B10M-62	Caetano Enigma	C49FT	2002	
PN02TJV	Volvo B12M	Sunsundegui Sideral	C49FT	2002	

Special event vehicles

FAP9	Bedford OB	Duple Vista	C29F	1949	Hursts of Wigan, 1995
LTF346	Bedford OB	Duple Vista	C29F	1950	Topp Line, Liverpool, 1995

Previous registrations:

6SVK	L210GJO	NIL7914	F266KTN
824HAO	K615EEO	NIL9581	F265KTN
2954XI	M338EEC	NIL9932	F485CKU
3770RU	M208SCK	OET309	WIA20
4150RU	N610REC	OW5371	M339EEC
5129UA	E902UNW, RIB5093	UD1100	N282OYE
6137RU	K36OUY		
6267UA	N281OYE	WX7622	N781PEC
6682WY	L213GJO		
7606UR	M209SCK	XJF386	E901UNW, RIB5092
7962IL	N160GRN	Y2EEC	Y874XEO
9201FH	N48MDW	Y3EEC	Y875XEO
BYP985	C174KET	XDO32	L211GJO
KBZ5749	A287FEC	YFG333	F477WFX, 9530RU, F515WFA, 4150RU
LSU939	N751CYA		

Livery: Trafalgar - R171SUT, R791NEC, T61LEC, T62LEC, T63LEC, T64LEC, W148EEC, W149EEC, W151EEC, Y2EE Y693HEC, Y724HEC, PN02SVJ, PN02SVK, PN02TJV.

TYRER BUS

Tyrer Tours Ltd, 2 Whiteholme Mill, Skipton Road, Trawden, Colne, BB8 8RA

GIL2409	Volvo B10M-61	Plaxton Paramount 3500	C53F	1983	Senior, Witney, 1998
VIA197	Leyland Tiger TRCTL11/3RZ	Van Hool Alizée H	C57F	1985	Shearings, 1991
F365BUA	Mercedes-Benz 811D	Optare StarRider	B32F	1988	Buzz, Harlow, 1997
G170FJC	Mercedes-Benz 709D	Reeve Burgess	BC25F	1989	Arriva Cymru, 2000
G176FJC	Mercedes-Benz 709D	Reeve Burgess	BC25F	1989	Arriva Cymru, 2000
G236FJC	Mercedes-Benz 709D	Robin Hood	B25F	1989	Arriva Cymru, 2001
H543EVM	Mercedes-Benz 709D	Made-to-Measure	B28F	1990	Metcalfe, Nelson, 1999
H521VWA	Mercedes-Benz 811D	Whitaker Europa	B31F	1990	Coakley Bus, Motherwell, 1999
MAZ7092	DAF MB230LT615	Van Hool Alizée H	C49FT	1991	Gath, Dewsbury, 2000
J214KTT	Mercedes-Benz 709D	Reeve Burgess Beaver	B25F	1991	Plymouth Citybus, 1999
J216KTT	Mercedes-Benz 709D	Reeve Burgess Beaver	B25F	1991	Plymouth Citybus, 1999
J224KTT	Mercedes-Benz 709D	Reeve Burgess Beaver	B25F	1991	Plymouth Citybus, 1999
J946JJR	Optare MetroRider MR03	Optare	B26F	1991	Go-Ahead Northern, 2001
7529UK	DAF MB230LT615	Van Hool Alizée H	C51FT	1992	TLC Coaches, Irlam, 2000
1606UK	DAF SB3000DKVF601	Van Hool Alizée H	C51FT	1992	Barnard, Kirton-in-Lindsey, 1998
K157BRF	Mercedes-Benz 709D	Dormobile Routemaker	B29F	1993	Arriva Cymru, 2001
N257DUR	Mercedes-Benz 709D	Plaxton Beaver	B27F	1996	First PMT, 2000
P2TYR	Volvo B10M-62	Plaxton Première 350	C49FT	1997	
P405MDT	Mercedes-Benz Vario 814D	Plaxton Beaver 2	BC32F	1997	Lakeland, Hurst Green, 2000
YJ51EKO	DAF DE02GSSB220	Ikarus Citibus	N44F	2001	
YJ51EKP	DAF DE02GSSB220	Ikarus Citibus	N44F	2001	

Previous Registrations

1606UK	K517RJX		GIL2409	A772HKA, FDJ75
			MAZ7092	J100SGT
7529UK	J833KHD		VIA197	B476UNB

Tyrer Bus operate in the Pendle area from a base in Colne. Seen in Burnley bus station, G236FJC is one of four Mercedes-Benz 709D purchased from Arriva Cymru, though the only one with Robin Hood bodywork. The vehicle has returned from Nelson at the time. *David Longbottom*

UK NORTH

UK North Enterprises Ltd, Gorton Lane, Gorton, Manchester M18 8DA

164	T164AUA	DAF DE02GSSB220	Ikarus Citibus	B43F	1999	Ludlows, Halesowen, 2000
176	W176CDN	DAF DE02GSSB220	Ikarus Citibus	N44F	2000	
177	W177CDN	DAF DE02GSSB220	Ikarus Citibus	N44F	2000	
178	W178CDN	DAF DE02GSSB220	Ikarus Citibus	N44F	2000	
220	E220WBG	Leyland Olympian ONCL10/1RZ	Alexander RL	B45/30F	1988	Arriva North West, 2001
230	E230WBG	Leyland Olympian ONCL10/1RZ	Alexander RL	B45/30F	1988	Arriva North West, 2001
247	F247YTJ	Leyland Olympian ONCL10/1RZ	Alexander RL	B45/30F	1988	Arriva North West, 2001
249	E249YTJ	Leyland Olympian ONCL10/1RZ	Alexander RL	B45/30F	1988	Arriva North West, 2001
317	P317KTW	DAF DE02RSDB250	Northern Counties Palatine II	B47/30F	1996	East Thames Buses, 2001
396	R396XDA	DAF DE02GSSB220	Plaxton Prestige	N42F	1997	Arriva Bus & Coach, 1999
397	R397XDA	DAF DE02GSSB220	Plaxton Prestige	N42F	1997	Arriva Bus & Coach, 1999
440	F440AKB	Leyland Olympian ONCL10/2RZ	Northern Counties	B51/34F	1988	Arriva North Western, 2001
605	M605RCP	DAF SB220LT550	Ikarus Citibus	B49F	1995	Simonds, Botesdale, 1999
630	M630RCP	DAF SB220LT550	Northern Counties Paladin	B49F	1995	Fuggles, Benenden, 1999
651	V651LWT	DAF DE02RSDB250	Alexander ALX400	N45/23F	1999	
652	V652LWT	DAF DE02RSDB250	Alexander ALX400	N45/23F	1999	
654	V654LWT	DAF DE02RSDB250	Alexander ALX400	N45/23F	1999	
655	V655LWT	DAF DE02RSDB250	Alexander ALX400	N45/23F	1999	
763	M763RCP	DAF SB220LT550	Ikarus Citibus	B49F	1995	First Edinburgh, 1999
822	M822RCP	DAF SB220LT550	Northern Counties Paladin	B49F	1995	First Manchester, 2000
833	M833RCP	DAF SB220LT550	Ikarus Citibus	B49F	1995	First Edinburgh, 1999
845	M845RCP	DAF SB220LT550	Northern Counties Paladin	B49F	1995	Fuggles, Benenden, 1999
902	P902PWW	DAF SB220LT550	Northern Counties Paladin	B49F	1996	Speedlink, 1999
909	P909PWW	DAF SB220LT550	Northern Counties Paladin	B49F	1996	Speedlink, 1999
L302	G302UYK	Leyland Olympian ONCL10/1RZ	Leyland	B47/31F	1989	London United, 2001
L305	G305UYK	Leyland Olympian ON2R50C13Z4	Leyland	B47/31F	1989	London United, 2001
L309	G309UYK	Leyland Olympian ON2R50C13Z4	Leyland	B47/31F	1989	London United, 2001
L310	G310UYK	Leyland Olympian ON2R50C13Z4	Leyland	B47/31F	1989	London United, 2001
T663	NUW663Y	Leyland Titan TNLXB2RR	Leyland	B44/27F	1982	Stagecoach South East, 2001
T784	OHV784Y	Leyland Titan TNLXB2RR	Leyland	B44/27F	1982	Stagecoach South East, 2001
T823	A823SUL	Leyland Titan TNLXB2RR	Leyland	B44/26F	1983	Stagecoach South East, 2001

Four Alexander-bodied DAF double-decks were delivered to UK North in 1999, providing the operator with modern buses that meet the requirements of the Greater Manchester tendering authority. Seen operating route 43, 654, V654LWT was pausing in Manchester's Piccadilly when pictured. *Richard Godfrey*

VALE of MANCHESTER

Vales Coaches (Manchester) Ltd, 49 Broughton Street, Manchester M8 8AN

w	F623YCW	Iveco Daily 49.10	Northern Counties	BC22F	1989	
	G820KWF	Mercedes-Benz 811D	Reeve Burgess Beaver	B31F	1989	Stagecoach East Midlands, 2001 .
	G826KWF	Mercedes-Benz 811D	Reeve Burgess Beaver	B31F	1989	Stagecoach East Midlands, 2001
	G97MRN	Mercedes-Benz 811D	Reeve Burgess Beaver	B31F	1990	Stagecoach Ribble, 2001
	H522FSB	Mercedes-Benz 709D	Reeve Burgess Beaver	B23F	1990	Timeline, Leigh, 1997
	H564OOK	Mercedes-Benz 709D	Carlyle	B27F	1991	Timeline, Leigh, 1997
	K881UDB	Mercedes-Benz 709D	Plaxton Beaver	B27F	1993	Derwent, Swalwell, 1997
	K883UDB	Mercedes-Benz 709D	Plaxton Beaver	B27F	1993	G M North, 1997
	L644DNA	Mercedes-Benz 709D	Plaxton Beaver	B27F	1993	Cooper, Dukinfield, 1996
	L645DNA	Mercedes-Benz 709D	Plaxton Beaver	B27F	1993	Cooper, Dukinfield, 1996
	N416CBU	Mercedes-Benz 709D	Plaxton Beaver	B27F	1996	
	N417CBU	Mercedes-Benz 709D	Plaxton Beaver	B27F	1996	
	P418HNF	Mercedes-Benz 709D	Alexander Sprint	B23F	1996	
	P419HNF	Mercedes-Benz 709D	Alexander Sprint	B23F	1996	
	P298PVR	Mercedes-Benz 709D	Plaxton Beaver	B27F	1997	City Nippy, Middleton, 2000
	P299PVR	Mercedes-Benz 709D	Plaxton Beaver	B27F	1997	City Nippy, Middleton, 2000
	S737RNE	Mercedes-Benz Vario O814	Plaxton Beaver 2	B27F	1998	
	S738RNE	Mercedes-Benz Vario O814	Plaxton Beaver 2	B27F	1998	
	S739RNE	Mercedes-Benz Vario O814	Plaxton Beaver 2	B27F	1998	
	T291ROF	Mercedes-Benz Vario O814	Plaxton Beaver 2	B31F	1999	Jim Stones, Leigh, 2000

Previous Registrations

P298PVR	P1JPT		P299PVR	P2JPT

Bury interchange is the location for this view of N416CBU, one of the Plaxton Beaver-bodied minibuses operated by Vale of Manchester. Following the withdrawal of the last Iveco, the fleet now entirely comprises Mercedes-Benz stock. *Mark Doggett*

WALTON'S

Walton's Coach Hire, 111 Bush Lane, Freckleton, Preston, PR1 1UN

AVK175W	Leyland Atlantean AN68A/2R	Alexander AL	B49/37F	1980	Go-Ahead Northern, 2000
LFJ854W	Bristol VRT/SL3/6LXB	Eastern Coach Works	B43/31F	1980	Redline, Penwortham, 1999
LFJ868W	Bristol VRT/SL3/6LXB	Eastern Coach Works	B43/31F	1980	Redline, Penwortham, 2000
VUA471X	Bristol VRT/SL3/6LXB	Eastern Coach Works	B43/31F	1980	Happy Als, Birkenhead, 1999
LFR872X	Leyland National 2 NL106AL11/1R		B44F	1981	Stagecoach North West, 2000
B168WRN	Leyland Tiger TRCTL11/3RH	Duple Laser 2	C53F	1985	Grange, Canning Town, 1990
NXI1610	Neoplan N122/3	Neoplan Skyliner	C57/20CT	1987	Trathens, Plymouth, 1997
TIB4568	Bova FHD12.290	Bova Futura	C34FT	1989	Jumbo Ambulance Project, 1996
MIL8741	DAF SB2305DHS585	Jonckheere Jubilee	C52FT	1990	Alec Head, Lutton, 2001
G729XLO	Mercedes-Benz 609D	Reeve Burgess Beaver	BC19F	1991	Reline, Penwortham, 1996
J323HVV	EOS E180Z	EOS 90	C53FT	1992	Boorman, Henlow, 1998
K530EHE	Scania K93CRB	Plaxton Paramount 3200 III	C51FT	1993	Swanbrook, Cheltenham, 1995
W381WGE	Mercedes-Benz Vario O814	Plaxton Cheetah	C33F	2000	Redline, Penwortham, 2001
MW51PJW	Ayats	Ayats Alpha	C57FT	2001	

Previous registrations:

J323HVV	J323HVV, 173HKH	TIB4568	F940MBB
MIL8741	G184UAV, A8EAD	W381WGE	W381WGE, 14RED
NXI1610	E111KFA		

Depot: Naze Lane Industrial Estate, Freckleton, Preston

As well as undertaking coaching activities, employing the first Ayats Alpha in the UK, Walton's operate a number of double-decks on school contract work in the area. Seen here are Alexander-bodied Atlantean AVK175V and Bristol VR VUA471X. *Bob Downham*

WRIGHT BROS

Wright Brothers (Coaches) Ltd, Central Garage Nenthead, Alston, Cumbria, CA9 3NP

UGE807W	Volvo B10M-61	Plaxton Supreme IV	C57F	1981	McPhail, Newarthill, 1992
LTG271X	Volvo B58-56	Plaxton Supreme IV	C53F	1981	Capitol, Cwmbran, 1994
SAO466X	Bedford YNT	Plaxton Supreme V Express	C53F	1982	
SAO467X	Bedford YMP	Plaxton Supreme V Express	C45F	1982	
MJI6406	Volvo B10M-56	Plaxton Viewmaster IV	C51F	1982	Thandi S, Rowley Regis, 1998
A431ESO	Volvo B10M-56	Plaxton Paramount 3200	C53F	1983	Dereham, East Dereham, 1998
KIW8608	Volvo B10M-61	Plaxton Paramount 3200	C53F	1985	Price, Shareshill, 1999
C363SVV	Volvo B10M-53	Jonckheere Jubilee P90	C52/6FT	1986	Team Travel, Horsforth, 1992
D478VSA	Volvo B10M-56	Plaxton Paramount 3200	C53F	1986	Owen, Yateley, 2000
NIL9247	Volvo B10M-61	Plaxton Paramount 3200	C53F	1988	Hearn, Harrow Weald, 2001
SJI8113	Scania K112CRB	Jonckheere Jubilee P599	C12FT	1988	Buddens, Romsey , 1996
TSV807	Scania K113TRB	Van Hool Astrobel	C--/16DT	1990	Busways, 1994
H917PTG	Volvo B10M-60	Ikarus Blue Danube 358	C53FT	1991	Thames Transit, 1995
J499MOD	Volvo B10M-60	Ikarus Blue Danube 358	C49FT	1991	Thames Transit, 1997
K400CAP	Volvo B10M-60	Plaxton Première 320	C53F	1993	Airlinks, 2002
V3WBC	Mercedes-Benz Vario O814	Autobus Nouvelle 2	C31F	1999	

Special event vehicle:

FUN319	Crossley SD42/7	Burlingham	C33F	1949	Patterson, Beadnell, 1959
RRM915M	Bedford YRQ	Plaxton Panorama Elite III Exp	C45F	1974	

Previous registrations:

C363SVV	C363SVV, UDX921	MJI6406	KNP5X
D478VSA	D478VSA, ONY837	NIL9247	E361NEG
J499MOD	J499MOD, CIW290	SJI8113	E517KNV
KIW8608	B61RNX	TSV807	G31WTY,813VPU, G852NUP

Named after the famous river that flows through Hungary, where the Ikarus factory is located, two Blue Danube coaches reside in the fleet of Wright Bros, a long-established operator in the Penrith area. Here J499MOD is seen waiting time in Keswick prior to working the return leg on service 888 which links the town with Penrith, Newcastle, Alston and Hexham. *J C Walton*

YELLOW BUZZ

Dreamline Travel Ltd, 9 Stancliffe Industrial Estate, Blackburn, BB2 2QR

HFH202	Neoplan N116/3	Neoplan Cityliner	C50F	1996	Ebdon, Sidcup, 1998
CTT826T	Mercedes-Benz L307D	Devon Conversions	C12F	1987	Woodstock, Chadderton, 1996
LDA430W	Ford R1114	Plaxton Supreme IV	C28FT	1980	non-pcv, Mount Sorrell, 1994
E48UKL	Mercedes-Benz 609D	Reeve Burgess Beaver	B20F	1987	Arriva Scotland West, 2000
E60UKL	Mercedes-Benz 609D	Reeve Burgess Beaver	B20F	1987	Arriva Scotland West, 2000
F68GTU	Mercedes-Benz 609D	North West CS	B24F	1989	Ribble Valley, Padiham, 2000
WJI7688	DAF SB3000DKV601	Van Hool Alizée	C49FT	1989	Henshaw, Nottingham, 2001
M29HNY	Volvo B12T	Jonckheere Monaco	C(47)FT	1994	Hats Coaches, Chippenham, 2000
1598PH	MAN 18.370 HOCL - R	Caetano Algarve II	C49FT	1995	Smith, Bedford, 2001

Previous registration

1598PH	M843LFP	LDA430W	PLA74W, TOY285W, PNT501, GOH1N
HFH202	L955MWB,	WJI7688	F891PNA, DUI672, F591UVW, 1245FM, F98RAR

Yellow Buzz is the new operating name for Blackburn operator Dreamline Travel. Illustrating the new order is E48UKL which was new to Maidstone & District. *Bob Downham*

The Lancashire, Cumbria and Manchester Bus Handbook

Vehicle index

Reg	Operator	Reg	Operator	Reg	Operator	Reg	Operator
5AAX	Homeswood	A4HWD	Homeswood	A708DAU	Blackpool	B37PJA	First
6SVK	Travellers' Choice	A5FWS	Staintons	A709DAU	Blackpool	B38PJA	First
10RU	Finglands	A15TVL	Sim's Travel	A710DAU	Blackpool	B39PJA	Stagecoach Manchester
152ENM	Homeswood	A16TVL	Sim's Travel	A719YFS	Blackburn	B40PJA	First
184XNO	Homeswood	A19HWD	Homeswood	A720YFS	Blackburn	B41PJA	First
188TAE	Titterington	A20HWD	Homeswood	A721YFS	Blackburn	B42PJA	First
201SC	Homeswood	A20JDA	Archway	A745DRM	Robinson's	B43MAO	Stagecoach NW
212VPF	Titterington	A21HNC	Stagecoach Manchester	A823SUL	UK North	B43PJA	First
219DLV	Sim's Travel	A22HNC	Stagecoach Manchester	A855SUL	Stagecoach NW	B44PJA	First
289BUA	Mayne	A23HNC	Stagecoach Manchester	A914RRN	Homeswood	B45NDX	Northern Blue
296HFM	Homeswood	A24HNC	Stagecoach Manchester	A975OST	Burnley & Pendle	B45PJA	First
368SHX	Titterington	A25HNC	Stagecoach Manchester	AAX300A	Homeswood	B47PJA	First
403BGO	Mayne	A26JBV	Blackburn	AAX589A	Titterington	B49PJA	Stagecoach Manchester
464HYB	Homeswood	A26ORJ	Stagecoach Manchester	ABV939Y	Fishwick	B53PJA	Stagecoach Manchester
466YMG	Homeswood	A27ORJ	Stagecoach Manchester	ACH942A	Grayway	B54PJA	First
515VTB	Hulme Hall	A28JBV	Blackburn	AFB597V	South Lancs Travel	B55PJA	Stagecoach Manchester
629LFM	Homeswood	A28ORJ	Stagecoach Manchester	AFM5W	Blackburn	B56PJA	Stagecoach Manchester
647JOE	Finglands	A29JBV	Blackburn	AHG331V	Blackpool	B57PJA	Stagecoach Manchester
716GRM	Homeswood	A29ORJ	Stagecoach Manchester	AHG332V	Blackpool	B58PJA	Stagecoach Manchester
817GTA	Battersby	A30ORJ	Stagecoach Manchester	AHG333V	Blackpool	B60PJA	Stagecoach Manchester
824HAO	Travellers' Choice	A31ORJ	Stagecoach Manchester	AHG334V	Blackpool	B61PJA	First
848AFM	Homeswood	A32ORJ	Stagecoach Manchester	AHG336V	Blackpool	B62PJA	First
890TTE	Titterington	A33MRN	Preston Bus	AHG337V	Blackpool	B64PJA	First
906GAU	Mayne	A33ORJ	Stagecoach Manchester	AHG338V	Blackpool	B65PJA	Stagecoach Manchester
990ENR	Robinson's	A70KDU	Brownriggs	AHG339V	Blackpool	B66PJA	First
1359UP	Battersby	A101DPB	Mayne	AHG340V	Blackpool	B67PJA	Stagecoach Manchester
1598PH	Yellow Buzz	A102DAO	Stagecoach NW	ALZ6244	Homeswood	B68PJA	First
1606UK	Tyrer Bus	A132FDC	Pilkington	ANA151Y	First	B69PJA	Stagecoach Manchester
2954XI	Travellers' Choice	A138MRN	Stagecoach NW	ANA172Y	First	B70PJA	Stagecoach Manchester
3267HX	Battersby	A142MRN	Lancashire United	ANA181Y	First	B71PJA	First
3353RU	Homeswood	A143MRN	Lancashire United	ANA183Y	First	B72PJA	Stagecoach Manchester
3402FM	Frazer Eagle	A145OFR	Lancashire United	ANA187Y	First	B74PJA	Stagecoach Manchester
3770RU	Travellers' Choice	A156OFR	Lancashire United	ANA538Y	M R Travel	B76PJA	First
3937TR	Robinson's	A157OFR	Lancashire United	ASV237	Homeswood	B77PJA	Stagecoach Manchester
4148VZ	Battersby	A158OFR	Burnley & Pendle	AUP380W	Northern Blue	B78PJA	First
4150RU	Travellers' Choice	A159OFR	Lancashire United	AVK138V	Northern Blue	B80PJA	Stagecoach Manchester
4360WF	Battersby	A227MDD	Brownriggs	AVK150V	Northern Blue	B81PJA	First
4761TR	Robinson's	A247GAO	Stagecoach NW	AVK158V	Northern Blue	B82PJA	Stagecoach Manchester
5096WF	Battersby	A280ROW	R Bullock	AVK175W	Walton's	B83PJA	First
5108VX	Battersby	A355HHG	Blackpool	AYR324T	Blackburn	B84SJA	Stagecoach Manchester
5129UA	Travellers' Choice	A356HHG	Blackpool	B1BUS	Jim Stones	B86SJA	Stagecoach Manchester
5287FM	Frazer Eagle	A357HHG	Blackpool	B1JYM	Jim Stones	B87SJA	Stagecoach Manchester
5692FM	Frazer Eagle	A358HHG	Blackpool	B10JYM	Jim Stones	B88SJA	Stagecoach Manchester
5096VW	Homeswood	A359HHG	Blackpool	B10MHC	Alfa	B89SJA	Stagecoach Manchester
5137RU	Travellers' Choice	A360HHG	Blackpool	B10MNC	Alfa	B90PJA	First
5267UA	Travellers' Choice	A361HHG	Blackpool	B11JYM	Jim Stones	B91SJA	Stagecoach Manchester
5682WY	Travellers' Choice	A362HHG	Blackpool	B14JYM	Jim Stones	B91WUV	Stagecoach NW
017UN	Battersby	A431ESO	Wright Brothers	B16TYG	Jim Stones	B92PJA	First
7121RU	Battersby	A462LFV	Fishwick	B21TVU	Stagecoach Manchester	B93PJA	First
7144FN	Battersby	A499MHG	Jim Stones	B22TVU	Stagecoach Manchester	B94SJA	Stagecoach Manchester
7345FM	Frazer Eagle	A545HAC	Stagecoach NW	B23TVU	Stagecoach Manchester	B95SJA	Stagecoach Manchester
7501FM	Frazer Eagle	A581HDB	Lancashire United	B24TVU	Stagecoach Manchester	B96PJA	First
529UK	Tyrer Bus	A582HDB	Lancashire United	B25TVU	Stagecoach Manchester	B98SJA	First
506UR	Travellers' Choice	A583HDB	Lancashire United	B26TVU	Stagecoach Manchester	B100WUV	Stagecoach NW
522UK	Battersby	A584HDB	Burnley & Pendle	B27TVU	Stagecoach Manchester	B101SJA	First
845UG	Battersby	A585HDB	Stagecoach Manchester	B28TVU	Stagecoach Manchester	B103SJA	First
062IL	Travellers' Choice	A671HNB	Finglands	B29TVU	Stagecoach Manchester	B104SJA	First
074FM	Frazer Eagle	A679HNB	Northern Blue	B30TVU	Stagecoach Manchester	B105SJA	First
350WU	Battersby	A703YFS	Blackburn	B34PJA	Stagecoach Manchester	B106SJA	First
201FH	Travellers' Choice	A704YFS	Blackburn	B35PJA	Stagecoach Manchester	B107SJA	First
484TR	Robinson's	A707DAU	Blackpool	B36PJA	Stagecoach Manchester	B107UAT	Northern Blue

Reg	Operator	Reg	Operator	Reg	Operator	Reg	Operator
B108SJA	First	B893UAS	Stagecoach NW	C122PNV	Homeswood	C213CBU	Stagecoach NW
B109SJA	First	B895UAS	Stagecoach NW	C124CAT	Northern Blue	C214CBU	Stagecoach Manchester
B110SJA	Stagecoach Manchester	B896UAS	Stagecoach NW	C125CAT	Northern Blue	C215CBU	Stagecoach Manchester
B110WUV	Stagecoach NW	B899UAS	Stagecoach NW	C129CAT	Northern Blue	C216CBU	Stagecoach Manchester
B111SJA	First	B900WRN	Stagecoach NW	C156YBA	Stagecoach Manchester	C217CBU	First
B112SJA	First	B901TVR	Stagecoach Manchester	C158YBA	Stagecoach Manchester	C218CBU	First
B113SJA	First	B902TVR	Stagecoach Manchester	C159YBA	First	C219CBU	First
B114SJA	Stagecoach Manchester	B903TVR	Stagecoach Manchester	C160YBA	First	C220CBU	First
B116TVU	First	B904TVR	Stagecoach Manchester	C161YBA	First	C221CBU	Stagecoach Manchester
B117TVU	Stagecoach NW	B905TVR	Stagecoach Manchester	C163YBA	First	C221HJN	Buzy Buz
B118TVU	Stagecoach Manchester	B906TVR	Stagecoach Manchester	C164YBA	Stagecoach Manchester	C223CBU	First
B119TVU	Stagecoach Manchester	B907TVR	Stagecoach Manchester	C165YBA	Stagecoach Manchester	C224CBU	Stagecoach Manchester
B120TVU	First	B908TVR	Stagecoach Manchester	C166YBA	Stagecoach Manchester	C225CBU	First
B121TVU	Stagecoach Manchester	B909BGA	Kirkby Lonsdale	C167YBA	Stagecoach Manchester	C226ENE	Stagecoach Manchester
B122TVU	Stagecoach Manchester	B909TVR	Stagecoach Manchester	C168YBA	First	C227ENE	First
B123TVU	First	B910TVR	Stagecoach Manchester	C169YBA	Stagecoach Manchester	C229ENE	First
B124TVU	Stagecoach Manchester	B911TVR	Stagecoach Manchester	C170ECK	Stagecoach NW	C230ENE	Stagecoach Manchester
B125TVU	Stagecoach Manchester	B912TVR	Stagecoach Manchester	C170YBA	Stagecoach Manchester	C231ENE	First
B126WNB	Stagecoach Manchester	B913TVR	Stagecoach Manchester	C171YBA	First	C232ENE	First
B127TVU	First	B914TVR	Stagecoach Manchester	C172YBA	Stagecoach Manchester	C233ENE	First
B128WNB	First	B915TVR	Stagecoach Manchester	C173ECK	Lancashire United	C234ENE	Stagecoach Manchester
B129WNB	First	B916TVR	Stagecoach Manchester	C173YBA	Stagecoach Manchester	C235ENE	First
B130WNB	First	B917TVR	Stagecoach Manchester	C174ECK	Stagecoach NW	C236EVU	Stagecoach Manchester
B131WNB	First	B918TVR	Stagecoach Manchester	C174YBA	Stagecoach Manchester	C237EVU	First
B132WNB	Stagecoach Manchester	B919TVR	Stagecoach Manchester	C175ECK	Stagecoach NW	C238EVU	First
B133WNB	Stagecoach Manchester	B920TVR	Stagecoach Manchester	C175YBA	Stagecoach Manchester	C239EVU	First
B134WNB	First	B931YCW	Darwen Coach	C176ECK	Stagecoach NW	C240EVU	First
B135WNB	Stagecoach Manchester	BCA126W	Homeswood	C176YBA	Stagecoach Manchester	C241EVU	First
B136WNB	First	BCB340	Blackburn	C177ECK	Stagecoach NW	C243EVU	First
B137WNB	Stagecoach Manchester	BFV861R	Blackburn	C177YBA	First	C244EVU	First
B138WNB	Stagecoach Manchester	BHF291A	Homeswood	C178ECK	Lancashire United	C245EVU	First
B140WNB	First	BTB928	Blackpool	C178YBA	Stagecoach Manchester	C246FRJ	First
B141WNB	First	BUI1133	R Bullock	C179ECK	Stagecoach NW	C247FRJ	First
B142WNB	First	BUI1424	R Bullock	C179YBA	Stagecoach Manchester	C248FRJ	First
B143WNB	Stagecoach Manchester	BUI1484	R Bullock	C181YBA	Stagecoach Manchester	C249FRJ	First
B144WNB	First	BUI1610	R Bullock	C183YBA	First	C250FRJ	First
B145WNB	Stagecoach Manchester	BUI1675	R Bullock	C184YBA	Stagecoach Manchester	C251FRJ	First
B146XNA	Stagecoach Manchester	BUS1N	Jim Stones	C185YBA	Stagecoach Manchester	C252FRJ	First
B147XNA	Stagecoach Manchester	BUS1S	Jim Stones	C186YBA	First	C253FRJ	First
B148XNA	First	BUS1T	Jim Stones	C187YBA	First	C254FRJ	First
B149XNA	Stagecoach Manchester	BUS51T	Jim Stones	C188YBA	First	C255FRJ	Stagecoach Manchester
B150XNA	Stagecoach Manchester	BVP807V	Blackburn	C189YBA	First	C281BBP	R Bullock
B151WRN	Stagecoach NW	BVR100T	Mayne	C190YBA	First	C285BBP	R Bullock
B152TRN	Lancashire United	BYP985	Travellers' Choice	C191YBA	Stagecoach Manchester	C363SVV	Wright Brothers
B152XNA	First	BYW361V	Blackburn	C192YBA	First	C382SAO	Stagecoach NW
B153NKB	Grayway	BYW379V	R Bullock	C193YBA	Stagecoach Manchester	C383SAO	Stagecoach NW
B153WRN	Stagecoach NW	BYX205V	Archway	C195YBA	Stagecoach Manchester	C410VVN	M & M Coaches
B153XNA	Stagecoach Manchester	BYX280V	Archway	C196YBA	Stagecoach Manchester	C419VVN	Buzy Buz
B154XNA	Stagecoach Manchester	BYX295V	Archway	C197YBA	Stagecoach Manchester	C454GKE	Homeswood
B155XNA	Stagecoach Manchester	C34CHM	Rossendale	C198YBA	Stagecoach Manchester	C472CAP	Brownriggs
B168WRN	Walton's	C39CHM	Rossendale	C199YBA	Stagecoach Manchester	C481CBU	First
B351PJA	First	C40CHM	Rossendale	C200CBU	First	C482CBU	First
B363UBV	Blackpool	C84CHM	Rossendale	C201CBU	First	C483CBU	First
B364UBV	Blackpool	C85CHM	Rossendale	C202CBU	First	C613LFT	Stagecoach Manchester
B446WKE	Homeswood	C88CHM	Rossendale	C203CBU	First	C631LFT	Stagecoach Manchester
B571RWY	First	C89CHM	Rossendale	C203FVU	First	C659PCX	Cosgrove's
B572RWY	First	C90CHM	Rossendale	C204CBU	First	C752CWX	Archway
B694BPU	Homeswood	C93CHM	Rossendale	C205CBU	Stagecoach Manchester	C752OCN	JP Trave
B737GSC	Blackburn	C96CHM	Rossendale	C206CBU	First	C857EML	Ashalls
B738GSC	Blackburn	C110OHH	Brownriggs	C207CBU	Stagecoach Manchester	C858EML	Ashalls
B739GSC	Blackburn	C110UBC	Mayne	C208CBU	Stagecoach Manchester	C875CYX	Collinsor
B740GSC	Blackburn	C111UBC	Mayne	C208FVU	First	C888REG	Ashalls
B741GSC	Blackburn	C112CAT	Northern Blue	C209CBU	First	C959LWJ	R Bulloc
B829VJT	Homeswood	C112UBC	Mayne	C210CBU	Stagecoach Manchester	CAZ2051	Stainton
B874XWR	Homeswood	C113UBC	Mayne	C211CBU	First	CAZ6835	Stainton
B892UAS	Stagecoach NW	C120PNV	Homeswood	C212CBU	Stagecoach Manchester	CHA460K	Robinson'

Reg	Operator	Reg	Operator	Reg	Operator	Reg	Operator
CKC624X	Stagecoach NW	D312LNB	First	E101EVM	Darwen Coach	F57YCW	Collinson
CKC626X	Stagecoach NW	D313LNB	First	E101JFV	Burnley & Pendle	F68GTU	Yellow Buzz
CLZ8353	Homeswood	D314LNB	First	E102EVM	Darwen Coach	F73FKK	M & M Coaches
CSF160W	Blue Bus	D315LNB	First	E102JFV	Burnley & Pendle	F74DCW	Lancashire United
CTT826T	Darwen Coach	D316LNB	First	E103JNH	M & M Coaches	F74SMC	Archway
CTT826T	Yellow Buzz	D317LNB	First	E107DJR	Bluebird	F102GRM	First
CUB72Y	Stagecoach NW	D318LNB	First	E113FNU	Homeswood	F103XCW	Lancashire United
CUI925	Titterington	D319LNB	First	E113RBO	Lancashire United	F104XCW	Lancashire United
CUL179V	Stagecoach NW	D320LNB	First	E114SDW	Lancashire United	F105XCW	Lancashire United
CWR526Y	Burnley & Pendle	D324YNO	Blackburn	E115SDW	Burnley & Pendle	F106XCW	Lancashire United
CYJ492Y	Brownriggs	D331VVV	Archway	E131ORP	Stagecoach NW	F107XCW	Lancashire United
D25VCW	Fishwick	D337VBB	JP Travel	E132ORP	Stagecoach NW	F108XCW	Lancashire United
D27XFL	Ashalls	D367JJD	Blackburn	E133ORP	Stagecoach NW	F109XCW	Lancashire United
D30VCW	Fishwick	D375DCK	Stagecoach NW	E133VOK	JP Travel	F110XCW	Lancashire United
D32MWN	Pilkington	D380XRS	Stagecoach NW	E134ORP	Stagecoach NW	F111XCW	Lancashire United
D32YCW	Fishwick	D381XRS	Stagecoach NW	E135ORP	Stagecoach NW	F112HNC	Mayne
D33YCW	Fishwick	D384XAO	Stagecoach NW	E142ERA	Buzy Buz	F112XCW	Lancashire United
D41SNE	Stagecoach Manchester	D431SNC	Stagecoach Manchester	E177UWF	Darwen Coach	F113HNC	Mayne
D44UAO	M & M Coaches	D438TMB	Homeswood	E218WBG	JP Travel	F119JTO	Buzy Buz
D45UAO	M & M Coaches	D474SNC	Stagecoach Manchester	E220WBG	UK North	F128KTV	Homeswood
D56SNE	Stagecoach Manchester	D475SNC	Stagecoach Manchester	E222WBG	JP Travel	F130AEL	Sim's Travel
D103TTJ	M & M Coaches	D478VSA	Wright Brothers	E230WBG	UK North	F135SPX	Stagecoach NW
D109NDW	Burnley & Pendle	D497NYS	First	E249YTJ	UK North	F136SPX	Stagecoach NW
D116NUS	Buzy Buz	D501LNA	First	E260CVR	Stagecoach Manchester	F137SPX	Stagecoach NW
D118NUS	Buzy Buz	D504LNA	First	E269CVR	Stagecoach Manchester	F152HAT	First
D133FYM	Blackburn	D513XAO	Stagecoach NW	E293PDC	Stagecoach Manchester	F152XYG	First
D137NUS	Battersby	D528RCK	M & M Coaches	E328WYS	M & M Coaches	F153HAT	First
D141FYM	Blackburn	D672SHH	Darwen Coach	E331EVH	Cosgrove's	F154HAT	First
D144FYM	Blackburn	D682SEM	Darwen Coach	E357KPO	JP Travel	F155HAT	First
D145FYM	Blackburn	D683MHS	JP Travel	E373FKX	Grayway	F156HAT	First
D239NCS	Darwen Coach	D683SEM	Darwen Coach	E415EPE	M & M Coaches	F157HAT	First
D240SNC	Stagecoach Manchester	D685SEM	Darwen Coach	E423AFT	M & M Coaches	F167SMT	Lancashire United
D256JVR	First	D689SEM	Darwen Coach	E424AFT	M & M Coaches	F168SMT	Burnley & Pendle
D257JVR	First	D752DLO	First	E426AFT	Buzy Buz	F171SMT	Lancashire United
D258JVR	First	D765XFR	Cosgrove's	E430AFT	M & M Coaches	F187PFV	Aspden
D259JVR	First	D836KWT	Grayway	E470SON	First	F201FHH	Stagecoach Manchester
D260JVR	Stagecoach Manchester	DBV24W	Stagecoach NW	E473SON	Finglands	F202FHH	Stagecoach Manchester
D261FUL	Homeswood	DBV100W	Stagecoach NW	E474SON	Finglands	F210YHG	Preston Bus
D261JVR	First	DBV132Y	Burnley & Pendle	E476SON	Finglands	F211YHG	Preston Bus
D262JVR	First	DBV134Y	Stagecoach NW	E480UOF	Finglands	F212YHG	Preston Bus
D263JVR	First	DCZ2326	Northern Blue	E514HHN	Buzy Buz	F213YHG	Preston Bus
D264JVR	First	DK02GCU	Shearings	E602TBS	Darwen Coach	F220RSE	Battersby
D265JVR	First	DK02GDF	Shearings	E671FSH	Grayway	F231YTJ	R Bullock
D266JVR	First	DK02GJU	Shearings	E687UNE	M R Travel	F232YTJ	R Bullock
D267JVR	First	DK02GMV	Shearings	E694UNE	M R Travel	F233YTJ	R Bullock
D268JVR	Stagecoach Manchester	DK02GNY	Shearings	E702UEM	M & M Coaches	F235YTJ	R Bullock
D269JVR	Stagecoach Manchester	DPX685W	Hulme Hall	E755VJO	Brownriggs	F236YTJ	R Bullock
D270JVR	First	DRN173Y	Preston Bus	E758OWY	R Bullock	F237YTJ	R Bullock
D271JVR	First	DRN174Y	Preston Bus	E775WEC	Travellers' Choice	F238YTJ	R Bullock
D272JVR	Stagecoach Manchester	DRN175Y	Preston Bus	E928KYR	R Bullock	F239YTJ	R Bullock
D273JVR	First	DRN176Y	Preston Bus	E941CDS	Homeswood	F240YTJ	R Bullock
D274JVR	First	DRN177Y	Preston Bus	E968CVM	Stagecoach Manchester	F242MBA	Finglands
D275JVR	First	E46HFE	Brownriggs	ECB96W	Aspden	F245MVW	First
D276JVR	First	E47CHH	Stagecoach NW	EGB53T	Stagecoach NW	F245YTJ	JP Travel
D277JVR	Stagecoach Manchester	E48CHH	Stagecoach NW	EJR105W	Northern Blue	F246MVW	First
D301JVR	First	E48UKL	Yellow Buzz	EKA215V	Stagecoach NW	F247YTJ	UK North
D302JVR	First	E49CHH	Stagecoach NW	EKA220Y	Stagecoach NW	F254RHK	First
D303JVR	First	E50CHH	Stagecoach NW	ENJ917V	Collinson	F258DAG	Travellers' Choice
D304JVR	First	E57HFE	Brownriggs	ESK807	Homeswood	F258RHK	First
D305JVR	First	E60UKL	Yellow Buzz	ESU913	Brownriggs	F278DRJ	First
D306JVR	First	E60WDT	Lancashire United	ESU920	Brownriggs	F279DRJ	First
D307JVR	First	E61WDT	Lancashire United	ESU926	Lakeland	F279NHJ	First
308JVR	First	E63WDT	Burnley & Pendle	EUK978	Mayne	F280DRJ	First
309JVR	First	E87KGV	Lancashire United	EXI2455	Blackburn	F280NHJ	First
310JVR	First	E88HRN	Darwen Coach	EYE323V	Archway	F281DRJ	First
311LNB	First	E100MFV	Fishwick	F32AHG	Preston Bus	F281NHJ	First

F282DRJ	Stagecoach Manchester	F608GVO	Finglands	G60RND	First	G283OGE	First
F282NHJ	First	F608WBV	First	G61RND	South Lancs Travel	G284OGE	First
F283DRJ	Stagecoach Manchester	F609GVO	Finglands	G61SMC	South Lancs Travel	G286OGE	First
F283NHJ	First	F610GVO	Finglands	G62RND	First	G287OGE	First
F284DRJ	First	F611GVO	Finglands	G62SMC	South Lancs Travel	G291OGE	First
F284NHJ	First	F621OHD	Coastlinks	G63SMC	South Lancs Travel	G293OGE	First
F285DRJ	Stagecoach Manchester	F623YCW	Vale of Manchester	G64RND	First	G293TSL	Stagecoach NW
F285NHJ	First	F639HVU	JP Travel	G65RND	First	G294OGE	First
F286DRJ	First	F674XMS	JP Travel	G67RND	First	G294TSL	Stagecoach NW
F286NHJ	First	F678YOG	JP Travel	G69RND	First	G295TSL	Stagecoach NW
F287DRJ	First	F682SRN	R Bullock	G70RND	First	G296KWY	Lancashire United
F287NHJ	First	F701ENE	Blue Bus	G94ERP	Northern Blue	G296OGE	First
F288DRJ	First	F705JCN	First	G96ERP	Northern Blue	G296TSL	Stagecoach NW
F288NHJ	First	F722LRG	Pilkington	G97MRN	Vale of Manchester	G297KWY	Lancashire United
F289DRJ	Stagecoach Manchester	F767FDV	Brownriggs	G99NBD	Northern Blue	G297OGE	First
F289GNB	Grayway	F769FDV	Brownriggs	G101NBV	Blackpool	G297TSL	Stagecoach NW
F289NHJ	First	F770FDV	Brownriggs	G102NBV	Blackpool	G298KWY	Lancashire United
F290DRJ	First	F792LSU	First	G103NBV	Blackpool	G298OGE	First
F290NHJ	First	F793FOS	Grayway	G104NBV	Blackpool	G298TSL	Stagecoach NW
F291DRJ	Stagecoach Manchester	F793LSU	First	G105NBV	Blackpool	G299OGE	First
F291NHJ	First	F795LSU	First	G106NBV	Blackpool	G299TSL	Stagecoach NW
F292DRJ	First	F803FAO	Stagecoach NW	G107FJW	First	G300TSL	Stagecoach NW
F293DRJ	First	F804FAO	Stagecoach NW	G107NBV	Blackpool	G301OGE	First
F293NHJ	First	F805FAO	Stagecoach NW	G108NBV	Blackpool	G302OGE	First
F294DRJ	Stagecoach Manchester	F806FAO	Stagecoach NW	G109YRE	First	G302UYK	UK North
F294NHJ	First	F807FAO	Stagecoach NW	G115SBA	Mayne	G304UYT	Rossendale
F295DRJ	Stagecoach Manchester	F808FAO	Stagecoach NW	G116SBA	Mayne	G305UYK	UK North
F296DRJ	Stagecoach NW	F809FAO	Stagecoach NW	G117SBA	Mayne	G307UYT	Rossendale
F297DRJ	Stagecoach NW	F810FAO	Stagecoach NW	G121PGT	South Lancs Travel	G309UYK	UK North
F298DRJ	Stagecoach Manchester	F811FAO	Stagecoach NW	G129NRC	Homeswood	G310UYK	UK North
F299DRJ	First	F816OVU	Blue Bus	G155NRC	Northern Blue	G312UYT	Rossendale
F300DRJ	Stagecoach Manchester	F840HAP	Darwen Coach	G156NRC	Darwen Coach	G313UYT	Rossendale
F301DRJ	Stagecoach Manchester	F842EHH	Robinson's	G157NRC	Northern Blue	G314UYT	Rossendale
F301JNC	Finglands	F902JBB	Blue Bus	G164LWN	Coastlinks	G330XRE	Collinson
F302DRJ	First	F905YWY	Darwen Coach	G170FJC	Tyrer Bus	G376NRC	Homeswood
F302JNC	Finglands	F914XWY	South Lancs Travel	G176FJC	Tyrer Bus	G378NRC	Homeswood
F303DRJ	First	F915KCA	Homeswood	G176JYG	First	G384OGD	First
F304DRJ	Stagecoach Manchester	F915YWY	Darwen Coach	G177JYG	First	G385OGD	First
F305DRJ	First	F927YWY	Collinson	G178JYG	First	G386OGD	First
F332FWW	Pilkington	FAO427V	Stagecoach NW	G178PAO	Stagecoach NW	G387OGD	First
F338VSD	Rossendale	FAP9	Travellers' Choice	G180PAO	Stagecoach NW	G388OGD	First
F339VSD	Rossendale	FBV524S	Fishwick	G187JHG	Stagecoach NW	G389OGD	First
F341XFR	Aspden	FCK24Y	Blackburn	G188JHG	Stagecoach NW	G390OGD	First
F344ECK	Stagecoach NW	FCK25Y	Blackburn	G190PAO	Stagecoach NW	G392OGD	First
F362YTJ	First	FCK27Y	Blackburn	G192PAO	Stagecoach NW	G393OGD	First
F365BUA	Tyrer Bus	FDZ362	Lakeland	G214KRN	Preston Bus	G394OGD	First
F368AFR	Blackpool	FFR170S	Aspden	G215KRN	Preston Bus	G395OGD	First
F369AFR	Blackpool	FIL4988	Archway	G216KRN	Preston Bus	G396OGD	First
F370AFR	Blackpool	FN02VCP	Homeswood	G217KRN	Preston Bus	G397OGD	First
F371AFR	Blackpool	FN02VCT	Homeswood	G218KRN	Preston Bus	G398OGD	First
F372AFR	Blackpool	FUN319	Wright Brothers	G225HCP	Cosgrove's	G399OGD	First
F373AFR	Blackpool	FXI547	Grayway	G226HCP	Cosgrove's	G400OGD	First
F409KOD	Stagecoach Manchester	G24CSG	Buzy Buz	G236FJC	Tyrer Bus	G403OGD	First
F439AKB	R Bullock	G34OCK	Preston Bus	G25HDW	South Lancs Travel	G405OGD	First
F440AKB	UK North	G34TGW	JP Travel	G263TSL	Stagecoach NW	G406OGD	First
F452FDB	R Bullock	G35OCK	Preston Bus	G264TSL	Stagecoach NW	G407OGD	First
F514TPA	Pilkington	G35TGW	JP Travel	G265TSL	Stagecoach NW	G410OGD	First
F516TPA	Pilkington	G36OCK	Preston Bus	G266TSL	Stagecoach NW	G411OGD	First
F517TPA	Pilkington	G36TGW	JP Travel	G267TSL	Stagecoach NW	G412OGD	First
F523UVW	Homeswood	G37OCK	Preston Bus	G268TSL	Stagecoach NW	G414OGD	First
F580ONJ	Travellers' Choice	G37TGW	JP Travel	G269TSL	Stagecoach NW	G423SNF	R Bulloc
F601XWY	First	G51BEL	Buzy Buz	G275MWU	Bu-Val	G449LKW	Bu-Va
F602XWY	First	G57BEL	Buzy Buz	G276MWU	Bu-Val	G452FVX	Northern Blu
F603XWY	First	G58RND	First	G280OGE	First	G492XWS	South Lancs Trave
F604XWY	First	G59RND	South Lancs Travel	G281OGE	First	G520LWU	Stagecoach N
F605XWY	First	G60ATS	Mountain Goat	G282OGE	First		

Reg	Operator	Reg	Operator	Reg	Operator	Reg	Operator
G523RDS	First	GFR101W	Burnley & Pendle	H114SAO	Stagecoach NW	H196WFR	Stagecoach NW
G524RDS	First	GHG341W	Blackpool	H114YHG	Blackpool	H199ENC	Manchester Airport
G525RDS	First	GHG343W	Blackpool	H115ABV	Burnley & Pendle	H201ENC	Manchester Airport
G526RDS	First	GHG344W	Blackpool	H115MOB	Rossendale	H251ANE	Travellers' Choice
G530RDS	First	GHG345W	Blackpool	H115SAO	Stagecoach NW	H373OHK	First
G532RDS	First	GHG346W	Blackpool	H115YHG	Blackpool	H388MAR	First
G533RDS	First	GHG347W	Blackpool	H116MOB	Rossendale	H406BVR	Buzy Buzz
G566PRM	Stagecoach NW	GHG348W	Blackpool	H116SAO	Stagecoach NW	H407BVR	Kirkby Lonsdale
G567PRM	Stagecoach NW	GHG349W	Blackpool	H116YHG	Blackpool	H417FGS	Lancashire United
G570PRM	Stagecoach NW	GHG350W	Blackpool	H117MOB	Rossendale	H418FGS	Burnley & Pendle
G571PRM	Stagecoach NW	GIL2160	Mayne	H117SAO	Stagecoach NW	H461BEU	Grayway
G575PRM	Northern Blue	GIL2409	Tyrer Bus	H117YHG	Blackpool	H463GVM	Stagecoach Manchester
G607JUG	Travellers' Choice	GIL2781	Kirkby Lonsdale	H118CHG	Blackpool	H464GVM	Stagecoach Manchester
G613OTV	Finglands	GIL3112	Coastlinks	H118MOB	Rossendale	H465GVM	Stagecoach Manchester
G616OTV	Finglands	GND505N	Mayne	H118SAO	Stagecoach NW	H466GVM	Stagecoach Manchester
G617OTV	Finglands	GOG231W	Northern Blue	H119CHG	Blackpool	H467GVM	Stagecoach Manchester
G618OTV	Finglands	GRN895W	Fishwick	H119MOB	Rossendale	H521VWA	Tyrer Bus
G621CPS	South Lancs Travel	GSC636X	Collinson	H119SAO	Stagecoach NW	H522FSB	Vale of Manchester
G665PHH	Stagecoach NW	GSC637X	Collinson	H120CHG	Blackpool	H543EVM	Tyrer Bus
G687PNS	First	GSU386	Grayway	H120MOB	Rossendale	H564OOK	Vale of Manchester
G688PNS	First	GSU859T	Stagecoach NW	H122CHG	Blackpool	H583JDB	Grayway
G689PNS	First	GYE254W	Stagecoach NW	H127MOB	Rossendale	H584JDB	Grayway
G690PNS	First	GYE281W	Stagecoach NW	H128MOB	Rossendale	H611MOM	Rossendale
G691PNS	First	GYE382W	Archway	H129MOB	Rossendale	H617ACK	Stagecoach NW
G694PNS	First	GYE445W	Archway	H130MOB	Rossendale	H618ACK	Stagecoach NW
G695PNS	First	H1FBT	Blackpool	H131GVM	Stagecoach Manchester	H619ACK	Stagecoach NW
G696PNS	First	H1JYM	Jim Stones	H131MOB	Rossendale	H620MOM	Rossendale
G697PNS	First	H2FBT	Blackpool	H132GVM	Stagecoach Manchester	H621MOM	Rossendale
G698PNS	First	H2HWD	Homeswood	H133GVM	Stagecoach Manchester	H622ACK	Stagecoach NW
G699PNS	First	H3FBT	Blackpool	H134GVM	Stagecoach Manchester	H623ACK	Stagecoach NW
G701PNS	First	H23YBV	Preston Bus	H135GVM	Stagecoach Manchester	H650VVV	Lancashire United
G703AEF	Ashalls	H24YBV	Preston Bus	H136GVM	Stagecoach Manchester	H651VVV	Lancashire United
G727JJC	Rossendale	H26YBV	Preston Bus	H137GVM	Stagecoach Manchester	H678GPF	South Lancs Travel
G728JJC	Rossendale	H27YBV	Preston Bus	H138GVM	Stagecoach Manchester	H688YGO	Darwen Coach
G729XLO	Walton's	H28YBV	Preston Bus	H139GGS	Lancashire United	H691FNB	JP Travel
G801JRH	First	H29YBV	Preston Bus	H139GVM	Stagecoach Manchester	H701GVM	First
G802JRH	First	H64CCK	Fishwick	H139UUA	Northern Blue	H702GVM	First
G803JRH	First	H65CCK	Fishwick	H140GGS	Lancashire United	H703GVM	First
G804JRH	First	H79CFV	Lancashire United	H140GVM	Stagecoach Manchester	H704GVM	First
G805JRH	First	H85PTG	Kirkby Lonsdale	H140UUA	Northern Blue	H705GVM	First
G812BPG	Homeswood	H101BFR	Preston Bus	H141GGS	Lancashire United	H706GVM	First
G813RNC	Bluebird	H101EKR	South Lancs Travel	H142GGS	Lancashire United	H812AHS	Homeswood
G814BPG	Homeswood	H101VFV	Rossendale	H143GGS	Burnley & Pendle	H812WKH	First
G815BPG	Homeswood	H102BFR	Preston Bus	H144GGS	Lancashire United	H813WKH	First
G816BPG	Homeswood	H102MOB	Rossendale	H145GGS	Burnley & Pendle	H814WKH	First
G817BPG	Homeswood	H102VFV	Rossendale	H146GGS	Lancashire United	H815WKH	First
G820KWF	Vale of Manchester	H103BFR	Preston Bus	H147CBU	JP Travel	H816WKH	First
G826KWF	Vale of Manchester	H103VFV	Rossendale	H147GGS	Lancashire United	H840UUA	Northern Blue
G889TJA	JP Travel	H104BFR	Preston Bus	H149GGS	Lancashire United	H851GRE	First
G902WAY	Grayway	H104CHG	Rossendale	H151GGS	Lancashire United	H887UUA	Northern Blue
G911RPN	South Lancs Travel	H104MOB	Rossendale	H152GGS	Lancashire United	H917PTG	Wright Brothers
G911UPP	Coastlinks	H105CHG	Rossendale	H163DJU	Blue Bus	H918XUA	Bu-Val
G914RPN	South Lancs Travel	H108MOB	Rossendale	H174DVM	Timeline	H919SWF	Grayway
G915UPP	Rossendale	H109MOB	Rossendale	H177OSG	Rossendale	H929DRJ	Homeswood
G918DVX	R Bullock	H109YHG	Blackpool	H178OSG	Rossendale	HBV682	Aspden
G994VWV	Rossendale	H110MOB	Rossendale	H179OSG	Rossendale	HCS807N	Bluebird
G996VWV	Rossendale	H110YHG	Blackpool	H180OSG	Rossendale	HDZ5436	Buzy Buzz
GBU15V	First	H112MOB	Rossendale	H181OSG	Rossendale	HDZ5468	JP Travel
GBV152W	Preston Bus	H112SAO	Stagecoach NW	H182OSG	Rossendale	HDZ5490	Buzy Buzz
GBV156W	Preston Bus	H112YHG	Blackpool	H183OSG	Rossendale	HEK86G	Grayway
BZ8304	Coastlinks	H113ABV	Burnley & Pendle	H184OSG	Rossendale	HFH202	Yellow Buzz
CK428W	Fishwick	H113MOB	Rossendale	H185OSG	Rossendale	HHJ374Y	First
CK429W	Fishwick	H113SAO	Stagecoach NW	H186OSG	Rossendale	HIL5341	Blackpool
CK430W	Fishwick	H113YHG	Blackpool	H193WFR	Stagecoach NW	HIL5342	Blackpool
DZ3841	Mayne	H114ABV	Burnley & Pendle	H195WFR	Stagecoach NW	HIL5943	Blackpool
EY273	Aspden	H114MOB	Rossendale	H196JVT	M & M Coaches	HIL7745	Finglands

HIL7746	Finglands	J182WAX	Darwen Coach	J709ONF	First	K129DAO	Stagecoach NW
HIL9152	Blue Bus	J198HFR	Stagecoach NW	J710ONF	First	K129UFV	Blackpool
HOI7544	Homeswood	J199HFR	Stagecoach NW	J712BAO	Routledge	K130DAO	Stagecoach NW
HPF313N	Blackburn	J200BUL	R Bullock	J753MFP	Buzy Buz	K130UFV	Blackpool
HRN100N	Blackpool	J201HFR	Stagecoach NW	J754MFP	Buzy Buz	K131DAO	Stagecoach NW
HRN103N	Blackpool	J202HFR	Stagecoach NW	J796CNN	Homeswood	K132DAO	Stagecoach NW
HTU671X	Collinson	J203HFR	Stagecoach NW	J835JNP	Homeswood	K133DAO	Stagecoach NW
HWT64N	Collinson	J204HFR	Stagecoach NW	J867JNS	Grayway	K134DAO	Stagecoach NW
HXI311	Northern Blue	J205HFR	Stagecoach NW	J915OAY	Homeswood	K135DAO	Stagecoach NW
IAZ4775	Mayne	J206HFR	Stagecoach NW	J942MFT	Dennis's	K157BRF	Tyrer Bus
IAZ4776	Mayne	J207HFR	Stagecoach NW	J944MFT	Dennis's	K223MGT	Blackburn
IIL3476	Ashalls	J208HFR	Stagecoach NW	J946JJR	Tyrer Bus	K339ADB	Brownriggs
IIL4821	Pilkington	J209HFR	Stagecoach NW	J951MFT	Dennis's	K342PJR	M & M Coaches
IIL4822	Pilkington	J210HFR	Stagecoach NW	J952MFT	Dennis's	K366RTY	Dennis's
IIL5133	Homeswood	J214KTT	Tyrer Bus	J966JNL	Darwen Coach	K368RTY	Dennis's
J2HMT	Northern Blue	J216KTT	Tyrer Bus	J967CGK	Preston Bus	K369RTY	Dennis's
J5BUS	Jim Stones	J220XKY	Homeswood	J969CGK	Preston Bus	K374RTY	South Lancs Travel
J7JFS	Fishwick	J224KTT	Tyrer Bus	J976PRW	Preston Bus	K400CAP	Wright Brothers
J14JFS	Fishwick	J227JJR	M & M Coaches	JB51BUS	Jim Stones	K449YCW	Stagecoach NW
J24MCW	Stagecoach NW	J227OKX	Bluebird	JBV529	Aspden	K450YCW	Stagecoach NW
J25MCW	Stagecoach NW	J228OKX	Bu-Val	JDT432N	Blackburn	K454VVR	Northern Blue
J29LJA	Homeswood	J243LFR	Robinsons	JFR2W	Stagecoach NW	K455VVR	Northern Blue
J41GGB	Burnley & Pendle	J244LFR	Robinsons	JFR3W	Lancashire United	K480EUX	First
J42GGB	Burnley & Pendle	J245LFR	Robinsons	JFR5W	Burnley & Pendle	K481EUX	First
J101WSC	Lancashire United	J246LFR	Robinsons	JFR7W	Burnley & Pendle	K482EUX	First
J104WSC	Lancashire United	J247LFR	Robinsons	JFR8W	Burnley & Pendle	K483EUX	First
J105WSC	Lancashire United	J259NNC	Timeline	JFR10W	Burnley & Pendle	K484EUX	First
J107KCW	Preston Bus	J266NNC	Timeline	JFR11W	Burnley & Pendle	K485EUX	First
J108KCW	Preston Bus	J276NNC	Homeswood	JFR13W	Burnley & Pendle	K486EUX	First
J108WSC	Lancashire United	J293TFP	Homeswood	JHF824	Homeswood	K487BCY	Kirkby Lonsdale
J109KCW	Preston Bus	J323HVV	Walton's	JHF825	Homeswood	K487EUX	First
J109WSC	Lancashire United	J375GKH	JP Travel	JIL8204	R Bullock	K488EUX	First
J110KCW	Preston Bus	J376GKH	JP Travel	JIL8205	R Bullock	K489EUX	First
J112KCW	Preston Bus	J377GKH	JP Travel	JIL8209	R Bullock	K509RJX	M R Travel
J112WSC	Lancashire United	J378GKH	JP Travel	JJG907P	Blackburn	K512RJX	Alfa
J113KCW	Preston Bus	J418JBV	Blackburn	JPU817	Stagecoach NW	K513RJX	Alfa
J113WSC	Lancashire United	J419JBV	Blackburn	JSJ431W	Homeswood	K529EFL	Bu-Val
J114KCW	Preston Bus	J420JBV	Blackburn	JWG191P	Blackburn	K530EHE	Walton's
J114WSC	Lancashire United	J421JBV	Blackburn	K1BLU	Blue Bus	K563GSA	Stagecoach NW
J115WSC	Lancashire United	J422JBV	Blackburn	K2SLT	South Lancs Travel	K600BUL	R Bullock
J116WSC	Lancashire United	J455FSR	Homeswood	K3SLT	South Lancs Travel	K601LAE	First
J120AAO	Stagecoach NW	J461OVU	First	K4HWD	Homeswood	K602LAE	First
J120AHH	Stagecoach NW	J499MOD	Wright Brothers	K5HWD	Homeswood	K603LAE	First
J121AAO	Stagecoach NW	J567DFU	Grayway	K26WBV	Burnley & Pendle	K604LAE	First
J121AHH	Stagecoach NW	J584CUB	Rossendale	K27WBV	Burnley & Pendle	K605LAE	First
J122AAO	Stagecoach NW	J587CUB	Rossendale	K28XBA	Rossendale	K610UFR	Stagecoach NW
J123GRN	Blackpool	J588CUB	Rossendale	K29XBA	Rossendale	K611UFR	Stagecoach NW
J123XHH	Stagecoach NW	J589CUB	Rossendale	K75XCW	Northern Blue	K612UFR	Stagecoach NW
J124GRN	Blackpool	J606KCU	Dennis's	K84UND	JP Travel	K613UFR	Stagecoach NW
J124XHH	Stagecoach NW	J610KCU	Dennis's	K112XHG	Stagecoach NW	K614UFR	Stagecoach NW
J125GRN	Blackpool	J622KCU	Dennis's	K113XHG	Stagecoach NW	K615UFR	Stagecoach NW
J125XHH	Stagecoach NW	J623KCU	Dennis's	K114XHG	Stagecoach NW	K616UFR	Stagecoach NW
J126GRN	Blackpool	J627KCU	South Lancs Travel	K115XHG	Stagecoach NW	K618UFR	Stagecoach NW
J126XHH	Stagecoach NW	J628KCU	Dennis's	K116XHG	Stagecoach NW	K619UFR	Stagecoach NW
J127XHH	Stagecoach NW	J630KCU	Dennis's	K117XHG	Stagecoach NW	K620UFR	Stagecoach NW
J152YRM	First	J633KCU	Dennis's	K118XHG	Stagecoach NW	K622UFR	Stagecoach NW
J153YRM	First	J635KCU	South Lancs Travel	K120XHG	Stagecoach NW	K623UFR	Stagecoach NW
J154YRM	First	J638KCU	South Lancs Travel	K121XHG	Stagecoach NW	K624UFR	Stagecoach NW
J155YRM	First	J640KCU	Dennis's	K123AJA	JP Travel	K625UFR	Stagecoach NW
J156YRM	First	J694CGK	Blackburn	K124XHG	Stagecoach NW	K626UFR	Stagecoach NW
J157YRM	First	J701CGK	Blackburn	K125TCP	Manchester Airport	K699ERM	Stagecoach NW
J158YRM	First	J702CWT	Stagecoach NW	K126TCP	Manchester Airport	K700DAO	Stagecoach NW
J176WAX	Darwen Coach	J703CGK	Blackburn	K127TCP	Manchester Airport	K701DAO	Stagecoach N
J179WAX	Darwen Coach	J707ONF	First	K127UFV	Blackburn	K702DAO	Stagecoach N
J180WAX	Darwen Coach	J708CGK	Blackburn	K128DAO	Stagecoach NW	K703DAO	Stagecoach N
J181WAX	Darwen Coach	J708ONF	First	K128UFV	Blackpool	K704ERM	Stagecoach N

Reg	Operator	Reg	Operator	Reg	Operator	Reg	Operator
K705DAO	Stagecoach NW	K772DAO	Stagecoach NW	L1JFS	Fishwick	L449HTM	Burnley & Pendle
K706DAO	Stagecoach NW	K773DAO	Stagecoach NW	L4BLU	Bluebird	L491JFU	Homeswood
K707DAO	Stagecoach NW	K774DAO	Stagecoach NW	L5HWD	Homeswood	L501KSA	First
K708DAO	Stagecoach NW	K775DAO	Stagecoach NW	L6HWD	Homeswood	L502KSA	First
K709DAO	Stagecoach NW	K776DAO	Stagecoach NW	L8SLT	R Bullock	L503KSA	First
K710DAO	Stagecoach NW	K777DAO	Stagecoach NW	L10BUL	R Bullock	L504KSA	First
K711DAO	Stagecoach NW	K778DAO	Stagecoach NW	L18HWD	Homeswood	L505KSA	First
K712DAO	Stagecoach NW	K779DAO	Stagecoach NW	L20BUL	R Bullock	L506KSA	First
K713DAO	Stagecoach NW	K780DAO	Stagecoach NW	L26FNE	Rossendale	L506MAO	Brownriggs
K714DAO	Stagecoach NW	K781DAO	Stagecoach NW	L27FNE	Rossendale	L507KSA	First
K715DAO	Stagecoach NW	K783DAO	Stagecoach NW	L42DBC	R Bullock	L508KSA	First
K716DAO	Stagecoach NW	K784DAO	Stagecoach NW	L107SDY	Burnley & Pendle	L509KSA	First
K717DAO	Stagecoach NW	K785DAO	Stagecoach NW	L114DNA	Mayne	L510KSA	First
K718DAO	Stagecoach NW	K786DAO	Stagecoach NW	L119DRN	Stagecoach NW	L510MAO	Brownriggs
K719DAO	Stagecoach NW	K787DAO	Stagecoach NW	L122DRN	Stagecoach NW	L511KSA	First
K720DAO	Stagecoach NW	K788DAO	Stagecoach NW	L123DRN	Stagecoach NW	L512KSA	First
K721DAO	Stagecoach NW	K833HUM	Lakeland	L125DRN	Stagecoach NW	L513KSA	First
K722DAO	Stagecoach NW	K838HUM	Grayway	L125NAO	Stagecoach NW	L514KSA	First
K723DAO	Stagecoach NW	K857PCN	Dennis's	L126DRN	Stagecoach NW	L547KRE	Brownriggs
K724DAO	Stagecoach NW	K865PCN	Dennis's	L126NAO	Stagecoach NW	L562FND	Timeline
K725DAO	Stagecoach NW	K871GHH	Stagecoach NW	L127DRN	Stagecoach NW	L563FND	Timeline
K726DAO	Stagecoach NW	K872GHH	Stagecoach NW	L127NAO	Stagecoach NW	L564FND	Timeline
K727DAO	Stagecoach NW	K873GHH	Stagecoach NW	L128DRN	Stagecoach NW	L565FND	Timeline
K728DAO	Stagecoach NW	K874GHH	Stagecoach NW	L143BFV	Stagecoach NW	L629BFV	Stagecoach NW
K729DAO	Stagecoach NW	K875GHH	Stagecoach NW	L149BFV	Burnley & Pendle	L630BFV	Stagecoach NW
K730DAO	Stagecoach NW	K875ODY	Stagecoach NW	L152BFV	Stagecoach NW	L631BFV	Stagecoach NW
K731DAO	Stagecoach NW	K876GHH	Stagecoach NW	L154BFV	Stagecoach NW	L632BFV	Stagecoach NW
K732DAO	Stagecoach NW	K876ODY	Stagecoach NW	L157BFV	Lancashire United	L633BFV	Stagecoach NW
K733DAO	Stagecoach NW	K877GHH	Stagecoach NW	L160CCW	Stagecoach NW	L634BFV	Stagecoach NW
K734DAO	Stagecoach NW	K877ODY	Stagecoach NW	L161CCW	Stagecoach NW	L635BFV	Stagecoach NW
K735DAO	Stagecoach NW	K878GHH	Stagecoach NW	L179LHG	Northern Blue	L636BFV	Stagecoach NW
K736DAO	Stagecoach NW	K878ODY	Stagecoach NW	L188SDY	Stagecoach NW	L644DNA	Vale of Manchester
K737DAO	Stagecoach NW	K881UDB	Vale of Manchester	L190DDW	Northern Blue	L645DNA	Vale of Manchester
K738DAO	Stagecoach NW	K883UDB	Vale of Manchester	L191DDW	Northern Blue	L653MYG	South Lancs Travel
K739DAO	Stagecoach NW	K888BFG	First	L196DVM	JP Travel	L654MYG	Blue Bus
K740DAO	Lancashire United	K888BWU	First	L225LRM	Brownriggs	L657MYG	South Lancs Travel
K741DAO	Stagecoach NW	K888ELR	First	L237CCW	Stagecoach NW	L658MSF	Stagecoach NW
K742DAO	Stagecoach NW	K888LAD	First	L243SDY	Stagecoach NW	L659MYG	Burnley & Pendle
K743DAO	Stagecoach NW	K888PFD	First	L244SDY	Stagecoach NW	L662MSF	Stagecoach NW
K744DAO	Stagecoach NW	K888TKS	First	L245SDY	Stagecoach NW	L665MSF	Stagecoach NW
K745DAO	Stagecoach NW	K888TTT	First	L248JBV	Robinsons	L680GNA	Dennis's
K746DAO	Stagecoach NW	K888TWY	First	L249JBV	Robinsons	L681GNA	Dennis's
K748DAO	Stagecoach NW	K977JWW	Manchester Airport	L250JBV	Robinsons	L682GNA	Travellers' Choice
K749DAO	Stagecoach NW	K978JWW	Manchester Airport	L252CCK	Stagecoach NW	L683GNA	Dennis's
K750DAO	Stagecoach NW	KAZ1363	Finglands	L255CCK	Stagecoach NW	L708LKY	JP Travel
K751DAO	Stagecoach NW	KBV310	Aspden	L256CCK	Stagecoach NW	L800BUL	R Bullock
K752DAO	Stagecoach NW	KBZ5749	Travellers' Choice	L266JPY	Titterington	L803FBA	Bu-Val
K753DAO	Stagecoach NW	KDB137V	Mayne	L269GBU	First	L804FBA	Bu-Val
K754DAO	Stagecoach NW	KIW8608	Wright Brothers	L270LHH	Stagecoach NW	L813KCW	Rossendale
K755DAO	Stagecoach NW	KPJ286W	M R Travel	L271LHH	Stagecoach NW	L814KCW	Rossendale
K756DAO	Stagecoach NW	KRM431W	Stagecoach NW	L272LHH	Stagecoach NW	L881SDY	Stagecoach NW
K757DAO	Stagecoach NW	KRM435W	Stagecoach NW	L273LHH	Stagecoach NW	L882SDY	Stagecoach NW
K758DAO	Stagecoach NW	KUM537L	Titterington	L274LHH	Stagecoach NW	L883SDY	Stagecoach NW
K759DAO	Stagecoach NW	KYN306X	Blackburn	L275JAO	Stagecoach NW	L884SDY	Stagecoach NW
K760DAO	Stagecoach NW	KYV311X	Stagecoach NW	L276JAO	Stagecoach NW	L885SDY	Stagecoach NW
K761DAO	Stagecoach NW	KYV340X	Stagecoach NW	L277JAO	Stagecoach NW	L886SDY	Stagecoach NW
K762DAO	Stagecoach NW	KYV465X	Blackburn	L278JAO	Stagecoach NW	L887SDY	Stagecoach NW
K763DAO	Stagecoach NW	KYV508X	Blackburn	L281JAO	Stagecoach NW	L911ECW	Rossendale
K764DAO	Stagecoach NW	KYV512X	Stagecoach NW	L282JAO	Stagecoach NW	L912ECW	Rossendale
K765DAO	Stagecoach NW	KYV517X	Blackburn	L283JAO	Stagecoach NW	L950NWW	Grayway
K766DAO	Stagecoach NW	KYV521X	Blackburn	L323NRF	First	LBZ4071	Blue Bus
K767DAO	Stagecoach NW	KYV525X	Blackburn	L335PWX	Homeswood	LDA430W	Yellow Buzz
K768DAO	Stagecoach NW	KYV526X	Blackburn	L345ERU	Blackburn	LDZ2951	Blue Bus
K769DAO	Stagecoach NW	KYV533X	Blackburn	L388YNV	Homeswood	LFJ854W	Walton's
K770DAO	Stagecoach NW	KYV544X	Blackburn	L392LNA	Stagecoach Manchester	LFJ868W	Walton's
K771DAO	Stagecoach NW	KYV545X	Blackburn	L412CDB	Grayway	LFR872X	Walton's

LHE254W	Homeswood	M233TBV	Lancashire United	M423RRN	Finglands	M522RSS	First
LIB804	Homeswood	M234TBV	Lancashire United	M424RRN	Finglands	M523RSS	First
LIB3768	Staintons	M234VWU	First	M425RRN	Finglands	M524RSS	First
LIB3769	Staintons	M235TBV	Stagecoach NW	M426RRN	Finglands	M529RHG	Rossendale
LIB6437	Mayne	M236TBV	Stagecoach NW	M427RRN	Finglands	M530RHG	Rossendale
LIB6438	Homeswood	M237VWU	First	M439ECS	Titterington	M533RCW	Blackburn
LIB6439	Mayne	M238VWU	First	M451VCW	Stagecoach NW	M534RCW	Blackburn
LIB6440	Homeswood	M239VWU	First	M452VCW	Stagecoach NW	M535RCW	Blackburn
LIJ749	Northern Blue	M245VWU	First	M453VCW	Burnley & Pendle	M536RCW	Blackburn
LIL2831	JP Travel	M247VWU	First	M454VCW	Stagecoach NW	M586TSO	First
LIL3061	Grayway	M248VWU	First	M454VHE	Stagecoach NW	M598RFS	Grayway
LIL5947	Grayway	M251NVM	First	M455VCW	Stagecoach NW	M598RFS	JP Travel
LIL5948	Grayway	M252NVM	First	M455VHE	Stagecoach NW	M601ORJ	Shearings
LIL6147	Grayway	M253NVM	First	M456VCW	Stagecoach NW	M602ORJ	Shearings
LIL6149	Grayway	M254NVM	First	M456VHE	Stagecoach NW	M603ORJ	Shearings
LJA474P	Collinson	M255NVM	First	M457UUR	Lancashire United	M604ORJ	Shearings
LJY145	Stagecoach NW	M256NVM	First	M457VCW	Stagecoach NW	M605ORJ	Shearings
LRN552N	Blackburn	M257NVM	First	M457VHE	Stagecoach NW	M605RCP	UK North
LSU939	Travellers' Choice	M258NVM	First	M458VCW	Stagecoach NW	M606ORJ	Shearings
LTF346	Travellers' Choice	M259NVM	First	M458VHE	Stagecoach NW	M607ORJ	Shearings
LTG271X	Wright Brothers	M260KWK	First	M459UUR	Lancashire United	M608ORJ	Shearings
LUF549	Blackburn	M260NVM	First	M459VCW	Stagecoach NW	M608SBA	First
M1BUS	Jim Stones	M261SVU	First	M459VHE	Stagecoach NW	M609ORJ	Shearings
M2BLU	Blue Bus	M262SVU	First	M460UUR	Lancashire United	M609SBA	First
M2JPT	JP Travel	M263SVU	First	M460VHE	Stagecoach NW	M610ORJ	Shearings
M5BLU	Bu-Val	M264SVU	First	M461UUR	Lancashire United	M610SBA	First
M6BLU	Bu-Val	M265SVU	First	M461VHE	Stagecoach NW	M611ORJ	Shearings
M6MGH	Mountain Goat	M266SVU	First	M462VHE	Stagecoach NW	M611SBA	First
M6OAT	Mountain Goat	M267SVU	First	M463VCW	Stagecoach NW	M612ORJ	Shearings
M8BLU	Bluebird	M268SVU	First	M465RVO	Kirkby Lonsdale	M612SBA	First
M8MGH	Mountain Goat	M269SVU	First	M500GSM	Homeswood	M613ORJ	Shearings
M9BLU	Bu-Val	M270SVU	First	M501GRY	First	M613SBA	First
M10BLU	Bluebird	M335KRY	Homeswood	M501PNA	First	M614ORJ	Shearings
M10MGH	Mountain Goat	M347MCY	Rossendale	M502GRY	First	M614SBA	First
M12BLU	Bu-Val	M348MCY	Rossendale	M502PNA	First	M615ORJ	Shearings
M20MGH	Mountain Goat	M351MRU	Blackburn	M503GRY	First	M617SBA	First
M29HNY	Yellow Buzz	M359OBU	Manchester Airport	M503PNA	First	M618SBA	First
M31KAX	Homeswood	M360OBU	Manchester Airport	M504GRY	First	M627WBV	Blackburn
M42ONF	Mayne	M361OBU	Manchester Airport	M504PNA	First	M628WBV	Blackburn
M68LAG	Ashalls	M362OBU	Manchester Airport	M505PNA	First	M629WBV	Blackburn
M88SLT	South Lancs Travel	M364LFX	Homeswood	M506GRY	First	M630RCP	UK North
M99SLT	South Lancs Travel	M367CUF	Bu-Val	M506PNA	First	M630WFR	Blackburn
M101RRJ	First	M374SCK	Blackpool	M507GRY	First	M631WFR	Blackburn
M102RRJ	First	M375SCK	Blackpool	M507PNA	First	M632WFR	Blackburn
M103RRJ	First	M376SCK	Blackpool	M508GRY	First	M634FJF	Stagecoach Manchester
M104RRJ	First	M377SCK	Blackpool	M508PNA	First	M639RCP	Cosgrove's
M105RRJ	First	M378SCK	Blackpool	M509GRY	First	M677KVU	Shearings
M106RRJ	First	M379SCK	Blackpool	M509PNA	First	M678KVU	Shearings
M113RNK	Mayne	M379TJA	Stagecoach Manchester	M510GRY	First	M679KVU	Shearings
M164SCK	Stagecoach NW	M384VWX	Burnley & Pendle	M510PNA	First	M680KVU	Shearings
M165SCK	Stagecoach NW	M385VWX	Burnley & Pendle	M511PNA	First	M680TDB	Stagecoach Manchester
M166LNC	South Lancs Travel	M401TCK	Preston Bus	M512PNA	First	M681KVU	Shearings
M167LNC	South Lancs Travel	M402TCK	Preston Bus	M513PNA	First	M681TDB	Stagecoach Manchester
M204VWF	Brownriggs	M403TCK	Preston Bus	M514PNA	First	M682TDB	Stagecoach Manchester
M207VWU	First	M404TCK	Preston Bus	M515PNA	First	M683TDB	Stagecoach Manchester
M209VWU	First	M405TCK	Preston Bus	M516PNA	First	M684TDB	Stagecoach Manchester
M210NDB	Mayne	M406BFG	Stagecoach NW	M516RSS	First	M685TDB	Stagecoach Manchester
M211NDB	Mayne	M406TCK	Preston Bus	M517PNA	First	M686TDB	Stagecoach Manchester
M211VWU	First	M407TCK	Preston Bus	M517RSS	First	M687TDB	Stagecoach Manchester
M213VWU	First	M408TCK	Preston Bus	M518PNA	First	M688TDB	Stagecoach Manchester
M215VWU	First	M409TCK	Preston Bus	M518RSS	First	M689TDB	Stagecoach Manchester
M218VWU	First	M410RND	First	M519PNA	First	M690TDB	Stagecoach Manchester
M223VWU	First	M410TCK	Preston Bus	M519RSS	First	M691TDB	Stagecoach Manchester
M230TBV	Stagecoach NW	M415RND	First	M520PNA	First	M692TDB	Stagecoach Manchester
M231TBV	Lancashire United	M416RND	First	M520RSS	First	M693TDB	Stagecoach Manchester
M232TBV	Lancashire United	M422RRN	Finglands	M521RSS	First	M694TDB	Stagecoach Manchester

The Lancashire, Cumbria and Manchester Bus Handbook

M695TDB	Stagecoach Manchester	MF51MBU	Finglands	MV02UMT	Shearings	MV02VDP	First
M696TDB	Stagecoach Manchester	MF51MBV	Finglands	MV02UMU	Shearings	MV02VDR	First
M699TDB	Stagecoach Manchester	MF51MBX	Finglands	MV02UMW	Shearings	MV02VDT	First
M728MBU	Dennis's	MF51TVV	Blue Bus	MV02UMX	Shearings	MV02VDX	First
M729MBU	Dennis's	MF51TVW	Blue Bus	MV02VAA	First	MV02VDY	First
M730MBU	Dennis's	MF51TVX	Blue Bus	MV02VAD	First	MV02VDZ	First
M733BSJ	Stagecoach NW	MF51TVY	Blue Bus	MV02VAE	First	MV02VEA	First
M734BSJ	Stagecoach NW	MIL8741	Walton's	MV02VAF	First	MV02VEB	First
M741PRS	Stagecoach NW	MIL9576	Homeswood	MV02VAH	First	MV02VEF	First
M742PRS	Stagecoach NW	MJI5765	Mayne	MV02VAJ	First	MV02VEH	First
M743PRS	Stagecoach NW	MJI6406	Wright Brothers	MV02VAK	First	MV02VEK	First
M744PRS	Stagecoach NW	MK02EFV	Stagecoach Manchester	MV02VAM	First	MV02VEL	First
M745PRS	Stagecoach NW	MK02EFW	Stagecoach Manchester	MV02VAO	First	MV02VEM	First
M746PRS	Stagecoach NW	MK02EFX	Stagecoach Manchester	MV02VAU	First	MV02XYH	Blue Bus
M748PRS	Stagecoach NW	MK02EFY	Stagecoach Manchester	MV02VAX	First	MV02XYJ	Blue Bus
M749PRS	Stagecoach NW	MK02EFZ	Stagecoach Manchester	MV02VAY	First	MV02XYK	Blue Bus
M750PRS	Stagecoach NW	MK02EGC	Stagecoach Manchester	MV02VBA	First	MW51PJW	Walton's
M763RCP	UK North	MK02EGD	Stagecoach Manchester	MV02VBB	First	N4BLU	Blue Bus
M782PRS	Lancashire United	MK02EGE	Stagecoach Manchester	MV02VBC	First	N7BLU	Bluebird
M783PRS	Lancashire United	MK02EGF	Stagecoach Manchester	MV02VBD	First	N13BLU	Bu-Val
M786NBA	R Bullock	MK02EHC	Stagecoach Manchester	MV02VBE	First	N14BLU	Bu-Val
M788NBA	R Bullock	MK02EHD	Stagecoach Manchester	MV02VBF	First	N17BLU	Bluebird
M789NBA	R Bullock	ML02EGG	Stagecoach Manchester	MV02VBG	First	N30SHB	Brownriggs
M790NBA	R Bullock	ML02EGU	Stagecoach Manchester	MV02VBJ	First	N47ANE	Finglands
M794PRS	Lancashire United	ML02EGY	Stagecoach Manchester	MV02VBK	First	N67YVR	Mayne
M795PRS	Lancashire United	ML02RWF	R Bullock	MV02VBL	First	N68YVR	Mayne
M796PRS	Lancashire United	ML02RWJ	Stagecoach Manchester	MV02VBM	First	N71YNF	First
M797NFJ	Northern Blue	ML02RWN	Stagecoach Manchester	MV02VBN	First	N78CVP	Homeswood
M797PRS	Lancashire United	ML02RWN	Stagecoach Manchester	MV02VBO	First	N91WVC	Homeswood
M798PRS	Lancashire United	ML02RWO	Stagecoach Manchester	MV02VBP	First	N94BNF	Blue Bus
M799PRS	Burnley & Pendle	ML02RWU	Stagecoach Manchester	MV02VBT	First	N95BNF	Blue Bus
M822RCP	UK North	ML02RWV	Stagecoach Manchester	MV02VBU	First	N103YHH	Mountain Goat
M827RCP	Cosgrove's	ML02RWW	Stagecoach Manchester	MV02VBX	First	N106LCK	Rossendale
M832HNS	Grayway	ML02RWX	Stagecoach Manchester	MV02VBY	First	N107LCK	Rossendale
M832HVC	Finglands	MRJ35W	First	MV02VBZ	First	N108LCK	Rossendale
M833RCP	UK North	MRJ50W	First	MV02VCA	First	N109HRH	Brownriggs
M845RCP	UK North	MRJ61W	First	MV02VCC	First	N109LCK	Rossendale
M846HDF	Stagecoach NW	MV02ULK	Shearings	MV02VCD	First	N110LCK	Rossendale
M847PRS	Stagecoach NW	MV02ULL	Shearings	MV02VCE	First	N116YHH	Stagecoach NW
M911OVR	Homeswood	MV02ULM	Shearings	MV02VCF	First	N117YHH	Stagecoach NW
M924TYG	Blackpool	MV02ULN	Shearings	MV02VCG	First	N118YHH	Stagecoach NW
M943JBO	Burnley & Pendle	MV02ULO	Shearings	MV02VCJ	First	N119YHH	Stagecoach NW
M944JBO	Burnley & Pendle	MV02ULP	Shearings	MV02VCK	First	N120YHH	Stagecoach NW
M944SRE	First	MV02ULR	Shearings	MV02VCL	First	N121YHH	Stagecoach NW
M945JBO	Burnley & Pendle	MV02ULS	Shearings	MV02VCM	First	N122YHH	Stagecoach NW
M946SRE	First	MV02ULT	Shearings	MV02VCN	First	N123YHH	Stagecoach NW
M947JBO	Burnley & Pendle	MV02ULU	Shearings	MV02VCO	First	N124YHH	Stagecoach NW
M947OVC	First	MV02ULW	Shearings	MV02VCP	First	N125YHH	Stagecoach NW
M947SRE	First	MV02ULX	Shearings	MV02VCT	First	N126YRM	Stagecoach NW
M948JBO	Burnley & Pendle	MV02ULY	Shearings	MV02VCU	First	N127YRM	Stagecoach NW
M948SRE	First	MV02ULZ	Shearings	MV02VCW	First	N128VAO	Stagecoach NW
M949RHH	Titterington	MV02UMA	Shearings	MV02VCX	First	N128YRM	Stagecoach NW
M950RHH	Titterington	MV02UMB	Shearings	MV02VCY	First	N129VAO	Stagecoach NW
M958VWY	Manchester Airport	MV02UMC	Shearings	MV02VCZ	First	N129YRM	Stagecoach NW
M963XVT	First	MV02UMD	Shearings	MV02VDA	First	N130VAO	Stagecoach NW
M965XVT	First	MV02UME	Shearings	MV02VDC	First	N130YRM	Stagecoach NW
M966XVT	First	MV02UMF	Shearings	MV02VDD	First	N131VAO	Stagecoach NW
MAZ4969	Bluebird	MV02UMG	Shearings	MV02VDE	First	N131YRM	Stagecoach NW
MAZ4970	Bluebird	MV02UMH	Shearings	MV02VDF	First	N132VAO	Stagecoach NW
MAZ7092	Tyrer Bus	MV02UMJ	Shearings	MV02VDG	First	N132YRM	Stagecoach NW
MBR438T	Collinson	MV02UMK	Shearings	MV02VDJ	First	N133YRM	Stagecoach NW
MC02BLU	Bluebird	MV02UML	Shearings	MV02VDK	First	N176LCK	Lancashire United
MD02BLU	Bluebird	MV02UMM	Shearings	MV02VDL	First	N177LCK	Lancashire United
MEF823W	Hulme Hall	MV02UMO	Shearings	MV02VDM	First	N178LCK	Lancashire United
MF51LZW	Finglands	MV02UMR	Shearings	MV02VDN	First	N179LCK	Lancashire United
F51LZZ	Finglands	MV02UMS	Shearings	MV02VDO	First	N180LCK	Lancashire United

Reg	Operator	Reg	Operator	Reg	Operator	Reg	Operator
N194LFV	Stagecoach NW	N337NPN	Stagecoach NW	N428GBV	Preston Bus	N554WVR	First
N195LFV	Stagecoach NW	N338NPN	Stagecoach NW	N428WVR	Stagecoach Manchester	N556WVR	First
N196LFV	Stagecoach NW	N339NPN	Stagecoach NW	N429GBV	Preston Bus	N557BNF	First
N197LFV	Stagecoach NW	N340NPN	Stagecoach NW	N429WVR	Stagecoach Manchester	N558BNF	First
N198LFV	Stagecoach NW	N343CJA	First	N430GBV	Preston Bus	N559BNF	First
N199LFV	Stagecoach NW	N344CJA	First	N431GBV	Preston Bus	N561BNF	First
N200BLU	Blue Bus	N347CJA	First	N443WUX	Homeswood	N562BNF	First
N201LFV	Stagecoach NW	N348CJA	First	N447XVA	Stagecoach NW	N585GRN	Blackpool
N201UHH	Stagecoach NW	N352BKK	Rossendale	N451NWY	Lancashire United	N586GRN	Blackpool
N202LFV	Stagecoach NW	N354TTH	Titterington	N452VOD	Stagecoach NW	N587GRN	Blackpool
N202UHH	Stagecoach NW	N372CJA	First	N453NWY	Lancashire United	N588GRN	Blackpool
N203UHH	Stagecoach NW	N373CJA	First	N454NWY	Lancashire United	N589GRN	Blackpool
N204UHH	Stagecoach NW	N374CJA	First	N455NWY	Lancashire United	N590GRN	Blackpool
N205UHH	Stagecoach NW	N375CJA	First	N455VOD	Stagecoach NW	N591GRN	Blackpool
N206UHH	Stagecoach NW	N376CJA	First	N461VOD	Stagecoach NW	N592GRN	Blackpool
N207UHH	Stagecoach NW	N377CJA	First	N462VOD	Stagecoach NW	N593LFV	Blackpool
N207WBA	First	N378CJA	First	N463VOD	Stagecoach NW	N594LFV	Blackpool
N208UHH	Stagecoach NW	N379CJA	First	N465VOD	Stagecoach NW	N595LFV	Blackpool
N208WBA	First	N380CJA	First	N466VOD	Stagecoach NW	N596DWY	Cosgrove's
N209UHH	Stagecoach NW	N381CJA	First	N467VOD	Stagecoach NW	N596LFV	Blackpool
N209WBA	First	N382CJA	First	N519BJA	Stagecoach NW	N599XRJ	Manchester Airport
N210UHH	Stagecoach NW	N383CJA	First	N521WVR	First	N601XJM	First
N210WBA	First	N384CJA	First	N522WVR	First	N601XRJ	Manchester Airport
N211UHH	Stagecoach NW	N385CRJ	First	N523WVR	First	N602XJM	First
N211WBA	First	N386CRJ	First	N524WVR	First	N602XRJ	Manchester Airport
N212UHH	Stagecoach NW	N391EUG	First	N525VSA	First	N603XJM	First
N212WBA	First	N398CNB	Travellers' Choice	N525WVR	First	N604XJM	First
N213UHH	Stagecoach NW	N401WVR	Stagecoach Manchester	N526VSA	First	N606XJM	First
N214HWX	Titterington	N402WVR	Stagecoach Manchester	N526WVR	First	N607XJM	First
N214UHH	Stagecoach NW	N403WVR	Stagecoach Manchester	N527VSA	First	N608XJM	First
N215UHH	Stagecoach NW	N404WVR	Stagecoach Manchester	N527WVR	First	N609XJM	First
N224THO	Blackburn	N405HVT	First	N528VSA	First	N610XJM	First
N251KFR	Robinsons	N405WVR	Stagecoach Manchester	N528WVR	First	N613VSS	Stagecoach NW
N252KFR	Robinsons	N406WVR	Stagecoach Manchester	N529VSA	First	N614VSS	Stagecoach NW
N253KFR	Robinsons	N407WVR	Stagecoach Manchester	N529WVR	First	N615VSS	Stagecoach NW
N254KFR	Robinsons	N408WVR	Stagecoach Manchester	N530VSA	First	N616VSS	Stagecoach NW
N255DUR	Buzy Buz	N409WVR	Stagecoach Manchester	N530WVR	First	N617VSS	Stagecoach NW
N256THO	Sim's Travel	N410HVT	First	N531VSA	First	N619CDB	First
N257DUR	Tyrer Bus	N410WVR	Stagecoach Manchester	N531WVR	First	N619VSS	Stagecoach NW
N258DUR	South Lancs Travel	N411WVR	Stagecoach Manchester	N532VSA	First	N620CDB	First
N298VRM	Sim's Travel	N412WVR	Stagecoach Manchester	N532WVR	First	N621CDB	First
N300EST	Rossendale	N413WVR	Stagecoach Manchester	N533VSA	First	N621XBU	R Bullock
N301WNF	First	N414WVR	Stagecoach Manchester	N533WVR	First	N622CDB	First
N302WNF	First	N415WVR	Stagecoach Manchester	N534VSA	First	N623CDB	First
N303WNF	First	N416CBU	Vale of Manchester	N534WVR	First	N624CDB	First
N304WNF	First	N416WVR	Stagecoach Manchester	N535WVR	First	N625CDB	First
N305WNF	First	N417CBU	Vale of Manchester	N536WVR	First	N626CDB	First
N306WNF	First	N417WVR	Stagecoach Manchester	N537WVR	First	N627CDB	First
N320YNC	Dennis's	N418WVR	Stagecoach Manchester	N538WVR	First	N628CDB	First
N321YNC	Dennis's	N419WVR	Stagecoach Manchester	N539WVR	First	N629CDB	First
N322YNC	Dennis's	N420GBV	Preston Bus	N540WVR	First	N630CDB	First
N325HUA	First	N420WVR	Stagecoach Manchester	N541WVR	First	N631CDB	First
N325NPN	Stagecoach NW	N421GBV	Preston Bus	N542WVR	First	N632CDB	First
N326NPN	Stagecoach NW	N421WVR	Stagecoach Manchester	N543WVR	First	N633CDB	First
N327NPN	Stagecoach NW	N422GBV	Preston Bus	N544WVR	First	N633LFR	Blackburn
N327XRP	Stagecoach NW	N422WVR	Stagecoach Manchester	N545WVR	First	N634CDB	First
N328NPN	Stagecoach NW	N423GBV	Preston Bus	N546WVR	First	N634LFR	Blackburn
N328XRP	Stagecoach NW	N423WVR	Stagecoach Manchester	N547SJF	Homeswood	N634XBU	R Bullock
N329NPN	Stagecoach NW	N424GBV	Preston Bus	N547WVR	First	N635CDB	First
N329XRP	Stagecoach NW	N424WVR	Stagecoach Manchester	N548WVR	First	N635LFR	Blackburn
N330NPN	Stagecoach NW	N425GBV	Preston Bus	N549WVR	First	N636CDB	First
N331NPN	Stagecoach NW	N425WVR	Stagecoach Manchester	N550WVR	First	N636LFR	Blackburn
N332NPN	Stagecoach NW	N426GBV	Preston Bus	N551WVR	First	N637CDB	First
N334NPN	Stagecoach NW	N426WVR	Stagecoach Manchester	N552WVR	First	N638CDB	First
N335NPN	Stagecoach NW	N427GBV	Preston Bus	N553WVR	First	N640CDB	First
N336NPN	Stagecoach NW	N427WVR	Stagecoach Manchester	N554SOA	Mountain Goat	N641CDB	First

Reg	Operator	Reg	Operator	Reg	Operator	Reg	Operator
N641VSS	Stagecoach NW	N744ANE	Finglands	OBV165X	Preston Bus	P130XCN	Stagecoach NW
N642CDB	First	N744VRM	Brownriggs	OCW13X	Blackburn	P131XCN	Stagecoach NW
N643CDB	First	N745ANE	Finglands	OED201	Mayne	P132XCN	Stagecoach NW
N644CDB	First	N746ANE	Finglands	OET309	Travellers' Choice	P133XCN	Stagecoach NW
N645CDB	First	N746YVR	Stagecoach Manchester	OFS684Y	Blackburn	P134XCN	Stagecoach NW
N645VSS	Stagecoach NW	N748ANE	Finglands	OFV14X	Lancashire United	P211DCK	Rossendale
N646CDB	First	N748YVR	Stagecoach Manchester	OFV15X	Burnley & Pendle	P211RUM	Alfa
N646VSS	Stagecoach NW	N753VCY	Ashalls	OFV16X	Stagecoach NW	P211RWR	Rossendale
N647CDB	First	N784ORY	Homeswood	OFV17X	Stagecoach NW	P212DCK	Rossendale
N647VSS	Stagecoach NW	N787EUB	First	OFV18X	Lancashire United	P212RUM	Alfa
N648CDB	First	N788EUB	First	OFV19X	Burnley & Pendle	P213DCK	Rossendale
N648VSS	Stagecoach NW	N789EUB	First	OFV21X	Burnley & Pendle	P213HRJ	First
N649CDB	First	N789VRM	Stagecoach NW	OFV22X	Burnley & Pendle	P213RUM	Alfa
N649VSS	Stagecoach NW	N790VRM	Stagecoach NW	OFV23X	Burnley & Pendle	P214RUM	Alfa
N650CDB	First	N796XRA	South Lancs Travel	OFV620X	Fishwick	P215RUM	Alfa
N650VSS	Stagecoach NW	N829REC	Mountain Goat	OFV621X	Fishwick	P224VCK	Stagecoach NW
N651CDB	First	N879AVV	Stagecoach Manchester	OHV684Y	Stagecoach NW	P225VCK	Stagecoach NW
N651VSS	Stagecoach NW	N880AVV	Stagecoach Manchester	OHV728Y	Stagecoach NW	P226VCK	Stagecoach NW
N652CDB	First	N881AVV	Stagecoach Manchester	OHV729Y	Stagecoach NW	P226YGG	Lakeland
N652VSS	Stagecoach NW	N882AVV	Stagecoach Manchester	OHV739Y	Stagecoach NW	P227VCK	Stagecoach NW
N653CDB	First	N883AVV	Stagecoach Manchester	OHV784Y	UK North	P228VCK	Stagecoach NW
N657AEO	Kirkby Lonsdale	N884AVV	Stagecoach Manchester	OHV809Y	Stagecoach NW	P229VCK	Stagecoach NW
N660VSS	Stagecoach Manchester	N885AVV	Stagecoach NW	OIB5403	Rossendale	P230VCK	Stagecoach NW
N663VSS	Stagecoach Manchester	N897KFA	Homeswood	OIW5804	Stagecoach NW	P231VCK	Stagecoach NW
N664VSS	Stagecoach Manchester	N899KFA	Homeswood	OJD899R	Pilkington	P232VCK	Stagecoach NW
N665VSS	Stagecoach Manchester	N910DWJ	Homeswood	OJI4371	Blackpool	P233VCK	Stagecoach NW
N701UVR	Shearings	N955DWJ	Lakeland	OJI4372	Blackpool	P234VCK	Stagecoach NW
N702UVR	Shearings	N962WJA	Manchester Airport	OJI4373	Blackpool	P235VCK	Stagecoach NW
N703UVR	Shearings	N963WJA	Manchester Airport	OJI4374	Blackpool	P248KND	South Lancs Travel
N704UVR	Shearings	N964WJA	Manchester Airport	ONF660R	Archway	P255YFR	Robinsons
N705UVR	Shearings	N976LWR	Brownriggs	ONF698R	Archway	P256YFR	Robinsons
N706UVR	Shearings	N990KUS	Cosgrove's	OSJ610R	Bluebird	P257YFR	Robinsons
N707UVR	Shearings	NDE916R	R Bullock	OTK802	Hulme Hall	P260VPN	Stagecoach NW
N708UVR	Shearings	NEH103V	Grayway	OTO555M	First	P261VPN	Stagecoach NW
N709UVR	Shearings	NEH104V	Grayway	OTO555M	First	P262VPN	Stagecoach NW
N710UVR	Shearings	NFR559T	Fishwick	OTO555M	First	P263VPN	Stagecoach NW
N711UVR	Shearings	NFR560T	Fishwick	OW5371	Travellers' Choice	P270VPN	Stagecoach NW
N712UVR	Shearings	NHH358W	Manchester Airport	OZ4688	Titterington	P271VPN	Stagecoach NW
N713UVR	Shearings	NHH359W	Manchester Airport	P2HWD	Homeswood	P272VPN	Stagecoach NW
N714UVR	Shearings	NIB3261	Mayne	P2TYR	Tyrer Bus	P273VPN	Stagecoach NW
N715UVR	Shearings	NIB4162	Mayne	P4HWD	Homeswood	P274VPN	Stagecoach NW
N716UVR	Shearings	NIL5675	Homeswood	P5HWD	Homeswood	P275VPN	Stagecoach NW
N717UVR	Shearings	NIL6108	Brownriggs	P6JPT	JP Travel	P298PVR	Vale of Manchester
N718UVR	Shearings	NIL7914	Travellers' Choice	P8JPT	JP Travel	P299PVR	Vale of Manchester
N719UVR	Shearings	NIL8256	Mayne	P13BLU	Bluebird	P301LND	First
N720UVR	Shearings	NIL8258	Mayne	P14BLU	Bluebird	P302LND	First
N721UVR	Shearings	NIL8663	Brownriggs	P20BLU	Bluebird	P303LND	First
N722UVR	Shearings	NIL9247	Wright Brothers	P30BLU	Bluebird	P304LND	First
N723UVR	Shearings	NIL9581	Travellers' Choice	P40BLU	Bluebird	P305LND	First
N724UVR	Shearings	NIL9773	Mayne	P50BLU	Bluebird	P305VWR	Shearings
N725UVR	Shearings	NIL9774	Mayne	P50HWD	Homeswood	P306LND	First
N726UVR	Shearings	NIL9932	Travellers' Choice	P101HNC	Mayne	P306VWR	Shearings
N727UVR	Shearings	NIW6515	Coastlinks	P102HNC	Mayne	P307LND	First
N728UVR	Shearings	NJI1250	Finglands	P103HNC	Mayne	P308LND	First
N729UVR	Shearings	NJI5504	Blackpool	P104HNC	Mayne	P309LND	First
N730UVR	Shearings	NJI5505	Blackpool	P108DCW	Stagecoach NW	P310LND	First
N731UVR	Shearings	NMX643	Mayne	P109DCW	Stagecoach NW	P311LND	First
N732UVR	Shearings	NST162Y	Collinson	P110DCW	Stagecoach NW	P312LND	First
N733UVR	Shearings	NUS333Y	Robinson's	P112DCW	Stagecoach NW	P312VWR	Grayway
N734UVR	Shearings	NUW663Y	UK North	P112OJA	Dennis's	P313LND	First
N735UVR	Shearings	NXI1610	Walton's	P113DCW	Stagecoach NW	P314LND	First
N740VBA	Finglands	OBV142	Aspden	P113OJA	Dennis's	P315LND	First
N741VBA	Finglands	OBV158X	Preston Bus	P114DCW	Stagecoach NW	P316LND	First
N742GKH	First	OBV159X	Preston Bus	P127XCN	Stagecoach NW	P317KTW	UK North
N742VBA	Finglands	OBV161X	Collinson	P128XCN	Stagecoach NW	P317LND	First
N743VBA	Finglands	OBV162X	Collinson	P129XCN	Stagecoach NW	P318LND	First

P319LND	First	P514LND	First	P564PNE	Stagecoach Manchester	P853GND	Stagecoach Manchester
P320LND	First	P515LND	First	P565PNE	Stagecoach Manchester	P854GND	Stagecoach Manchester
P321LND	First	P516LND	First	P566PNE	Stagecoach Manchester	P855GND	Stagecoach Manchester
P322LND	First	P517LND	First	P637ARN	Blackburn	P856GND	Stagecoach Manchester
P323LND	First	P518LND	First	P638ARN	Blackburn	P857GND	Stagecoach Manchester
P324LND	First	P519LND	First	P639ARN	Blackburn	P858GND	Stagecoach Manchester
P325LND	First	P520LND	First	P640ARN	Blackburn	P859GND	Stagecoach Manchester
P334VWR	Homeswood	P521LND	First	P704CRM	Homeswood	P860GND	Stagecoach Manchester
P335JND	Burnley & Pendle	P522LND	First	P716GND	Stagecoach Manchester	P861GND	Stagecoach Manchester
P336JND	Lancashire United	P523LND	First	P717GND	Stagecoach Manchester	P862GND	Stagecoach Manchester
P337JND	Burnley & Pendle	P524LND	First	P718GND	Stagecoach Manchester	P863GND	Stagecoach Manchester
P338JND	Burnley & Pendle	P525LND	First	P719GND	Stagecoach Manchester	P864GND	Stagecoach Manchester
P339JND	Lancashire United	P526LND	First	P720GND	Stagecoach Manchester	P865GND	Stagecoach Manchester
P340JND	Burnley & Pendle	P527LND	First	P721GND	Stagecoach Manchester	P866GND	Stagecoach Manchester
P341JND	Lancashire United	P528LND	First	P722GND	Stagecoach Manchester	P867GND	Stagecoach Manchester
P342JND	Lancashire United	P529LND	First	P723GND	Stagecoach Manchester	P868GND	Stagecoach Manchester
P343JND	Burnley & Pendle	P530LND	First	P724GND	Stagecoach Manchester	P871TAV	First
P344JND	Burnley & Pendle	P530PNE	Stagecoach Manchester	P725GND	Stagecoach Manchester	P872TAV	First
P345JND	Lancashire United	P531PNE	Stagecoach Manchester	P726GND	Stagecoach Manchester	P875MNE	Stagecoach Manchester
P346JND	Lancashire United	P532FPM	Homeswood	P727GND	Stagecoach Manchester	P876MNE	Stagecoach Manchester
P347JND	Lancashire United	P532PNE	Stagecoach Manchester	P728GND	Stagecoach Manchester	P876PWW	JP Travel
P348JND	Lancashire United	P533PNE	Stagecoach Manchester	P729GND	Stagecoach Manchester	P877MNE	Stagecoach Manchester
P349JND	Burnley & Pendle	P534PNE	Stagecoach Manchester	P730GND	Stagecoach Manchester	P878MNE	Stagecoach Manchester
P405MDT	Tyrer Bus	P535PNE	Stagecoach Manchester	P801GBA	Shearings	P878PWW	JP Travel
P411TFR	Preston Bus	P536PNE	Stagecoach Manchester	P802GBA	Shearings	P879MNE	Stagecoach Manchester
P412TFR	Preston Bus	P537PNE	Stagecoach Manchester	P803GBA	Shearings	P880MNE	Stagecoach Manchester
P413TFR	Preston Bus	P538PNE	Stagecoach Manchester	P804GBA	Shearings	P881MNE	Stagecoach Manchester
P414TFR	Preston Bus	P539PNE	Stagecoach Manchester	P805GBA	Shearings	P882MNE	Stagecoach Manchester
P415TFR	Preston Bus	P540BSS	First	P806GBA	Shearings	P884CHH	Routledge
P416TFR	Preston Bus	P540PNE	Stagecoach Manchester	P807GBA	Shearings	P893MNE	Stagecoach Manchester
P417HVR	South Lancs Travel	P541BSS	First	P808GBA	Shearings	P894MNE	Stagecoach Manchester
P418HNF	Vale of Manchester	P541PNE	Stagecoach Manchester	P809GBA	Shearings	P902PWW	UK North
P419HNF	Vale of Manchester	P542BSS	First	P810GBA	Shearings	P909PWW	UK North
P422MEH	First	P542ESA	Stagecoach NW	P811GBA	Shearings	P914JBC	Timeline
P423MEH	First	P542PNE	Stagecoach Manchester	P812GBA	Shearings	P915XUG	Rossendale
P424MEH	First	P543BSS	First	P813GBA	Shearings	P916XUG	Rossendale
P425MEH	First	P543ESA	Stagecoach NW	P814GBA	Shearings	P962SFR	Lakeland
P426MEH	First	P543PNE	Stagecoach Manchester	P815GBA	Shearings	P977UBV	Stagecoach NW
P427MEH	First	P544BSS	First	P816GBA	Shearings	P978LNB	Dennis's
P459EFL	M R Travel	P544ESA	Stagecoach NW	P817GBA	Shearings	P978UBV	Stagecoach NW
P480HBA	R Bullock	P544PNE	Stagecoach Manchester	P818GBA	Shearings	P979LNB	Dennis's
P481HBA	R Bullock	P545BSS	First	P819GBA	Shearings	P979UBV	Stagecoach NW
P482HBA	R Bullock	P545ESA	Stagecoach NW	P820GBA	Shearings	P980LNB	Dennis's
P483HBA	R Bullock	P545PNE	Stagecoach Manchester	P821GBA	Shearings	PBV779	Aspden
P484HBA	R Bullock	P546BSS	First	P822GBA	Shearings	PBZ7052	Homeswood
P485HBA	R Bullock	P546ESA	Stagecoach NW	P823GBA	Shearings	PCB24	Blackburn
P486HBA	R Bullock	P546PNE	Stagecoach Manchester	P824GBA	Shearings	PCK335	Stagecoach NW
P501HEG	Buzy Buz	P547BSS	First	P825GBA	Shearings	PE51YHF	Preston Bus
P501LND	First	P547ESA	Stagecoach NW	P826GBA	Shearings	PE51YHG	Preston Bus
P501UFR	Blackpool	P547HVM	Dennis's	P827GBA	Shearings	PE51YHH	Preston Bus
P502LND	First	P547PNE	Stagecoach Manchester	P828GBA	Shearings	PE51YHJ	Preston Bus
P502UFR	Blackpool	P548BSS	First	P829GBA	Shearings	PE51YHK	Preston Bus
P503LND	First	P548PNE	Stagecoach Manchester	P830GBA	Shearings	PE51YHL	Preston Bus
P503UFR	Blackpool	P549BSS	First	P831GBA	Shearings	PE51YHM	Preston Bus
P504LND	First	P549PNE	Stagecoach Manchester	P832GBA	Shearings	PE51YHN	Preston Bus
P504UFR	Blackpool	P550PNE	Stagecoach Manchester	P833GBA	Shearings	PF51KHB	Battersby
P505GHH	Sim's Travel	P551PNE	Stagecoach Manchester	P834GBA	Shearings	PF51KHC	Battersby
P505LND	First	P552PNE	Stagecoach Manchester	P835GBA	Shearings	PF51KMM	Rossendale
P506LND	First	P553PNE	Stagecoach Manchester	P845GND	Stagecoach Manchester	PF51KMO	Rossendale
P507LND	First	P554PNE	Stagecoach Manchester	P846GND	Stagecoach Manchester	PF51KMU	Rossendale
P508LND	First	P556PNE	Stagecoach Manchester	P847GND	Stagecoach Manchester	PF51KMV	Rossendale
P509LND	First	P557PNE	Stagecoach Manchester	P848GND	Stagecoach Manchester	PF51KMX	Rossendale
P510LND	First	P558PNE	Stagecoach Manchester	P849GND	Stagecoach Manchester	PFC514W	Hulme Hall
P511LND	First	P559PNE	Stagecoach Manchester	P850GND	Stagecoach Manchester	PFC515W	Hulme Hall
P512LND	First	P562PNE	Stagecoach Manchester	P851GND	Stagecoach Manchester	PIB1125	Pilkington
P513LND	First	P563PNE	Stagecoach Manchester	P852GND	Stagecoach Manchester	PIB3488	Pilkington

Accrington Buses, the names used for local services by Pilkingtons, carry a number of 'PIL' index marks. Seen working route 3 is PIL8560, a Gardner-engined Leyland National new to Cumberland. *David Heath*

PIB4290	Pilkington	PJ02PYG	Blackpool	PN02TJV	Travellers' Choice	PRN424X	Aspden
PIB5507	Pilkington	PJ02PYH	Blackpool	PO51BXT	Travellers' Choice	PRN909	Preston Bus
PIB5823	Pilkington	PJ02PYL	Blackpool	PO51BXU	Kirkby Lonsdale	PSU787	Stagecoach NW
PIB5952	Pilkington	PJ02PYO	Blackpool	PO51MTE	Lancashire United	PUS158W	Blackburn
PIB6434	Pilkington	PJ02PYP	Blackpool	PO51MTF	Lancashire United	Q580GRJ	Manchester Airport
PIB6667	Pilkington	PJ02PYS	Blackpool	PO51MTK	Lancashire United	R1BLU	Bluebird
PIB6945	Pilkington	PJ02PYT	Blackpool	PO51MTU	Lancashire United	R1LCB	First
PIB7014	Pilkington	PJI9170	Rossendale	PO51MTV	Lancashire United	R2LCB	First
PIB7256	Pilkington	PJI9171	Rossendale	PO51MTX	Lancashire United	R3HWD	Homeswood
PIB8076	Pilkington	PJI9172	Rossendale	PO51MTY	Lancashire United	R3LCB	First
PIB8301	Pilkington	PJI9173	Rossendale	PO51MTZ	Lancashire United	R4HWD	Homeswood
PIB9051	Pilkington	PJI9174	Rossendale	PO51MUA	Lancashire United	R4LCB	First
PIB9189	Pilkington	PJI9175	Rossendale	PO51MUB	Lancashire United	R5BSL	Alfa
PIB9482	Pilkington	PJI9176	Rossendale	PO51MUC	Lancashire United	R5LCB	First
PIB9536	Pilkington	PJI9177	Rossendale	PO51MUE	Lancashire United	R6BLU	Blue Bus
PIL2755	Pilkington	PJI9178	Rossendale	PO51MUP	Lancashire United	R6HWD	Homeswood
PIL4921	Pilkington	PJI9179	Rossendale	PO51MUU	Lancashire United	R6LCB	First
PIL5941	Pilkington	PJT267R	Blackburn	PO51MUV	Lancashire United	R7BLU	Blue Bus
PIL6617	Pilkington	PK51LJN	Blackburn	PO51MUW	Lancashire United	R7BOS	Homeswood
PIL6726	Pilkington	PK51LJO	Blackburn	PO51MUY	Lancashire United	R7LCB	First
PIL7012	Pilkington	PK51LJU	Blackburn	PO51MVA	Lancashire United	R8BLU	Blue Bus
PIL7013	Pilkington	PK51LJV	Blackburn	PO51WEC	Rossendale	R8LCB	First
PIL7395	Brownriggs	PK51LJX	Blackburn	PO51WLF	Stagecoach NW	R9LCB	First
PIL7752	Mayne	PK51LJY	Blackburn	PO51WLG	Stagecoach NW	R10LCB	First
PIL8380	Pilkington	PN02HVV	Lancashire United	PO51WLH	Stagecoach NW	R15BLU	Bluebird
PIL8381	Pilkington	PN02HVW	Lancashire United	PO51WLJ	Stagecoach NW	R16BLU	Bluebird
PIL8560	Pilkington	PN02HVX	Lancashire United	PO51WLK	Stagecoach NW	R18BLU	Bluebird
PIL9546	Pilkington	PN02HVZ	Lancashire United	PO51WLL	Stagecoach NW	R19BLU	Bluebird
PIL9562	Pilkington	PN02SVJ	Travellers' Choice	PO51WLN	Stagecoach NW	R24YNC	Mayne
PJ02PYD	Blackpool	PN02SVK	Travellers' Choice	PO51WLP	Stagecoach NW	R2SOH	Staintons
PJ02PYF	Blackpool	PN02SVL	Travellers' Choice	PO51WLR	Stagecoach NW	R32GNW	Fishwick

Reg	Operator	Reg	Operator	Reg	Operator	Reg	Operator
R33GNW	Blue Bus	R256NBV	Stagecoach NW	R448FWT	Homeswood	R649CVR	First
R36LSO	Stagecoach NW	R256SBA	First	R473MCW	Stagecoach NW	R650CVR	First
R44BLU	Blue Bus	R257NBV	Stagecoach NW	R474MCW	Stagecoach NW	R651CVR	First
R45CDB	Mayne	R257SBA	First	R475MCW	Stagecoach NW	R653HCD	Stagecoach Manchester
R46CDB	Mayne	R258NBV	Stagecoach NW	R476MCW	Stagecoach NW	R654CVR	First
R47CDB	Mayne	R258SBA	First	R477MCW	Stagecoach NW	R661GCA	South Lancs Travel
R48CDB	Mayne	R259NBV	Stagecoach NW	R478MCW	Stagecoach NW	R668LFV	Lancashire United
R49CDB	Mayne	R259SBA	First	R484YVV	Routledge	R669LFV	Lancashire United
R62MEW	Collinson	R260NBV	Stagecoach NW	R501UWL	Stagecoach Manchester	R670LFV	Stagecoach NW
R103BDB	Dennis's	R260SBA	First	R502UWL	Stagecoach Manchester	R671LFV	Lancashire United
R108YBA	Mayne	R261NBV	Stagecoach NW	R503UWL	Stagecoach Manchester	R672LFV	Stagecoach NW
R109YBA	Mayne	R261SBA	First	R504UWL	Stagecoach Manchester	R672NFR	Lakeland
R116GNW	Alfa	R262NBV	Stagecoach NW	R505UWL	Stagecoach Manchester	R674HCD	Stagecoach Manchester
R117GNW	Alfa	R262SBA	First	R506UWL	Stagecoach Manchester	R677HCD	Stagecoach Manchester
R118GNW	Alfa	R263NBV	Stagecoach NW	R507UWL	Stagecoach Manchester	R701YWC	Stagecoach Manchester
R119GNW	Alfa	R263SBA	First	R508RCH	Northern Blue	R702YWC	Stagecoach Manchester
R120GNW	Alfa	R264NBV	Stagecoach NW	R508UWL	Stagecoach Manchester	R703YWC	Stagecoach Manchester
R120VFR	Stagecoach NW	R264SBA	First	R509UWL	Stagecoach Manchester	R704YWC	Stagecoach Manchester
R121GNW	Alfa	R265NBV	Stagecoach NW	R510UWL	Stagecoach Manchester	R705YWC	Stagecoach Manchester
R165ESG	South Lancs Travel	R265SBA	First	R511UWL	Stagecoach Manchester	R706YWC	Stagecoach Manchester
R166ESG	South Lancs Travel	R266NBV	Stagecoach NW	R512BUA	Travellers' Choice	R707YWC	Stagecoach Manchester
R171SUT	Travellers' Choice	R266SBA	First	R512UWL	Stagecoach Manchester	R708YWC	Stagecoach Manchester
R207JSF	Timeline	R267NBV	Stagecoach NW	R513UWL	Stagecoach Manchester	R709YWC	Stagecoach Manchester
R214SBA	First	R267SBA	First	R540ESA	Stagecoach NW	R710YWC	Stagecoach Manchester
R215SBA	First	R268NBV	Stagecoach NW	R541ESA	Stagecoach NW	R711YWC	Stagecoach Manchester
R216SBA	First	R268SBA	First	R561NBL	Homeswood	R712YWC	Stagecoach Manchester
R217SBA	First	R269SBA	First	R562NBL	Homeswood	R713YWC	Stagecoach Manchester
R218SBA	First	R270SBA	First	R570ANB	Rossendale	R714YWC	Stagecoach Manchester
R219AOR	Bu-Val	R271SBA	First	R571YNC	First	R715YWC	Stagecoach Manchester
R219SBA	First	R272SBA	First	R572ABA	Dennis's	R716YWC	Stagecoach Manchester
R220SBA	First	R273SBA	First	R572SBA	First	R717YWC	Stagecoach Manchester
R221SBA	First	R274SBA	First	R573ABA	Dennis's	R718YWC	Stagecoach Manchester
R223SBA	First	R275SBA	First	R573SBA	First	R720EGD	Ashalls
R234SBA	First	R276CBU	Stagecoach Manchester	R574ABA	Dennis's	R744DRJ	Stagecoach Manchester
R235SBA	First	R276SBA	First	R574SBA	First	R745DRJ	Stagecoach Manchester
R236SBA	First	R277CBU	Stagecoach Manchester	R575ABA	Dennis's	R746DRJ	Stagecoach Manchester
R237SBA	First	R277SBA	First	R575SBA	First	R747DRJ	Stagecoach Manchester
R238SBA	First	R278SBA	First	R576SBA	First	R748DRJ	Stagecoach Manchester
R239SBA	First	R279SBA	First	R577SBA	First	R749DRJ	Stagecoach Manchester
R240SBA	First	R280SBA	First	R578SBA	First	R751DRJ	Stagecoach Manchester
R241SBA	First	R290CVM	R Bullock	R579SBA	First	R752DRJ	Stagecoach Manchester
R242SBA	First	R291CVM	R Bullock	R580SBA	First	R753DRJ	Stagecoach Manchester
R243SBA	First	R292CVM	R Bullock	R581SBA	First	R754DRJ	Stagecoach Manchester
R244SBA	First	R293CVM	R Bullock	R582SBA	First	R755DRJ	Stagecoach Manchester
R245SBA	First	R296PTF	Sim's Travel	R583SBA	First	R756DRJ	Stagecoach Manchester
R246NBV	Stagecoach NW	R300BLU	Blue Bus	R621CVR	First	R757DRJ	Stagecoach Manchester
R246SBA	First	R357URM	Robinson's	R622CVR	First	R758DRJ	Stagecoach Manchester
R247NBV	Stagecoach NW	R396XDA	UK North	R623CVR	First	R759DRJ	Stagecoach Manchester
R247SBA	First	R397XDA	UK North	R624CVR	First	R760DRJ	Stagecoach Manchester
R248NBV	Stagecoach NW	R399CVR	South Lancs Travel	R625CVR	First	R761DRJ	Stagecoach Manchester
R248SBA	First	R417RCW	Preston Bus	R626CVR	First	R762DRJ	Stagecoach Manchester
R249NBV	Stagecoach NW	R418RCW	Preston Bus	R627CVR	First	R763DRJ	Stagecoach Manchester
R249SBA	First	R419EOS	Travellers' Choice	R629CVR	First	R765DRJ	Stagecoach Manchester
R250NBV	Stagecoach NW	R419RCW	Preston Bus	R630CVR	First	R776PRM	Routledge
R250SBA	First	R432NFR	Preston Bus	R631CVR	First	R791NEC	Travellers' Choice
R251NBV	Stagecoach NW	R433NFR	Preston Bus	R632CVR	First	R791PAO	Stagecoach NW
R251SBA	First	R434FWT	Battersby	R633CVR	First	R792PAO	Stagecoach NW
R252KWY	Rossendale	R434NFR	Preston Bus	R633EYS	Kirkby Lonsdale	R793URM	Stagecoach NW
R252NBV	Stagecoach NW	R435NFR	Preston Bus	R641OBV	Blackburn	R794URM	Stagecoach NW
R252SBA	First	R436NFR	Preston Bus	R642OBV	Blackburn	R795URM	Stagecoach NW
R253NBV	Stagecoach NW	R437NFR	Preston Bus	R643OBV	Blackburn	R801WJA	Bu-Va
R253SBA	First	R438RCW	Preston Bus	R644OBV	Blackburn	R805WJA	Bu-Va
R254NBV	Stagecoach NW	R439RCW	Preston Bus	R645CVR	First	R807WJA	Bu-Va
R254SBA	First	R440RCW	Preston Bus	R646CVR	First	R809WJA	M R Trave
R255NBV	Stagecoach NW	R446YNF	Stagecoach Manchester	R647CVR	First	R845VEC	Fishwic
R255SBA	First	R447YNF	Stagecoach Manchester	R648CVR	First	R846VEC	Fishwic

OMNIBUS
SOCIETY

The Omnibus Society North Western & Yorkshire Branch would like to meet serious bus, coach and light rail enthusiasts for fun days out. All ages considered.

With national affiliations we can offer regular day and weekend tours, talks by top speakers, a local area bulletin, national magazine, library and archive.

All you need to do is contact the Branch Secretary at:
10 Bradley Close,
Timperley,
Altrincham WA15 6SH
for a free fact pack.

Reg	Operator	Reg	Operator	Reg	Operator	Reg	Operator
R847VEC	Fishwick	R928XVM	Stagecoach Manchester	R964XVM	Stagecoach Manchester	S4BLU	Bluebird
R848VEC	Fishwick	R928YBA	Shearings	R965XVM	Stagecoach Manchester	S4HWD	Homeswood
R853WRM	Sim's Travel	R929XVM	Stagecoach Manchester	R966XVM	Stagecoach Manchester	S5BLU	Bluebird
R895XVM	Stagecoach Manchester	R929YBA	Shearings	R967XVM	Stagecoach Manchester	S6BLU	Bluebird
R896XVM	Stagecoach Manchester	R930XVM	Stagecoach Manchester	R968XVM	Stagecoach Manchester	S8BOS	Homeswood
R897XVM	Stagecoach Manchester	R930YBA	Shearings	R969XVM	Stagecoach Manchester	S9BLU	Blue Bus
R898AVM	Stagecoach Manchester	R931XVM	Stagecoach Manchester	R970XVM	Stagecoach Manchester	S9BOS	Homeswood
R898XVM	Stagecoach Manchester	R931YBA	Shearings	R971XVM	Stagecoach Manchester	S11BLU	Bluebird
R899AVM	Stagecoach Manchester	R932XVM	Stagecoach Manchester	R972XVM	Stagecoach Manchester	S43BLU	Blue Bus
R899XVM	Stagecoach Manchester	R932YBA	Shearings	R973XVM	Stagecoach Manchester	S45BLU	Blue Bus
R901AVM	Stagecoach Manchester	R933XVM	Stagecoach Manchester	R974XVM	Stagecoach Manchester	S57TNA	Mayne
R901WEC	Battersby	R933YBA	Shearings	R975XVM	Stagecoach Manchester	S63TNA	Mayne
R901XVM	Stagecoach Manchester	R934XVM	Stagecoach Manchester	R976XVM	Stagecoach Manchester	S101TRJ	Stagecoach Manchester
R901YBA	Shearings	R934YBA	Shearings	R977XVM	Stagecoach Manchester	S102TNB	First
R902WEC	Battersby	R935XVM	Stagecoach Manchester	R978XVM	Stagecoach Manchester	S102TRJ	Stagecoach Manchester
R902XVM	Stagecoach Manchester	R935YNF	Shearings	R979XVM	Stagecoach Manchester	S103TNB	First
R902YBA	Shearings	R936XVM	Stagecoach Manchester	R980XVM	Stagecoach Manchester	S103TRJ	Stagecoach Manchester
R903XVM	Stagecoach Manchester	R936YNF	Shearings	R981XVM	Stagecoach Manchester	S104TNB	First
R903YBA	Shearings	R937XVM	Stagecoach Manchester	R982XVM	Stagecoach Manchester	S104TRJ	Stagecoach Manchester
R904XVM	Stagecoach Manchester	R937YNF	Shearings	R983XVM	Stagecoach Manchester	S105TNB	First
R904YBA	Shearings	R938XVM	Stagecoach Manchester	R984XVM	Stagecoach Manchester	S105TRJ	Stagecoach Manchester
R905XVM	Stagecoach Manchester	R938YNF	Shearings	R985XVM	Stagecoach Manchester	S106TNB	First
R905YBA	Shearings	R939XVM	Stagecoach Manchester	R986XVM	Stagecoach Manchester	S106TRJ	Stagecoach Manchester
R906XVM	Stagecoach Manchester	R939YNF	Shearings	R987XVM	Stagecoach Manchester	S107TNB	First
R906YBA	Shearings	R940XVM	Stagecoach Manchester	R988XVM	Stagecoach Manchester	S107TRJ	Stagecoach Manchester
R907XVM	Stagecoach Manchester	R940YNF	Shearings	R989XVM	Stagecoach Manchester	S108TNB	First
R907YBA	Shearings	R941XVM	Stagecoach Manchester	R990XVM	Stagecoach Manchester	S108TRJ	Stagecoach Manchester
R908XVM	Stagecoach Manchester	R941YNF	Shearings	R991ANB	Shearings	S109TNB	First
R908YBA	Shearings	R942XVM	Stagecoach Manchester	R991XVM	Stagecoach Manchester	S110TNB	First
R909CAU	Timeline	R943XVM	Stagecoach Manchester	R992XVM	Stagecoach Manchester	S111FML	First
R909XVM	Stagecoach Manchester	R943YNF	Shearings	R993XVM	Stagecoach Manchester	S112TNB	First
R909YBA	Shearings	R944XVM	Stagecoach Manchester	R994XVM	Stagecoach Manchester	S113TNB	First
R910XVM	Stagecoach Manchester	R944YNF	Shearings	R995XVM	Stagecoach Manchester	S113TRJ	Stagecoach Manchester
R910YBA	Shearings	R945XVM	Stagecoach Manchester	R996XVM	Stagecoach Manchester	S114KRN	Rossendale
R912XVM	Stagecoach Manchester	R945YNF	Shearings	RAZ5171	Mayne	S114TNB	First
R912YBA	Shearings	R946AMB	Bu-Val	RAZ5172	Homeswood	S114TRJ	Stagecoach Manchester
R913XVM	Stagecoach Manchester	R946YNF	Shearings	RAZ7353	Brownriggs	S115KRN	Rossendale
R913YBA	Shearings	R947XVM	Stagecoach Manchester	RAZ8628	Dennis's	S115TNB	First
R914XVM	Stagecoach Manchester	R947YNF	Shearings	RBZ4221	Kirkby Lonsdale	S115TRJ	Stagecoach Manchester
R914YBA	Shearings	R948AMB	South Lancs Travel	RBZ5459	Stagecoach NW	S116KRN	Rossendale
R915XVM	Stagecoach Manchester	R948XVM	Stagecoach Manchester	RDZ4278	Pilkington	S116TRJ	Stagecoach Manchester
R915YBA	Shearings	R948YNF	Shearings	RHG95T	Blackpool	S117KRN	Rossendale
R916XVM	Stagecoach Manchester	R949AMB	South Lancs Travel	RHG189X	Aspden	S117TRJ	Stagecoach Manchester
R916YBA	Shearings	R949XVM	Stagecoach Manchester	RIB7856	Grayway	S118KRN	Rossendale
R917XVM	Stagecoach Manchester	R949YNF	Shearings	RIB8747	Homeswood	S118TRJ	Stagecoach Manchester
R917YBA	Shearings	R950XVM	Stagecoach Manchester	RIL1026	Kirkby Lonsdale	S119KRN	Rossendale
R918XVM	Stagecoach Manchester	R950YNF	Shearings	RIL1744	Brownriggs	S119TRJ	Stagecoach Manchester
R918YBA	Shearings	R951XVM	Stagecoach Manchester	RIL5084	Stagecoach NW	S120KRN	Rossendale
R919XVM	Stagecoach Manchester	R951YNF	Shearings	RIL5085	Stagecoach NW	S120TRJ	Stagecoach Manchester
R919YBA	Shearings	R952XVM	Stagecoach Manchester	RIL8160	Mayne	S121KRN	Rossendale
R920XVM	Stagecoach Manchester	R952YNF	Shearings	RIW9059	Brownriggs	S121TRJ	Stagecoach Manchester
R920YBA	Shearings	R953XVM	Stagecoach Manchester	RJA809R	Archway	S122KRN	Rossendale
R921XVM	Stagecoach Manchester	R953YNF	Shearings	RJI2161	Blue Bus	S122TRJ	Stagecoach Manchester
R921YBA	Shearings	R954RCH	Travellers' Choice	RJI2162	Staintons	S123KRN	Rossendale
R922XVM	Stagecoach Manchester	R954XVM	Stagecoach Manchester	RJI6861	Pilkington	S124TRJ	Stagecoach Manchester
R922YBA	Shearings	R954YNF	Shearings	RJI6862	Northern Blue	S125TRJ	Stagecoach Manchester
R923XVM	Stagecoach Manchester	R955XVM	Stagecoach Manchester	RJI8711	Frazer Eagle	S126TRJ	Stagecoach Manchester
R923YBA	Shearings	R956XVM	Stagecoach Manchester	RJI8720	Rossendale	S127TRJ	Stagecoach Manchester
R924XVM	Stagecoach Manchester	R957XVM	Stagecoach Manchester	RJI8722	Rossendale	S128TRJ	Stagecoach Manchester
R924YBA	Shearings	R958XVM	Stagecoach Manchester	RRM915M	Wright Brothers	S129TRJ	Stagecoach Manchester
R925XVM	Stagecoach Manchester	R959XVM	Stagecoach Manchester	RUT131W	Archway	S130TRJ	Stagecoach Manchester
R925YBA	Shearings	R960XVM	Stagecoach Manchester	RUT842	Stagecoach NW	S131TRJ	Stagecoach Manchester
R926XVM	Stagecoach Manchester	R961XVM	Stagecoach Manchester	RYV77	Finglands	S132TRJ	Stagecoach Manchester
R926YBA	Shearings	R962XVM	Stagecoach Manchester	S2BLU	Bluebird	S133KRM	Stagecoach NW
R927XVM	Stagecoach Manchester	R963XVM	Stagecoach Manchester	S3BLU	Bluebird	S133TRJ	Stagecoach Manchester
R927YBA	Shearings			S3JPT	JP Travel	S134KRM	Stagecoach NW

S134TRJ	Stagecoach Manchester	S654RNA	First	SIA6180	Finglands	T116JBA	Shearings
S135TRJ	Stagecoach Manchester	S655NUG	First	SIB1287	Northern Blue	T117JBA	Shearings
S136TRJ	Stagecoach Manchester	S655RNA	First	SIB2014	Hulme Hall	T118JBA	Shearings
S137TRJ	Stagecoach Manchester	S656NUG	First	SIB2633	Staintons	T119JBA	Shearings
S138TRJ	Stagecoach Manchester	S656RNA	First	SIB8405	Blackpool	T120JBA	Shearings
S139TRJ	Stagecoach Manchester	S657NUG	First	SIL2732	Homeswood	T122JBA	Shearings
S140TRJ	Stagecoach Manchester	S658NUG	First	SIL2838	Homeswood	T124JBA	Shearings
S141TRJ	Stagecoach Manchester	S659NUG	First	SIL3856	Mayne	T125JBA	Shearings
S142TRJ	Stagecoach Manchester	S660NUG	First	SIW1909	Homeswood	T126JBA	Shearings
S143TRJ	Stagecoach Manchester	S661NUG	First	SIW2805	Brownriggs	T127JBA	Shearings
S144TRJ	Stagecoach Manchester	S662NUG	First	SJI5589	Collinson	T128JBA	Shearings
S145TRJ	Stagecoach Manchester	S663NUG	First	SJI8113	Wright Brothers	T129JBA	Shearings
S146TRJ	Stagecoach Manchester	S668SVU	First	SND114X	First	T130JBA	Shearings
S147TRJ	Stagecoach Manchester	S669SVU	First	SND115X	First	T131JBA	Shearings
S148TRJ	Stagecoach Manchester	S670SVU	First	SND126X	First	T132JBA	Shearings
S149TRJ	Stagecoach Manchester	S671SVU	First	SND129X	First	T154AUA	Fishwick
S150TRJ	Stagecoach Manchester	S737RNE	Vale of Manchester	SND138X	First	T160MVM	Stagecoach Manchester
S151TRJ	Stagecoach Manchester	S738RNE	Vale of Manchester	SND140X	First	T161MVM	Stagecoach Manchester
S152TRJ	Stagecoach Manchester	S739RNE	Vale of Manchester	SND149X	First	T162MVM	Stagecoach Manchester
S153TRJ	Stagecoach Manchester	S764RNE	First	SND437X	M R Travel	T163MVM	Stagecoach Manchester
S154TRJ	Stagecoach Manchester	S764SVU	Stagecoach Manchester	SND440X	M R Travel	T164AUA	UK North
S156TRJ	Stagecoach Manchester	S766RNE	First	SND451X	Stagecoach Manchester	T164MVM	Stagecoach Manchester
S157TRJ	Stagecoach Manchester	S766SVU	Stagecoach Manchester	SND455X	Stagecoach Manchester	T165MVM	Stagecoach Manchester
S158TRJ	Stagecoach Manchester	S767SVU	Stagecoach Manchester	SND472X	Stagecoach Manchester	T166MVM	Stagecoach Manchester
S159TRJ	Stagecoach Manchester	S768SVU	Stagecoach Manchester	SRJ757R	Blackpool	T167MVM	Stagecoach Manchester
S190RAO	Stagecoach NW	S769RVU	Stagecoach Manchester	SSV269	Mayne	T168MVM	Stagecoach Manchester
S191RAO	Stagecoach NW	S770RVU	Stagecoach Manchester	STM238W	Grayway	T169MVM	Stagecoach Manchester
S192RAO	Stagecoach NW	S771RVU	Stagecoach Manchester	T1KET	Jim Stones	T173MVM	Stagecoach Manchester
S193RAO	Stagecoach NW	S772RVU	Stagecoach Manchester	T2BLU	Bluebird	T178MVM	Stagecoach Manchester
S193UAO	Routledge	S773RVU	Stagecoach Manchester	T3FWS	Staintons	T179MVM	Stagecoach Manchester
S194RAO	Stagecoach NW	S774RVU	Stagecoach Manchester	T10BLU	Blue Bus	T180MVM	Stagecoach Manchester
S195RAO	Stagecoach NW	S775RVU	Stagecoach Manchester	T11BLU	Blue Bus	T181MVM	Stagecoach Manchester
S196RAO	Stagecoach NW	S776RVU	Stagecoach Manchester	T11SLT	South Lancs Travel	T182MVM	Stagecoach Manchester
S258JFR	Robinsons	S778RVU	Stagecoach Manchester	T42PVM	Blue Bus	T183MVM	Stagecoach Manchester
S259JFR	Robinsons	S779RVU	Stagecoach Manchester	T58AUA	Fishwick	T184MVM	Stagecoach Manchester
S260JFR	Robinsons	S780RVU	Stagecoach Manchester	T58JDB	Mayne	T185MVM	Stagecoach Manchester
S269KHG	Stagecoach NW	S781RVU	Stagecoach Manchester	T59AUA	Fishwick	T186MVM	Stagecoach Manchester
S270KHG	Stagecoach NW	S782RVU	Stagecoach Manchester	T61LEC	Travellers' Choice	T187MVM	Stagecoach Manchester
S299JRM	Routledge	S796KRM	Stagecoach NW	T62LEC	Travellers' Choice	T197JBA	Shearings
S309DLG	Bu-Val	S797KRM	Stagecoach NW	T63AUA	Dennis's	T198JBA	Shearings
S324JNW	Frazer Eagle	S798KRM	Stagecoach NW	T63LEC	Travellers' Choice	T199JBA	Shearings
S325JNW	Frazer Eagle	S799KRM	Stagecoach NW	T64JDB	Mayne	T210HCW	Blackpool
S369SND	Finglands	S884AGD	Collinson	T64LEC	Travellers' Choice	T211HCW	Blackpool
S445JTP	Kirkby Lonsdale	S903JHG	Stagecoach NW	T65JDB	Mayne	T212HCW	Blackpool
S446JTP	Kirkby Lonsdale	S904JHG	Stagecoach NW	T68FBN	R Bullock	T212TND	Stagecoach Manchester
S505LHG	Blackpool	S904LHG	Battersby	T69FBN	R Bullock	T213HCW	Blackpool
S506LHG	Blackpool	S905JHG	Stagecoach NW	T73JBA	M R Travel	T213TND	Stagecoach Manchester
S507LHG	Blackpool	S905LHG	Battersby	T78JBA	M R Travel	T214HCW	Blackpool
S508LHG	Blackpool	S906JHG	Stagecoach NW	T79JBA	M R Travel	T215HCW	Blackpool
S509LHG	Blackpool	S933SVM	Bu-Val	T85HFV	Mountain Goat	T216HCW	Blackpool
S510LHG	Blackpool	S934SVM	Bu-Val	T101JBA	Shearings	T217HCW	Blackpool
S511LHG	Blackpool	S957URJ	R Bullock	T102JBA	Shearings	T218HCW	Blackpool
S512LHG	Blackpool	S958URJ	R Bullock	T103JBA	Shearings	T222MTB	Blue Bus
S513LHG	Blackpool	S959URJ	R Bullock	T104JBA	Shearings	T223JND	Mayne
S514LHG	Blackpool	S960URJ	R Bullock	T105JBA	Shearings	T224JND	Mayne
S515LHG	Blackpool	S989EEC	Travellers' Choice	T106JBA	Shearings	T231JNC	Rossendale
S516LHG	Blackpool	S992UJA	First	T107JBA	Shearings	T232JNC	Rossendale
S517LHG	Blackpool	S993UJA	First	T108JBA	Shearings	T284PVM	Manchester Airport
S518LHG	Blackpool	S994UJA	First	T109JBA	Shearings	T291ROF	Vale of Manchester
S560JSE	First	S995UJA	First	T110JBA	Shearings	T341NBV	Rossendale
S561JSE	First	SAO466X	Wright Brothers	T112AUA	Alfa	T342NBV	Rossendale
S582RGA	Ashalls	SAO467X	Wright Brothers	T112JBA	Shearings	T343NBV	Rossendale
S651RNA	First	SBV16X	Blackburn	T113AUA	Alfa	T344NBV	Rossendale
S652RNA	First	SBV703	Aspden	T113JBA	Shearings	T370JVR	Finglands
S653RNA	First	SCK224X	Lancashire United	T114JBA	Shearings		
S654NUG	First	SHH124M	Stagecoach NW	T115JBA	Shearings		

T436EBD	Lakeland	TXJ540K	Bluebird	V127DJA	Mayne	V274HEC	Blackpool
T486CCK	Lakeland	TYT653	Titterington	V127DND	First	V275HEC	Blackpool
T487CCK	Lakeland	UCE665	Mayne	V128DJA	Mayne	V276HEC	Blackpool
T506JNA	First	UCW429X	Blackburn	V128DND	First	V301DRN	Battersby
T507JNA	First	UCW430X	Blackburn	V129DJA	Mayne	V302DRN	Battersby
T508JNA	First	UD1100	Travellers' Choice	V129DND	First	V330DBU	First
T509JNA	First	UGE807W	Wright Brothers	V130DND	First	V333ASH	Ashalls
T510JNA	First	UHG142V	Preston Bus	V131DND	First	V387HGG	Ashalls
T511JNA	First	UHG143V	Preston Bus	V132DND	First	V389HGG	Ashalls
T512JNA	First	UHG144V	Fishwick	V133DND	First	V389SVV	Lakeland
T513JNA	First	UHG147V	Fishwick	V134DND	First	V390HGG	Ashalls
T514JNA	First	UHG148V	Fishwick	V135DND	First	V428DND	Finglands
T515JNA	First	UHG149V	Fishwick	V136DND	First	V429DND	Finglands
T522JCA	Manchester Airport	UHG150V	Fishwick	V137DND	First	V614DJA	Stagecoach Manchester
T543EUB	Battersby	UHG351Y	Blackpool	V138DND	First	V615DJA	Stagecoach Manchester
T562BSS	First	UHG352Y	Blackpool	V138EAO	Routledge	V616DJA	Stagecoach Manchester
T563BSS	First	UHG353Y	Blackpool	V139DND	First	V617DJA	Stagecoach Manchester
T564BSS	First	UHG354Y	Blackpool	V140DND	First	V618DJA	Stagecoach Manchester
T565BSS	First	UJN883Y	Homeswood	V141DND	First	V619DJA	Stagecoach Manchester
T566BSS	First	ULS663T	Mayne	V142DND	First	V620DJA	Stagecoach Manchester
T567BSS	First	UOL337	Mayne	V151DFT	Stagecoach Manchester	V621DJA	Stagecoach Manchester
T581KGB	Ashalls	UOV721	Grayway	V152DFT	Stagecoach Manchester	V622DJA	Stagecoach Manchester
T612MNF	Stagecoach Manchester	URM801Y	Stagecoach NW	V153DFT	Stagecoach Manchester	V623DJA	Stagecoach Manchester
T613MNF	Stagecoach Manchester	URM802Y	Stagecoach NW	V154DFT	Stagecoach Manchester	V624DJA	Stagecoach Manchester
T674TSG	Blue Bus	URN168Y	Preston Bus	V155DFT	Stagecoach Manchester	V651HEC	Blackburn
T701PND	First	URN170Y	Preston Bus	V156DFT	Stagecoach Manchester	V651LWT	UK North
T702PND	First	URN172Y	Preston Bus	V157DFT	Stagecoach Manchester	V652HEC	Blackburn
T703PND	First	URN322V	Blackpool	V158DFT	Stagecoach Manchester	V652LWT	UK North
T704PND	First	URN323V	Blackpool	V159DFT	Stagecoach Manchester	V653HEC	Blackburn
T705PND	First	URN324V	Blackpool	V160DFT	Stagecoach Manchester	V654HEC	Blackburn
T706PND	First	URN325V	Blackpool	V161DFT	Stagecoach Manchester	V654LWT	UK North
T707PND	First	URN326V	Blackpool	V162DFT	Stagecoach Manchester	V655HEC	Blackburn
T708PND	First	URN327V	Blackpool	V163DFT	Stagecoach Manchester	V655LWT	UK North
T789JAO	Titterington	URN328V	Blackpool	V164DFT	Stagecoach Manchester	V656HEC	Blackburn
T916SSF	First	URN329V	Blackpool	V165DFT	Stagecoach Manchester	V657HEC	Blackburn
T917SSF	First	URN330V	Blackpool	V166DFT	Stagecoach Manchester	V658HEC	Blackburn
T918SSF	First	UTF119	Homeswood	V167DFT	Stagecoach Manchester	V659HEC	Blackburn
T919SSF	First	UWW5X	Blackpool	V168DFT	Stagecoach Manchester	V660HEC	Blackburn
T953JAO	Sim's Travel	UWW11X	Blackpool	V169DFT	Stagecoach Manchester	V674DHH	Routledge
T991JNW	Frazer Eagle	UWW15X	Blackpool	V170DFT	Stagecoach Manchester	V689FPB	JP Travel
T992JNW	Frazer Eagle	V3BLU	Bluebird	V171DFT	Stagecoach Manchester	V725AGD	Northern Blue
TAO154R	Titterington	V3JPT	JP Travel	V172DFT	Stagecoach Manchester	V801DFV	Stagecoach NW
TAZ5004	Brownriggs	V3WBC	Wright Brothers	V190EBV	Preston Bus	V802DFV	Stagecoach NW
TAZ5284	Kirkby Lonsdale	V4BLU	Bluebird	V191EBV	Preston Bus	V803DFV	Stagecoach NW
TAZ5285	Kirkby Lonsdale	V4HWD	Homeswood	V192EBV	Preston Bus	V804DFV	Stagecoach NW
TCW868T	Blackburn	V4JPT	JP Travel	V193EBV	Preston Bus	V806DFV	Stagecoach NW
TET746S	Mayne	V20CBC	Ashalls	V194EBV	Preston Bus	V807DFV	Stagecoach NW
TET747S	Mayne	V21BLU	Bluebird	V195EBV	Preston Bus	V808DFV	Stagecoach NW
THX555S	Mayne	V22BLU	Blue Bus	V196EBV	Preston Bus	V809DFV	Stagecoach NW
THX601S	Mayne	V22BLU	Bluebird	V206EBV	Blackburn	V811DFV	Stagecoach NW
TIA9275	Grayway	V22SLT	South Lancs Travel	V207EBV	Blackburn	V812DFV	Stagecoach NW
TIB4568	Walton's	V33BLU	Blue Bus	V208EBV	Blackburn	V928FMS	Blue Bus
TIL1173	South Lancs Travel	V33SLT	South Lancs Travel	V209EBV	Blackburn	V944DNB	M R Travel
TIL1180	Bluebird	V34ENC	Blue Bus	V210EBV	Blackburn	V951KAG	Blue Bus
TIL1182	Bluebird	V35ENC	Blue Bus	V261HEC	Blackpool	VAV257X	Grayway
TIL3971	Brownriggs	V41DJA	Blue Bus	V262HEC	Blackpool	VBG82V	Pilkington
TJI4823	Coastlinks	V41DTE	First	V263HEC	Blackpool	VBV18Y	Blackburn
TJI4826	Coastlinks	V42DTE	First	V264HEC	Blackpool	VBV21Y	Blackburn
TJI4830	Ashalls	V43DTE	First	V265HEC	Blackpool	VBV22Y	Blackburn
TJI4836	Ashalls	V82EVU	JP Travel	V266HEC	Blackpool	VEX291X	Hulme Hall
TJI4927	Homeswood	V122DND	First	V267HEC	Blackpool	VHG357V	Aspden
TJI7514	Pilkington	V124DND	First	V268HEC	Blackpool	VIA197	Tyrer Bus
TJN505R	Blackburn	V125DJA	Mayne	V269HEC	Blackpool	VJI6694	Hulme Hall
TKU540	Mayne	V125DND	First	V271HEC	Blackpool	VJI6850	Hulme Hall
TOF694S	Blackburn	V126DJA	Mayne	V272HEC	Blackpool	VKB708	Stagecoach NW
TSV807	Wright Brothers	V126DND	First	V273HEC	Blackpool	VLF578	Stagecoach NW

Reg	Operator	Reg	Operator	Reg	Operator	Reg	Operator
VLT104	Stagecoach NW	W284JBN	Shearings	W378JNE	First	WJI7688	Yellow Buzz
VOY182X	Rossendale	W285JBN	Shearings	W379JNE	First	WJI9072	Blue Bus
VRN827Y	Lancashire United	W286JBN	Shearings	W381WGE	Walton's	WJI9074	Blue Bus
VRN829Y	Stagecoach NW	W287JBN	Shearings	W387WGE	Cosgrove's	WLT980	Stagecoach NW
VRN830Y	Burnley & Pendle	W288JBN	Shearings	W425JBN	Mayne	WRN412V	Fishwick
VRR447	Stagecoach NW	W301GCW	Blackburn	W426JBN	Mayne	WRN413V	Fishwick
VUA471X	Walton's	W301JND	First	W427JBN	Mayne	WTU468W	Hulme Hall
VUA472X	Hulme Hall	W302JND	First	W428JBN	Mayne	WX7655	Travellers' Choice
W4FWS	Staintons	W303JND	First	W445CFR	Rossendale	WXI5865	Sim's Travel
W4HWD	Homeswood	W304JND	First	W446CFR	Rossendale	WYV56T	Stagecoach NW
W5BLU	Bluebird	W307JND	First	W531GCW	Dennis's	X2JPT	JP Travel
W5JPT	JP Travel	W308JND	First	W626RND	Stagecoach Manchester	X3MMC	M & M Coaches
W6BLU	Bluebird	W309JND	First	W627RND	Stagecoach Manchester	X4HWD	Homeswood
W6JPT	JP Travel	W311JND	First	W628RND	Stagecoach Manchester	X7BLU	Bluebird
W7JPT	JP Travel	W312JND	First	W629RND	Stagecoach Manchester	X13LUE	Blue Bus
W12LUE	Blue Bus	W313JND	First	W631RND	Stagecoach Manchester	X14LUE	Blue Bus
W19SLT	South Lancs Travel	W314JND	First	W632RND	Stagecoach Manchester	X23BLU	Blue Bus
W20SLT	South Lancs Travel	W315JND	First	W633RND	Stagecoach Manchester	X59YEC	Travellers' Choice
W44SLT	South Lancs Travel	W317JND	First	W634RND	Stagecoach Manchester	X118ABA	Mayne
W55SLT	South Lancs Travel	W319JND	First	W635RND	Stagecoach Manchester	X119ABA	Mayne
W81JBN	Mayne	W322JND	First	W636RND	Stagecoach Manchester	X131JCW	Rossendale
W82JBN	Mayne	W324JND	First	W637RND	Stagecoach Manchester	X132JCW	Rossendale
W83JBN	Mayne	W326JND	First	W638RND	Stagecoach Manchester	X133JCW	Rossendale
W142PSH	First	W327JND	First	W639RND	Stagecoach Manchester	X134JCW	Rossendale
W148EEC	Travellers' Choice	W329JND	First	W641RND	Stagecoach Manchester	X169GAW	M R Travel
W149EEC	Travellers' Choice	W331JND	First	W642RND	Stagecoach Manchester	X178XEC	Battersby
W151EEC	Travellers' Choice	W331RJA	First	W643RND	Stagecoach Manchester	X182RRN	Preston Bus
W152EEC	Travellers' Choice	W332JND	First	W644RND	Stagecoach Manchester	X183RRN	Preston Bus
W176CDN	UK North	W332RJA	First	W645RND	Stagecoach Manchester	X184RRN	Preston Bus
W177CDN	UK North	W334JND	First	W646RND	Stagecoach Manchester	X185RRN	Preston Bus
W178CDN	UK North	W334RJA	First	W647RND	Stagecoach Manchester	X186RRN	Preston Bus
W179BVP	First	W335JND	First	W648GBX	Homeswood	X187RRN	Preston Bus
W201JBN	Shearings	W335RJA	First	W652RCA	Shearings	X188RRN	Preston Bus
W202JBN	Shearings	W336JND	First	W663PTD	R Bullock	X189RRN	Preston Bus
W203JBN	Shearings	W336RJA	First	W664PTD	R Bullock	X197RRN	Preston Bus
W204JBN	Shearings	W337JND	First	W671PTD	R Bullock	X198RRN	Preston Bus
W207JBN	Shearings	W337RJA	First	W672PTD	R Bullock	X199RRN	Preston Bus
W208JBN	Shearings	W338JND	First	W672RCA	Shearings	X216BNE	Stagecoach Manchester
W209JBN	Shearings	W338RJA	First	W673PTD	R Bullock	X217BNE	Stagecoach Manchester
W211JBN	Shearings	W339JND	First	W674PTD	R Bullock	X218BNE	Stagecoach Manchester
W212JBN	Shearings	W339RJA	First	W675PTD	R Bullock	X219BNE	Stagecoach Manchester
W213JBN	Shearings	W341JND	First	W676PTD	R Bullock	X221BNE	Stagecoach Manchester
W214CDN	Alfa	W341RJA	First	W677PTD	R Bullock	X223BNE	Stagecoach Manchester
W214JBN	Shearings	W342RJA	First	W678PTD	R Bullock	X224BNE	Stagecoach Manchester
W215CDN	Alfa	W343RJA	First	W699RND	First	X226BNE	Stagecoach Manchester
W215JBN	Shearings	W345RJA	First	W701BFV	Lancashire United	X227BNE	Stagecoach Manchester
W216JBN	Shearings	W346RJA	First	W702BFV	Lancashire United	X228BNE	Stagecoach Manchester
W217CDN	Alfa	W347RJA	First	W715RCA	Shearings	X229BNE	Stagecoach Manchester
W217JBN	Shearings	W348RJA	First	W738RCA	Shearings	X231BNE	Stagecoach Manchester
W218JBN	Shearings	W349CCK	Lakeland	W743RCA	Shearings	X232BNE	Stagecoach Manchester
W219JBN	Shearings	W349RJA	First	W815AAY	Homeswood	X233BNE	Stagecoach Manchester
W221JBN	Shearings	W351RJA	First	W902JBA	Timeline	X234BNE	Stagecoach Manchester
W223CDN	Fishwick	W352RJA	First	W903JBA	Timeline	X235BNE	Stagecoach Manchester
W223JBN	Shearings	W353RJA	First	W912BEC	Battersby	X236BNE	Stagecoach Manchester
W224CDN	Fishwick	W354RJA	First	W913BEC	Battersby	X237BNE	Stagecoach Manchester
W224JBN	Shearings	W356RJA	First	W914BEC	Battersby	X238BNE	Stagecoach Manchester
W226JBN	Shearings	W357RJA	First	W916BEC	Battersby	X239BNE	Stagecoach Manchester
W227JBN	Shearings	W358RJA	First	W975BEC	Battersby	X241ATD	Stagecoach Manchester
W228JBN	Shearings	W359RJA	First	WAO645Y	Stagecoach NW	X242ATD	Stagecoach Manchester
W229JBN	Shearings	W361RJA	First	WCK124V	Aspden	X243ATD	Stagecoach Manchester
W261GBV	Robinsons	W361SNN	Kirkby Lonsdale	WDA1T	Brownriggs	X244ATD	Stagecoach Manchester
W262GBV	Robinsons	W362RJA	First	WDZ6975	M & M Coaches	X246ATD	Stagecoach Manchester
W263GBV	Robinsons	W363RJA	First	WEC263Y	Grayway	X253USH	First
W264GBV	Robinsons	W364RJA	First	WIB4053	Blue Bus	X256USH	First
W282JBN	Shearings	W365RJA	First	WIB4054	Blue Bus	X257USH	First
283JBN	Shearings	W366RJA	First	WJI3506	Pilkington	X261USH	First

X265USH	First	XAU703Y	Blackpool	Y171HRN	Burnley & Pendle	Y598KNE	First
X266USH	First	XAU704Y	Blackpool	Y172HRN	Burnley & Pendle	Y623RTD	First
X269USH	First	XAU705Y	Blackpool	Y173HRN	Lancashire United	Y633RTD	First
X271USH	First	XAU706Y	Blackpool	Y174HRN	Lancashire United	Y634RTD	First
X272USH	First	XCW957R	Fishwick	Y176HRN	Lancashire United	Y693HEC	Travellers' Choice
X287TAO	Sim's Travel	XDO32	Travellers' Choice	Y177HRN	Lancashire United	Y701HRN	Burnley & Pendle
X301AKY	Ashalls	XJF386	Travellers' Choice	Y178HRN	Lancashire United	Y702HRN	Burnley & Pendle
X371AVU	Finglands	XJI1301	Coastlinks	Y191KNB	Manchester Airport	Y703HRN	Burnley & Pendle
X401CSG	First	XJI1302	Coastlinks	Y192KNB	Manchester Airport	Y704HRN	Burnley & Pendle
X466KUT	Homeswood	XJI7908	M & M Coaches	Y193KNB	Manchester Airport	Y705HRN	Burnley & Pendle
X611NBU	First	XOU692	Titterington	Y194KNB	Manchester Airport	Y706HRN	Burnley & Pendle
X611OBN	First	XSU907	Northern Blue	Y195KNB	Manchester Airport	Y707HRN	Burnley & Pendle
X612OBN	First	XSU908	Northern Blue	Y196KNB	Manchester Airport	Y708HRN	Burnley & Pendle
X613OBN	First	XSU909	Northern Blue	Y266KCA	Shearings	Y709HRN	Burnley & Pendle
X614OBN	First	Y2EEC	Travellers' Choice	Y289KCA	Shearings	Y711HRN	Burnley & Pendle
X615OBN	First	Y2JPT	JP Travel	Y301KBN	Shearings	Y712HRN	Burnley & Pendle
X616OBN	First	Y3EEC	Travellers' Choice	Y302KBN	Shearings	Y713HRN	Burnley & Pendle
X617OBN	First	Y3JPT	JP Travel	Y303KBN	Shearings	Y714HRN	Burnley & Pendle
X618OBN	First	Y8BLU	Bluebird	Y304KBN	Shearings	Y715HRN	Burnley & Pendle
X619OBN	First	Y20BLU	Blue Bus	Y305KBN	Shearings	Y716HRN	Burnley & Pendle
X626JGE	Homeswood	Y21BLU	Blue Bus	Y306KBN	Shearings	Y716SUB	Frazer Eagle
X627OBN	First	Y36KNB	Blue Bus	Y307KBN	Shearings	Y717SUB	Frazer Eagle
X685REC	Lakeland	Y37KNB	Blue Bus	Y308KBN	Shearings	Y724HEC	Travellers' Choice
X721NSE	Stagecoach NW	Y38KNB	Blue Bus	Y309KBN	Shearings	Y774TNC	First
X761ABU	Finglands	Y42HHE	Homeswood	Y309KCA	Shearings	Y901KNB	First
X762ABU	Finglands	Y46ABA	Blue Bus	Y311KBN	Shearings	Y902KNB	First
X763ABU	Finglands	Y47ABA	Blue Bus	Y312KBN	Shearings	Y903KNB	First
X764ABU	Finglands	Y48ABA	Blue Bus	Y313KBN	Shearings	Y904KNB	First
X792JHG	Dennis's	Y66SLT	South Lancs Travel	Y314KBN	Shearings	Y905KNB	First
X793JHG	Dennis's	Y77SLT	South Lancs Travel	Y315KBN	Shearings	Y917XEC	Battersby
X805SRM	Stagecoach NW	Y98KRJ	Homeswood	Y317KBN	Shearings	Y918XEC	Battersby
X813SRM	Stagecoach NW	Y142HRN	Burnley & Pendle	Y319KBN	Shearings	Y919XEC	Battersby
X814SRM	Stagecoach NW	Y143HRN	Burnley & Pendle	Y343XBN	First	Y951XRN	Dennis's
X815SRM	Stagecoach NW	Y144HRN	Burnley & Pendle	Y344XBN	First	Y952XRN	Dennis's
X816SRM	Stagecoach NW	Y146HRN	Burnley & Pendle	Y347XBN	First	Y961XBU	First
X817SRM	Stagecoach NW	Y147HRN	Burnley & Pendle	Y356KCA	Shearings	Y962WAO	Titterington
X818SRM	Stagecoach NW	Y148HRN	Burnley & Pendle	Y364XBN	First	Y962XBU	First
X819SRM	Stagecoach NW	Y149HRN	Burnley & Pendle	Y373UOM	Staintons	Y984XEC	Travellers' Choice
X821NWX	Fishwick	Y149HWE	Staintons	Y374UOM	Staintons	YAZ6510	Brownriggs
X821SRM	Stagecoach NW	Y151HRN	Burnley & Pendle	Y387KBN	Shearings	YD02RHF	Fishwick
X822NWX	Fishwick	Y152HRN	Burnley & Pendle	Y388KBN	Shearings	YDG616	Stagecoach NW
X822SRM	Stagecoach NW	Y153HRN	Burnley & Pendle	Y389KBN	Shearings	YEV317S	Blackburn
X823NWX	Fishwick	Y154HRN	Burnley & Pendle	Y391KBN	Shearings	YEV324S	Blackburn
X823SRM	Stagecoach NW	Y157HRN	Burnley & Pendle	Y392KBN	Shearings	YFG333	Travellers' Choice
X824SRM	Stagecoach NW	Y158HRN	Burnley & Pendle	Y394RTD	First	YJ51EKO	Tyrer Bus
X825SRM	Stagecoach NW	Y159HRN	Burnley & Pendle	Y395RTD	First	YJ51EKP	Tyrer Bus
X826SRM	Stagecoach NW	Y161HRN	Burnley & Pendle	Y407XBU	Homeswood	YMB500W	Hulme Hall
X827SRM	Stagecoach NW	Y162HRN	Burnley & Pendle	Y431KCA	Shearings	YNC22X	Bu-Val
X936JDS	Homeswood	Y163HRN	Burnley & Pendle	Y431PBD	Manchester Airport	YPL764	Mayne
X939NBU	R Bullock	Y164HRN	Burnley & Pendle	Y432PBD	Manchester Airport	YT51KPT	Frazer Eagle
X983SHH	Routledge	Y165HRN	Burnley & Pendle	Y432WHH	Routledge	YTY867	Homeswood
X984SHH	Routledge	Y166HRN	Burnley & Pendle	Y448HUA	Fishwick	YXI7923	Homeswood
XAP956	Titterington	Y167HRN	Burnley & Pendle	Y477HUA	Fishwick		
XAU701Y	Blackpool	Y168HRN	Burnley & Pendle	Y500MRT	M R Travel		
XAU702Y	Blackpool	Y169HRN	Burnley & Pendle	Y597KNE	First		

ISBN 1 897990 77 4

© Published by *British Bus Publishing Ltd*, May 2002

British Bus Publishing Ltd, 16 St Margaret's Drive, Wellington, Telford, TF1 3PH
Telephone: 01952 255669 - Facsimile: 01952 222397

www.britishbuspublishing.co.uk - E-mail editorial@britishbuspublishing.co.uk